RESTITUTION AND THE POLITICS OF REPAIR

T0322387

To Cyril and Sava
And to their caretakers and educators,
in deep gratitude for care work

RESTITUTION AND THE POLITICS OF REPAIR

TROPES, IMAGINARIES, THEORY

Magdalena Zolkos

EDINBURGH
University Press

Edinburgh University Press is one of the leading university presses in the UK. We publish academic books and journals in our selected subject areas across the humanities and social sciences, combining cutting-edge scholarship with high editorial and production values to produce academic works of lasting importance. For more information visit our website: edinburghuniversitypress.com

© Magdalena Zolkos, 2020, 2022

Edinburgh University Press Ltd
The Tun – Holyrood Road, 12(2f) Jackson's Entry, Edinburgh EH8 8PJ

First published in hardback by Edinburgh University Press 2020

Typeset in 10/12.5 Adobe Sabon by
IDSUK (DataConnection) Ltd, and
printed and bound by CPI Group (UK) Ltd,
Croydon, CR0 4YY

A CIP record for this book is available from the British Library

ISBN 978 1 4744 5309 7 (hardback)
ISBN 978 1 4744 5310 3 (paperback)
ISBN 978 1 4744 5311 0 (webready PDF)
ISBN 978 1 4744 5312 7 (epub)

CONTENTS

ACKNOWLEDGEMENTS

The first part of this book was written at the Institute for Social Justice, ACU (now sadly discontinued). I thank the institute director, Nikolas Kompridis, for continuous encouragement for my work, for his intellectual generosity and for the optimism in dark times. Kiran Grewal and Allison Weir, for the many inspiring discussions, comments and feminist perspectives, always delivered with sophistication and rigour. Paula Gleeson and Lisa Tarantino were an endless source of support, solidarity and humour when it was most needed, and both became dear friends. Tina Dixson, Julie Macken and Riikka Prates, for intellectual companionship and inspiration; and the participants in my 2015 graduate seminar 'Politics of Suffering', where some of my ideas about restitution were presented. Jeanne Morefield offered prescient comments and support, and Jacqueline Rose welcomed me (and my baby) into her seminar on Freud's social thought, which deeply influenced my thinking about restitution and psychoanalysis.

The book was finalised during my stay as Humboldt Research Fellow at Frankfurt Memory Studies Platform at Goethe University. I thank Astrid Erll for her support and interest in my work, and all the FMSP group members for a warm welcome and a vibrant research environment. I acknowledge Alexander von Humboldt Stiftung for funding the fellowship.

This book has benefited greatly from discussions, feedback and the support of my academic peers: Karyn Ball, Peter Banki, Costica Bradatan, Simone Drichel (for the careful reading of Chapter 2 and the shared affection for the

Creature!), Joanne Faulkner, Katrina Jaworski, Fiona Jenkins, Andrew Kelly, Marguerite La Caze, Kitty Millet, Ahlam Mustafa, Gerda Roelvink, Michael Richardson, Jean-Marie Viljoen, Sonja van Wichelen and Jessica Whyte.

Victoria Hunt for her artistic and critical insights into indigenous dispossession and restitution.

It was privilege and pleasure to collaborate on this book with Jenny Daly, the Commissioning Editor for Politics at Edinburgh University Press; I thank her for the dedication and work during the editorial and publication process. Many thanks, too, to Sarah Foyle for her assistance.

I feel greatly indebted to a diverse group of people that performed pedagogic and care work within different institutional settings, and who supervised, taught and attended to the needs of my children with dedication and wisdom, enabling me to spend time on academic work. This book would never have happened without you: the educators at SDN Erskineville Children's Education and Care Centre, Erskineville Public School and IBMS Frankfurt. I hope that as a society we become capable of better recognising and valuing the importance of your work.

A wonderful group of friends, neighbours, and comrades in Sydney, including Jo Derry, Hande Loc Candemir, Bel Macedone, Megan Mackenzie, Eli Noir, Angela Spindler, Gillian Stokie and Emilia Subocz; also David Bitton, Candice Wild at Ella Guru Café (so much of that book was written over their great coffee!), the parental community of Erskineville Public School, the fabulous group of 'Erko Mums' and the Inner West Steiner Playgroup.

My parents, Teresa Żółkoś and Ryszard Żółkoś, for their support and care, and Monika Żółkoś, for continuous inspiration.

Finally, my loving thoughts go to two young people, who made little direct contribution to this book, and in fact were a source of constant distractions from it – Cyril and Sava. They ground and touch my life in ways that are nothing short of wondrous.

And Emilian, with love, always.

INTRODUCTION: IMAGINING RESTITUTION

Simon Curtis' 2015 film *Woman in Gold* narrates the struggle of Maria Altmann, a Jewish war refugee from Austria (played by Helen Mirren), to reclaim her family's property confiscated by the Nazis in a protracted court battle with the Austrian state (*Republic of Austria* v. *Altmann* 2004). Famously, her property included two paintings by Gustav Klimt of Altmann's aunt, Adele Bloch-Bauer, commissioned by Adele's husband before the war, and displayed at the Österreichische Galerie Belvedere since the 1940s. In the film, Altmann is invited to speak at a restitution conference in Vienna, held in connection with the 1998 *Kunstrückgabegesetz*, the Art Restitution Act, and the establishment of the Austrian Commission for Provenance Research (see Bazyler 2005; Bazyler and Alford 2006; Merryman 2010). During her speech, Altmann opens a dictionary and reads a definition of restitution: 'the return of something to its original state'. With this claim she both expands *and* complicates the dominant meaning of restitution as a remedial legal action of returning misappropriated things to the rightful owners. This claim also suggests that what Altmann sought to achieve in her restitutive struggle is itself rather complicated: while from the point of view of legal redress she wants to repossess her family's belongings, Altmann's narrative posturing discloses the existence of conflicted desires and melancholic investments, which the formal justice discourse will not, and cannot, address. Restitution also comes to signify for Altmann a reunification with her beloved aunt, as well as a return to the 'original state' – innocent, untainted by violence, prelapsarian – of her Vienna childhood. This 'original state' has both a temporal dimension (it is located in time *before* the 1938 annexation of Austria into Nazi Germany and the orchestrated expulsion and dispossession of the Jewish populations that ensued) and a phantasmatic one: it signifies a return to a condition of non-violent neighbourly coexistence that Altmann's experience reveals as being *always already* tentative, precarious and conditional.

Altmann's reference to restitution as the return to the original state also has a present-day provocative political resonance: by claiming the ownership of Adele's portraits and by introducing into the public discourse of art provenance and art restitution the familial and intimate meanings of these artefacts, she boldly asserts the Jewishness of 'the Mona Lisa of Austria'.[1] As such, she calls out the continuity of violence that the official Austrian discourse of *Rückvergütung* has relegated to the past (see Wodak 2009; Pelinka 2019). Altmann's return to Austria is narrated as her tracing of these violent remnants, both in the form of sensorially activated memories of Jewish persecution on the streets of Vienna that she witnessed as a child, and as present-day signs – sometimes ephemeral and gestural, and sometimes tangible, verbally articulated and explicit – of indifference to that difficult history, of the lack of remorse or expiation, and a disavowal of ethical responsibility. The response that Altmann repetitively received to her restitutive claim is that *Austria cannot part with Adele* – Klimt's paintings, though once shunned by the Nazis as overtly erotic and decadent, feature in the film as an *unrestitutable object*. Their removal would have meant a loss of something fundamental, perhaps foundational, in Austria, a gaping and unsuturable wound.

And yet, one could also ask, paraphrasing Achille Mbembe's prescient remarks on post-colonial art restitution in Europe,[2] whether Adele's portraits have *completed their task* in Austria – the task of signifying both the irreducible otherness of the neighbour *and* the neighbourly proximity of the other (cf. Žižek, Santner and Reinhard [2006] 2013). Adele in Klimt's paintings is the Jewish other; a Jewish woman whose alterity cannot be dissolved through assimilationism, nor can it be gotten rid of through violent expulsion outside of the borders of the nation-ideal, nor jealously robbed. In a moment of personal crisis, Maria Altmann confides in her lawyer, Eric Schoenberg: '[it is] I [who] would love to return to my original state', and with these words she momentarily blurs the apparent clarity of *what is the object*, and *who is the subject*, of restitution. The aporia of her restitutive desires is clearly revealed; while Altmann reclaims her family's objects and takes Adele's two portraits to America (where they are sold, respectively, to Neue Galerie in New York and to a private collector), the imagined passage into her childhood experience of the world void of genocidal violence will have remained barred.

The cinematic narrative of Altmann's struggle provides an entry-point into this book's opening question: what does the call for object restitution mean beyond the rights-based juridical framework of the return of confiscated[3] tangible things to the original owners? What imaginary and phantasmatic contents affix themselves to restitutive demands, so that their utterance also, perhaps inadvertently, activates the 'subcutaneous' restitutive motifs of the prelapsarian return – to the time and condition from before violence – and of renewal, rebirth and redemption?[4] While these obscured and suppressed idioms of restitution are not explicitly part of the secular liberal discourse,[5] they need to be considered, in that by undertaking and undergoing acts of restitution in the aftermath of state violence, the communities in question also embark on a project of *political imagining*; one in which historical meaning-making and the construction of a post-conflict future become tightly connected (cf. Rose 1996; Rose, in Clemens and Naparstek 2011: 346–59).[6] Through acts of restitution-making people come to envision themselves collectively and as a polity; the key term in this book, *restitutive imaginary*, invokes that sense of creative envisioning, and holding on to the promise of something not yet in existence, through drawing from and activating the repertoire of subcutaneously residing contents and motifs.[7]

I trace these retrocessive and prelapsarian tropes[8] of restitution in a selection of literary, philosophical, political and sociological European texts, which are brought together in this book under the heading of restitution theory. What these diverse texts have in common is that they articulate restitution alongside the motifs of the undoing of wrongs, as a reparative or curative procedure,[9] and as a return to a place, time or subjective condition *prior to* the event of violence. At the heart of the political fantasy of wiping out not simply *the consequences of the offence*, but of *the very fact of its occurrence* is an operation that Sigmund Freud called 'undoing-what-has-been-done' (*Ungeschehenmachen*), and which he related to obsessive enactments of magical procedures that annul undesirable actions ([1926] 2010; [1949] 1959; cf. Derrida 1996: 81).[10] Approaching it from a philosophic angle, Vladimir Jankélévitch wrote about 'metaphysical powerlessness' (*impuissance métaphysique*) to reverse the (fact of) 'having-done' or 'having-taken-place', or, as he put it, of changing the 'the *quoddity* of the misdeed' ([1967] 2019: 83; 2005: 47–8).[11]

Translating these psychoanalytic and philosophic insights into the language of restitution, I draw attention to the important clause, or a supplement, of 'prior to' in legal restitution speech, which specifies the restitutive aim as the subject's return to the state or condition that *would have existed* had the violence not occurred (cf. Avelar 1999; Torpey 2003). As such, restitution as a political practice interweaves three disparate impulses: reparative action; the undoing of wrongs; and return of the *status quo ante*. My ambition for this book is, in part, to disentangle these reparative, retrocessive and prelapsarian threads of the restitutive tapestry by bringing to the surface contents that have remained in the rear of restitution theory.[12] And, following from that, it is also to show that even in the case of texts considered paradigmatic of the liberal notion of restitution, such as Émile Durkheim's 1893 *The Division of Labor in Society*, it is possible to re-read them in a way that complicates the dominant meanings of restitution and their phantasmatic investments. Such re-reading requires attention to moments of hesitation and uncertainty in the authorial voice, to the internal tensions, contradictions or incongruities in the texts, and, sometimes, to what these texts are *not* saying.

* * *

The dominant theory of restitution in international politics and post-conflict studies concerns redress for expropriation that accompanied armed conflict, atrocity or/and systemic exploitation and impoverishment of minority groups, which is why restitution is conventionally classed within the rubric of reparative responses to justice.[13] As such, restitution is understood to reflect the 'legal obligations of a state, or individual(s) or groups, to reflect the consequences of violations' ('Reparations', ICTJ), together with such material and symbolic reparative measures as compensation,[14] rehabilitation, restoration of rights, invalidation of convictions, and others (De Greiff 2006a; Kyriakakis 2012: 113–39; May 2012b: 32–48; Bachmann and Frost 2015; Mégret and Vagliano 2017: 95–116). Recent scholarship has highlighted the connection between material expropriation of vulnerable groups during armed conflicts and the dynamics of expulsion and displacement; accordingly, international law and policy, and peace agreements, have linked the return of expropriated property with post-conflict return of displaced populations (Feldman, Geisler and Menon 2011; O'Mahony, Fox and Sweeney 2013; Carnoy 2014; 108–21; Chatty 2016).[15]

What that growing field of knowledge clearly shows is that restitution is not only a principle of transitional reparative justice and a corrective mechanism governing the re-acquisition of goods and resources, but also an established field of political practices, interventions and discourses, as well as is invested with symbolic, ritualistic and phantasmatic dimensions (Rotherham 2000; Cordial and Røsandhaug 2009; Ballard 2010; Lu 2018; 2019). To locate restitution solely within the purview of the procedures of formal justice is to reduce it to an inverse operation in relation to past offences within the rubric of returning to the *status quo ante* (cf. Williams 2007; Pantuliano and Elhawary 2009).[16] In contrast, by taking as its starting-point restitution as political action and performance that pivots upon the diverse and often competing ideas of return, or what I have called retrocessive and prelapsarian tropes of restitution, this book approaches restitutive theory as the interweaving of imaginaries and fantasies of undoing and repair within formal propositions about redress. What this approach reveals is that restitutive theorising, traced here across a variety of non-literary and literary texts, always involves envisioning – that is, *imaginatively calling into being* – particular kinds of post-conflict sociality, or, in the words of Steger and James (2013: 23), of patterning and convocation of 'the social whole' after political violence and atrocity.

What is characteristic of that imaginary restitutive formation in modern sociological and socio-legal literature is the motif of a *reversal event*. For instance, Antoine Buyse (2008: 131) uses expressions such as 'turn[ing] back the time' and 'magical wand' to capture the restitutive effect; John Torpey (2001; 2006) introduces the terminology of 'making whole [what has been smashed]'; and Berber Bevernage (2013) writes of 'irrevocable' past to capture the victim-centric subjective experiences of historical time. This retrocessive vernacular inadvertently echoes the first international ruling on restitution, issued in 1927 by the Permanent Court of International Justice in the *Chorzów Factory* case (*Germany* v. *Poland*), in that it was '[t]he essential principle contained in the actual notion of an illegal act . . . that reparation must, so far as possible, wipe out all the consequences of the illegal act and re-establish the situation which would, in all probability, have existed if that act had not been committed'. Commenting on the *Chorzów* ruling, Williams (2007: 1–2, 50) suggests that it affirmed restitution as 'not only . . . one possible form of reparations but as the preferred form', and that the language of *reversal* of wrongs connotes 'physically undoing (rather than simply mitigating) past harms . . . and restoring *status quo ante*' (see also Gray 1999). Here restitution as a *reversal event* is premised on an interjection 'so far as possible' (which, as I discuss in Chapter 3, is also important in Durkheim's conception of restitutive norms); this seemingly minor and innocuous qualifier is, I suggest, a pivot upon which the legal definition of restitution operates in relation to retrocessive and prelapsarian fantasies. On the one hand, it articulates an ideal of the subject's return to the original position; on the other hand, through the aforementioned qualifier ('so far as possible') it simultaneously presents this ideal as unachievable. The interjected phrase reveals what Derrida ([1976] 2016) has called 'the logic of the supplement' – while it appears to be secondary and auxiliary to the legal formulation of the restitutive ideal of the original state, and to merely *add* to it, refine, modify and condition it, the phrase is a form of substitution that troubles and destabilises the legal notion of restitution: it casts doubt on the restitutive possibility as a return to the original state at the very moment when it posits it.

The word 'restitution' in English comes from the Latin *restitutionem*, which is a nominalisation of the verb (*re-*)*statuere*, meanings 'to set up (again), to restore, to rebuild, to re-establish' (*Online Etymology Dictionary*). The image of firmly fixing an object in place, where, by assumption, it previously belonged, and which brings about an assumed state of equanimity, forms the backdrop of modern restitutive theorising. The Latin root *stō-* / *sistō-* derives from the Proto-Indo-European *stā-*, meaning 'to stand, set down, make, be firm'. The element *stā-* also forms two Greek words: *hístēmi* (ἵστημι), meaning 'put, place, cause to stand', and *stasis* (στάσις), meaning 'a standing still', and both connote placement, achieving stability and making firm.[17]

That etymology also hints at a semantic and philosophic link between restitution, restoration and reparation. In Chapter 4, I discuss Melanie Klein's use of the word *Wiederherstellung* ('restitution') in the description of her psychoanalytic observations of children in the 1930s and 1940s. In the English translations of her 1932 volume *The Psychoanalysis of Children*, the term *Wiederherstellung* appears as either 'restitution' or as 'restoration'. It has been a matter of a continuous polemic whether it carries associations with a reparative undertaking of Klein's key concept, *Wiedergutmachung*, reparation (cf. Sherwin-White 2018: 59–64). Outside the theory of psychoanalysis, *Wiederherstellung* has been defined as an act of making, procuring or producing again (*wieder herstellen*), with the aim of re-creating what has been subject to a destructive or erasing force. The Germanic root of *Wiederherstellung* also relates to the Proto-Indo-European *stā-*, and has associations to both place and movement. Interestingly, in Slavic languages the old term for 'restitution' (originating prior to the introduction of the Latin vocabulary) contains the lexical unit *nov* (the Old Church Slavonic *novъ*), meaning 'new', as in the Russian 'восстановление', the Polish 'odnowa' or the Bulgarian 'възстановяване'. This meaning of restitution as 'making new' (again) in nineteenth-century Slavic literature had perspicuous spiritual and religious collocations of a 'spiritual renewal' (cf. Greenleaf and Moeller-Sally 1998; Kalinowska 2004). Restitution as the action of positioning a thing in a *place* of its provenance, its original condition and its rightful belonging – a state from which the object had been removed or translocated – connotes in this context not only corrective and stabilising effects, but also a regenerative change of the subject–object relationship itself, with a distinctively Christian undertone (cf. Bowie 2003).

The 'Grammar' of Restitution

As a grammatical category, the action 'to restitute' can be both transitive and intransitive. In the first instance, it takes a direct object and captures an action of restoring that object to a subject that has been deprived of its prior ownership. In the second instance, it takes no direct object and describes the subject as simultaneously undertaking *and* undergoing the restitutive action.[18] As an intransitive verb, the restitutive action connotes that the subject *returns*, or *is returned* to, some prior status or condition (Zolkos 2017: 321–2). Legal theory of restitution has traditionally restricted its focus to restitution as a transitive action, that is, as a specific reparative measure that governs property return, or the reinstatement of the primary proprietary relationship. For instance, Birks (1989: 10) distinguishes between, on the one hand, 'restitution of a thing to a person', and, on the other hand, 'restitution of a thing or a person to an earlier condition' (though he also admits that these two meanings 'shade into one another').[19] However, while the literature on the international restitutive norm has included its consideration as, potentially, a *human* right, sometimes suggesting that restitution is the preferred redress mechanism for unlawful enrichment (see Williams 2007; Buyse 2008; Paglione 2008; Langford and Moyo 2010), less attention has been paid to legal interpellations into a position of the restitutive subject, that is, one that is returned, or restored, to the original status, position or condition.

These grammatical categories are operative in two international instruments on post-conflict reparations[20] and property return: the United Nations Basic Principles and Guidelines on the Right to a Remedy and Reparation for Victims of Gross Violations of International Human Right Law and Serious Violations of International Humanitarian Law;[21] and the United Nations Principles on Housing and Property Restitution for Refugees and Displaced Persons (the Pinheiro Principles).[22] The Pinheiro Principles address restitution in the context of conflict-related population displacement, defining it narrowly as a (transitive) process of returning illegally seized assets to their pre-conflict owners. In the Principles restitution thus means the restoration of 'any housing, land, and/or property of which [the refugees and displaced persons] were arbitrarily and unlawfully deprived' (Principle 2.1). Restitution is authorised through already existing human rights, including the right to privacy and respect for home, to peaceful enjoyment of possessions, to adequate housing and to freedom of movement (Principles 3–9). Situated within the grammatical outline of the transitive action of restitution, the Pinheiro Principles take as their aim exclusively the recovery and repossession of expropriated objects (land and dwellings), without further reference to the restitutive effects on post-conflict community-restoration and peace-building (or without putting into question the assumption about the universality of property). While the Principles do not exactly articulate restitution as a *human right* to property return, they are indicative, as Michelle J. Ballard suggests (2013: 12) of 'an emerging – albeit disputed – entitlement'.

In turn, the Basic Principles and Guidelines on the Right to a Remedy include restitution among a series of measures aimed at reparations provided to victims of rights violations, which also include compensation, rehabilitation, satisfaction and guarantees of non-repetition. The distinctive aim of restitution is to 'whenever possible,[23] *restore the victim to the original situation before the gross violations* of international human rights law or serious violations of international humanitarian law *occurred*' (Principle 18; emphasis mine). This definition expresses the restitutive sentiment I described earlier as a return to an original position – prior to and unsullied by violence. The principles articulating the right to a remedy envision restitution as both transitive *and* intransitive action, thereby broadening the understanding articulated in the 'Pinheiro Principles'. At hand is both the return of the misappropriated object to the victims of dispossession *and* the sense that the victims are themselves returned or restored, and thus somehow transformed, to an earlier proprietary status. As such, the Basic Principles and Guidelines define restitution as a specific *effect* on the subject, rather than as *a priori* defined norms, instruments and operations (see also Bassiouni 2006; Walker 2016).

<h3 style="text-align:center">CICATRIX, CORRECTION, RESURRECTION</h3>

According to Eglash (1959), the history of the concept of restitution concerns its development within three distinct disciplinary platforms or contexts, with little cross-fertilisation between them: legal, psychological and theological.[24] The legal tradition of restitution as a proprietary remedy emphasizes the action of 'giving up' and/or 'giving back' what one has gained in a situation identified as 'unjust enrichment' (Giglio 2004: 11–14; see also Birks 1989; Burrows 2011).[25] Restitution consists of acts of 'physical and legal restoration of wrongfully taken assets' (Williams 2012: 86).[26] Post-conflict and post-atrocity restitution is, on this account, differentiated from compensation, which is tied to the identification of the victim's loss, rather than the perpetrator's gain (De Greiff 2006b; Sabahi 2011; Walker 2016), and from those forms of reparative and remedial action where the 'symbolic' dimension is seen to prevail over the 'material' one, including rehabilitation, commemoration and apology (Galaway and Hudson 1972; Diner and Wunberg 2007; Waller 2016). Eglash (1959: 116) also suggests that as a legal norm restitution is characterised by both a 'repayment motive, distinct from revenge and retribution', and the 'use of authority or coercion, rather than an offender's desire [to restitute]'.[27]

In the legal tradition, the renewal of the prior relationship of belonging between the 'restituted thing' and the 'restituting person' has been confined to the institution of property and ownership.[28] One of the central premises of this book is that the formal juridical paradigm of restitution as a restoration of property relations has historically relied on the foundational epistemological distinction in Western law between 'persons' and 'things'. At the same time, in tracing the restitutive tropes and imaginaries in literary and philosophic texts, I also suggest that restitution can coincide with a curious moment of instability of that dichotomous distinction; perhaps, as in my earlier citation from *Woman in Gold*, even a confusion about who/what occupies the position of restitutive subject and object: who (what) is to initiate restitution?; what (who) is to be restituted? Roberto Esposito (2015; 2016) has argued that, following Gaius' *Institutions*, the Roman legal tradition has categorised its subjects as 'persons', who are capable of exerting control and mastery over inanimate 'things', including the right to use, derive profit from and to alienate them.[29] In turn, a thing has been viewed not as 'what it *is* but rather what someone *has*' (Esposito 2015: 18). From this perspective, *patrimonium* has meant both the totality of 'possessed "goods"' *and* a constellation of power relations between proprietaries and those devoid of property, signalling that there can be 'varying degrees of personhood' – and of 'thingness' (Esposito 2015: 23). The relevance of Esposito's insights for understanding the textual operations of restitution in the material at hand – and of its imaginary sub-cutis – is that Esposito not only alerts his readers to the foundational legal and epistemological status of the distinction between humans and inanimate objects, but that he also illuminates the political stakes of crossing the boundary between them. As Esposito argues (2015: 29), 'in ancient Rome nobody stayed a person for their whole life, from birth to death – everybody, for at least some period of time, passed through a condition not far removed from that of a possessed thing'. Talal Asad (2015) relates this conception of person-hood to the modern historical construct of the '"humanized" . . . modern self; [the] increasingly clear definition of the self as sole proprietor of itself, of self-ownership as the only basis for claiming to be the antithesis of thingness, something anyone may own'. In Chapters 1 and 3 I show that in theorising of restitution in their respective contexts (*ius post bellum* and legal sociology) Hugo Grotius and Émile Durkheim draw on the strong binary opposition of persons and material things and their fulfilment of the roles of restitutive subjects and objects. However, I also attempt to show that when approached through the heuristic prism of the prelapsarian and retrocessive imaginaries, these thinkers also complicate the binary opposition between persons and things in restitution due to their insight into the political effects of this dichotomy.

The spatial connotation of the act of restitution as *putting the translocated object in a place of its prior belonging*, is also noteworthy in regard to the figure of the hand as a synecdoche of such (restored) ownership. The 'place' to which the object is returned – in other words, the organ of re-appropriation – is the hand. The different expressions or modalities of ownership, including disposal, use and even potential destruction, are implied in the figuration of the hands; things are 'in the hands of [those] who possess them' and 'the hand that grasps and holds is one of the distinguishing features of the human species' (Esposito 2015: 28).[30] The use of hand figurations in restitutive theory is complex and ambiguous; it can denote – in line with Canetti, Irigaray and Esposito's critiques of appropriation[31] – the image of violence of grasping, seizing and claiming as exclusively one's own, and it can potentially invoke a set of different metaphors and associations, such as protection, custodianship, care and caress.[32]

Shifting now directions and disciplinary platforms from the legal domain to what Eglash calls 'psychological restitution', another context for the development of the concept of restitution has been the psychic mechanism of restoring a loss, or compensating for a loss, in contrast to both trauma theory and melancholia (see, for example, Abraham [1924] 1994; Loewald 1953; 1989; Lear 2014).[33] While trauma has been idiomatised as a *wound*, inflicted in the event of piercing through the subject's protective shield, which reveals the psyche's inability to absorb and process the 'overwhelming contents' at the time of the wounding, but only belatedly (Laplanche 1992; 1999; Caruth 1996; Luckhurst 2013; Pederson 2018), the figure of restitution is that of *cicatrix*. Cicatrix is the tissue that forms over a wound and subsequently develops into a scar; a sign of bodily healing and self-reparation. In psychoanalytic theory, one of the meanings of restitution has been the activation of defence mechanisms in response to guilt feelings; it has been also interpreted as the desire to restore relations, or to compensate for loss, by a way of atoning for destructive impulses and injurious desires (Rochlin 1953; Schnier 1957; Gottesman 1975/6). The *cicatrising effect* of restitution is akin to the 'reconstruct[ion] [of] a reality which has been lost' (Eglash 1959: 114); restitution re-establishes the subject's lost or abandoned libidinal investments in object representations (Moore and Fine 1990), or, in Freud's formulation ([1955] 2001), repairs the elapsed love of the world – the loss of *amor mundi*.[34]

In Judaic and Christian moral theology, restitution has been linked to atonement. In Judaism, the idea of restitutive endeavour correlates with the tradition of repentance for wrongdoing encompassed by the philosophy of *teshuvah* (Fackenheim 1994; Kravitz and Olizky 1995; Levine 2000; Celermajer 2009). In Christianity, restitution has been firmly placed within the tradition of commutative justice (Englard 2009). For example, St Thomas defined the event of *restitutio* as a corrective act in the course of which 'exact reparation as far as possible [was] made for an injury that [had] been done to another' (Slater 1911). The emphasis on the exactitude of the recompense is part of the Aristotelian 'arithmetic' approach to justice, which classifies restitution as a corrective response to wrongdoing, and places it within the framework of synallagma. The Greek word synallagma (συνάλλαγμα) means 'expressing reciprocal obligations' (*syn-* 'together with', and *allagma*, 'things taken in exchange'). In synallagmatic relations the parties are not defined by their social roles, but by the position they occupy vis-à-vis each other as contractually bound individuals: their paradigmatic examples are the roles of a 'debtor' and a 'creditor' (see Giglio 2004: 150). This suggests a symmetry between gain and loss. As Giglio puts it (2004: 150–1), wrongdoing causes 'an excess of gain on the agent's part and an excess of pain on the victim's part, for the one has done injustice and the other has suffered it', which in turn suggests that, just as in the Aristotelian arithmetic tradition, justice is 'a mean between loss and gain . . . The theory of mean requires that both the loss and the gain be nullified.'

That corrective function of justice is what Aristotle calls 'diorthosis' (διορθώσις), or 'rectification', meaning literally 'setting straight' or 'putting straight' that which is out of balance. St Thomas' *restitutio* exemplifies such diorthotic imaginary of justice that brings the victim back into his or her position prior to the offence. Specific to the tradition of corrective justice is the idea of sociality in a state of equipoise that becomes disturbed through acts of offence, and is subsequently recovered through acts of redress and recompense. Vladimir Jankélévitch (2005) used the expression 'myth of symmetry' to describe the idea of justice as a balance between injury and liability.[35] Jacques Derrida (1992) invokes the synallagmatic notion of restitution in his discussion of a gift: restitution is the figure of 'reciprocity, return, [and] exchange', against which he outlines the aporea of a gift that is not repaid or reciprocated (see also Derrida 2013: 351).[36] For Derrida, the restitutive logic assumes the equivalence of loss and gain (1992: 66–7). While restitution belongs to 'the economy of the proper, appropriation, expropriation, expropriation, and the coming or coming-back of an event . . .'; the gift '[does] not require restitution' (1992: 81) Rather, for Derrida the gift is the Aristotelian *dosis anapodotos*: 'giving [*dosis*] without something given in return [*anapodotos*]'.

Finally, I want to consider the meaning of restitution as a *return of life*; as a revival, re-animation, resurrection. The use of the word 'restitution' in this regenerative sense is scarce in contemporary English, but it has been preserved in Slavic and Germanic uses of the term in contexts ranging from conservation biology to building restoration. For instance, the German *Wiederherstellung* can be used in the sense of land revegetation (*Rekultivierung*); and the Polish word *restytucja* can be applied in broader contexts of conservationism as the restitution (regeneration) of endangered species (*restytucja gatunku*).[37] In Chapters 1, 2 and 4, I consider this restitutive trope of revitalisation more closely; it is evident that restitution as a return of abated aliveness is inseparable from its anthropocentrism: only humans are capable of restitution, and their belonging to the category of shared humanity is confirmed by that restitutive capacity. In discussing Hugo Grotius' incorporation of the Roman law of postliminium into his restitutive theory, I refer to the legal scholar H. C. Alexandrowicz, who defines restitution as a return to life of something that ceased to exist, namely, as 'the revival of a former condition of things' ([1969] 2017: 399). What is striking in Alexandrowicz's formulation is that the severance of the primary (proprietary) relation between persons and things is pictured as a kind of death, or as a loss or attenuation of aliveness. Subsequently, restitution invokes an event of rebirth or regeneration.

In his discussion of restitutive aspects of the creative process, Jacques Schnier (1957: 220) mentions the Dionysian celebrations of *Bouphonia*, the rite of 'ox-murder', which illustrates the link between restitution and resurrection. At the heart of *Bouphonia* was an event of bringing Dionysus back to life *after* he had adopted the form of an ox and was slain. The ritual operates upon a role reversal, and thus upon a semantic instability of the subject–object distinction; as the rite's participants 'emphatically denied their guilt in the murderous act', they eventually came to 'accuse . . . the axe used for the slaughter. Then, having partaken of the animal's flesh, they all acted out his resurrection' (Schnier 1957: 220). The point of the ritual was for the participants to 'act . . . and thus fantasize . . . themselves as the object which had previously been destroyed. By impersonating the destroyed animal, the dead were made to live again. Each person who wore the mask or animal skin felt he was, for the time being, the actual reincarnation of the dead . . .' (Schnier 1957: 220–1). In other words, the ritual emphasised the instability and uncertainty about *who was the subject* and *what was the object* of destruction and of subsequent rebirth and restitution. I have previously hinted at this uncertainty as a grammatical category of ambitransitivity in regard to two interwoven meanings of restitution, and I explore it at greater depth in Chapter 1 in the context of the law of postliminium and Hugo Grotius' theory of restitution. Schnier's reading of *Bouphonia* as a restitutive ritual operates upon a double substitution – first, the axe for the god Dionysus, and, next, of the axe's affordance for human culpability (cf. also Rotherham 2007). The return of the translocated material object into the place of its prior belonging opens up for the subject a passage to reunite with one's prelapsarian self, which, at the level of post-conflict imagination, means a phantasy of a polity *reconciled with itself*; returning to oneself from *before violence*.

RESTITUTION AND THE QUESTION OF POLITICAL SUBJECTIVITY

Tracing tropes and imaginaries of restitution in discourses on historical redress pivots on the identification of the key grammatical characteristic of restitution, namely, the transitive and intransitive actions of return: when the return of the lost object to the expropriated subject is at the same time an action upon the subjects themselves. This view of restitution resonates with the dual logic of dispossession as outlined by Athena Athanasiou and Judith Butler: speaking about the 'double valence' of dispossession, Butler argues that it means, first, 'what happens when populations lose their land, their citizenship, their means of livelihood, and become subject to military and legal violence' (Butler and Athanasiou 2013: 3, 4). At the same time, dispossession is also an important marker of her theory of subjectivity insofar as it signifies 'the limits of self-sufficiency' and 'establishes the self as social, as passionate, that is, as driven by passions it cannot fully consciously ground or know . . .' Deconstructing the link between these two modalities of dispossession (dispossession as deprivation of means and belongings, and dispossession as a 'negative' relational view of subjectivity), Athanasiou suggests that this 'double valence' of dispossession poses a problem – a problem that is political and linguistic, as well as philosophic – in that it relies on the assumption that dispossession is conceptually derivative of, and secondary to, the primary condition of (being in) 'possession' (Butler and Athanasiou 2013: 5). By adopting the language of restitution as the re-establishment of property rights to land, resources and cultural objects, the subject risks becoming inscribed within, and thus further legitimising, 'the exclusionary calculus of proprietariness in late liberal forms of power' (Butler and Athanasiou 2013: 7), which might have been a factor in their deprivation in the first place. Rather, it is 'important to think about *dispossession as a condition that is not simply countered by appropriation*, a term that re-establishes possession and property as the primary prerogative of self-authoring personhood' (Butler and Athanasiou 2013: 6; emphasis mine). Following recent critical post-colonial approaches to heritage and land return, I thus want to consider restitution as irreducible to the logic of re-appropriation and re-acquisition (see, for example, Bartels et al. 2017; Mbembe 2018; 2020; Sarr and Savoy 2018; Savoy 2018; Azoulay 2019).

One could perhaps speak of the 'double valence' of restitution, where, at one level, restitutive action denotes the political struggles of redressing past expropriations, and of countering the imperial and former colonial claims on confiscated objects in the present (objects that could be broadly categorised as spoils, grab and seizure, but that exceed the narrow definition of war plunder, cf. Azoulay 2019: 58–156). At another level, restitution is also a name for a distinctively political theory of subjectivity. While and Butler and Athanasiou's subject of dispossession affirms the 'constitutive self-displacement' in the emergence and consolidation of political subject positions, and prioritises moments of 'foreclosure and pre-emptive loss' (Butler and Athanasiou 2013: 5), the subject of restitution is tied to the return of the imaginary state or condition prior to the loss, and prior to violence, which references the goals of re-appropriation, as well as various other registers of 'making-good'. This is illustrated by the character of Maria Altmann from my opening paragraphs, who, through the re-possession of her family paintings, wants to be returned to the 'originary state' of childhood innocence, communion with her dead Jewish relatives, as well as revitalize the prospects of non-violent neighbourly co-existence of Jews and European host nations. And yet, as I show in tracing restitutive motives in Mary Shelly's *Frankenstein*, the subject of restitution also remains constitutively foreclosed in their attempts at undoing and reversal of past wrongs, and at the return of (to) the lost object. The terms 'aporetic restitution' and 'restitution without restitution' invoke restitutive theorising of subjectivity as something that emerges through the constitutive foreclosure of their desires, struggles and demands around the return of, or to, 'the original state'.

Idelber Avelar develops such an aporetic notion of restitution by situating it in conceptual proximity to mourning; he writes that '[a]ll mourning demands restitution' (Avelar 1999: 202). While mourning generally *does not* seek 'to restore the state prior to the loss', unless it morphs into melancholic fixations and attachments, as Avelar argues (1999: 202–3), it 'can run its course successfully only through a series of substitutive, metaphoric operations whereby the libido can reinvest new objects'. The idea of restitution as a 're-cathexis of object representations' is indebted to Freud's sketch of paranoid development of subject–object relations, which draws upon an autobiographic text by Daniel Paul Schreber, and where the final stage called 'restitution', or 'reconstruction', invokes the attempted counter-action to the previous withdrawal of libidinal investments in the world (Moore and Fine 1990: 169; see also Arlow and Brenner 1969). I return to this idea in Chapter 4, which analyses the psychoanalytic conceptualisations of restitution in the work of Sigmund Freud, Melanie Klein and others. For now, it is important to point out that Avelar's notion of restitution as an element and expression of mourning is a significant step in the direction of disconnecting restitution from the reinstatement of the status quo. On the contrary, from Avelar's perspective restitutive acts are moments of resistance to politics of substitution or exchangeability; rather than 'a transitory, ultimately surmountable phase of mourning', restitution is 'the very locus where mourning becomes an affirmative practice with clear political consequences', because 'the lost object [resists] any substitution [or] any metaphorical transaction' (Avelar 1999: 203).

RESTITUTIVE IMAGINARY

An important heuristic tool for the analysis of restitution in this book is the concept of social imaginary.[38] It includes restitutive norms and values, as well as institutional, discoursic and symbolic landscapes of repair, approached here as a political practice of envisioning, that is, of creating imaginal depictions of something that is not (yet) in existence. Imagining involves faculties of world-creating and pre-figuration. As Chiara Bottici argues (2014: 1), it entails 'the radical capacity to envisage things differently and construct alternative political projects', or, as Rabey puts it (2013: 2), it is 'the human impulse to transcend what exists in the direction of what might exist'. The Proto-Indo-European root of the Greek word for imagination, *phantasia*, is *bha* ('to shine'), which suggests semantic proximity between the action of imagining and the expressions 'bringing to light' and 'making appear' (*Online Etymology Dictionary*). In this book, imagination is defined as acts of granting social visibility to contents that have been occluded or concealed – 'subcutaneous' – in the liberal rights frameworks of restitution. To paraphrase Moira Gatens' idiom from *Imaginary Bodies* (1996: 126), such an approach focuses on the 'imaginary component' of restitutive theorising.

In tracing and analyzing restitutive motifs in selected literary, cultural, and socio-political texts, this book aims to sketch and scrutinise the process of *weaving of the modern restitutive imaginary*. As such, this book is part of the 'imaginal turn', or 'imaginal trend', in philosophy, championed by the work of Michèle Le Doeuff (1989; 2007; see also Deutscher 2001; La Caze 2003; 2008), and explored more broadly (see Gatens 1996; Pérez 1999; La Caze 2002; Naranch 2003; Geuss 2009; Bottici 2011; 2014; Murphy 2012). By acknowledging what Laurie E. Naranch (2003: 64) calls 'the power of images' to shape dominant conceptions of restitution and redress in ways that render the restitutive imaginary irreducible to the workings of ideology, this book signals the importance of visual idioms and pictorial references in political theorising. One example, which I explore in detail in Chapter 3, is the image of the clock, and specifically of turning-back the clock as a figure of self-reversing action, which has been central to Émile Durkheim's theory of restitutive law; another such example, discussed in Chapter 4, is the image of undoing by Freud's patient, Rat Man, who moved stones on the road, and then back to their original position, as an expression of the interspersed libidinal and aggressive impulses towards his fiancée. In these cases, the focus on images reveals the rich meanings affixed to restitution, which include the restoration of, or return to, the prelapsarian condition, and articulates the desire for a non-violent, paradisal neighbourly co-existence. Michèle Le Doeuff's approach of 'thinking in images' and 'iconographic investigation' counters the Western philosophical bias towards theoretical argument, and against imagery, depiction or figuration (1989: 1–2). Instead, Le Doeuff argues that a broad imaginary lexicon, including symbols, figures, metaphors, as well as scenes, stagings and spectacles, be recognised as valid philosophic productions. For Le Doeuff (1989: 8, 19) images and pictorial representations in theoretical texts are a 'sign that something important and troubling is seeking utterance'; they 'govern . . . the distinction between the thinkable and the unthinkable'. They can support the argument, articulate a difficulty or a friction within it, but they also can prove uncooperative, unruly, even destructive.[39] This book's focus on the restitutive imaginary, however, is not only about the use of images in social and political theory of reparation; rather, it also means that the politics of just redress for historical wrongs is itself *a work in imagination*. The concept and theory of restitution is, to paraphrase Gatens (1996: viii), '[a] product of subjective imagination [or] fantasy'.[40] Or, as Murphy argues, it 'informs and constrains the production of various forms of [political] subjectivity' and circumscribes 'domains of intelligibility and ethical entitlement' (Murphy 2012: 12).[41]

In this context, one also needs to note the close connection between the imaginary and fantasy. Laplanche and Pontalis ([1967] 1973: 314) explain the concept of fantasy (*Phantasie*) in psychoanalysis as an '[i]maginary scene in which the subject is a protagonist, representing the fulfilment of a wish . . . in a manner that is distorted to a greater or lesser extent by defensive processes'. Freud includes among fantasies such imaginary productions as 'day-dreams, scenes, episodes, romances or fictions'. Subsequently, the imaginary becomes 'inseparably bound with the primary function of phantasy, namely the *mise-en-scène* of desire – a *mise-en-scène* in which what is *prohibited* is always present in the actual formation of the wish' (Laplanche and Pontalis [1967] 1973: 314; emphasis in the original). The subject places themselves *within* the imaginary scene as a witness-participant, even in situations of dreams or fantasies where they appear to be conspicuously absent. Drawing on the psychoanalytic insights, the texts analysed in this book are approached from the perspective of staging of 'restitutive scenes'. Not unlike in the Dionysian *Bouphonia*, the intransitive dimension of restitution (where the subject of restitution becomes also its object) offers a way for the subject to become a witness-participant in restitution by *inserting themselves* within such scenes. Restitutive scenes consist of human participants, a location and material props. Drawing on the Freudian notion of *Verführungsszene*, 'the scene of seduction' (see [1896] 1962), I use the phrase 'restitutive scene' to signify a fantasised and affectively invested setting, in which the subjects of restitutive action not only procures the lost object, but also, through the act of re-acquisition, are themselves returned to the subject position prior to the event of violence. Bringing together the unlikely couple of 'seduction' and 'restitution' within the shared theatrical–psychoanalytic rubric of a scene allows me to tap into its semantic richness, which includes associations of spectatorship, imagination, fantasy and passive experience. In Laplanche's interpretation of Freud's *Verführungsszene*, seduction means an 'implantation' in the subject's unconsciousness of psychically unmetabolisable contents, or a 'foreign body' (1992; 1999). In relation to restitution, the question is what (and who) gets 'stuck', or is unprocessed, in this restitutive passage to 'the former condition of things', what kind of failure is unrestitutability, and what are its political effects?

*　*　*

Continuing with the theatrical–analytic terminology of scenes, this book offers not so much a comprehensive genealogy of restitution, but rather resembles a four-act play; as such, it stages, presents and sheds light on four restitutive scenarios in literature from the modern European period. The analysed texts represent different genres, and are involved in different disciplinary pursuits, creative moments and productions of knowledge; they do not stand for a homogeneous field of 'restitutive theory'. However, their differences notwithstanding, the texts included in the framework of this study bear a family resemblance in that they all participate in the unfolding of the European restitutive imaginary, and in its thematising as the undoing of wrongs, as a remedial and corrective practice, and as a return to a place, time or subjective condition prior to the event of violence.

With each of the four chapters I address a different 'problem' of restitution framed as the political desire for a prelapsarian return. The first such 'restitutive scene' is located in Hugo Grotius' writings on the conduct of war and on the *ante bellum* directives in his 1604/5 *De Iure Praedae* ([1901] 2001) and in the 1625 *De Iure Belli ac Pacis* ([1738] 2005). There are three elements in Grotius' restitution theory that I think are important for understanding the contents and logic of the modern restitutive imaginary. Situating restitution within the emerging international relations among the sovereign colonial states, Grotius, following in this regard Scholastic interpretations of the Aristotelian philosophy of justice, describes restitution as a corrective, compensatory and expletive justice response to wrongdoing. At the heart of restitution as such a corrective procedure of justice is the assumption that the wrongdoing becomes rectified, and that the dispossessed and injured subject's reinstatement to their previous proprietary position and status. Restitution is a legal and moral obligation that originates in Grotius' legitimisation of the institution of property, and as such in the close link that Grotius delineates between property and the subject's self-preservation. While Grotius articulates restitution in distinctively secular terms of natural law, he does weave into it the notion of return to an earlier state, which also denotes something unspoilt and unpolluted. While Grotius locates restitution within the domain of what he calls the 'justice of contracts' and within the synallagmatic relations between the offender and the victim, he also speculates about restitution in the context of the broader societal effects of dispossession.

The second aspect of Grotius' theory of justice concerns the relation between restitution and sociality. For Grotius restitution is one of the expressions of a *uniquely human* desire for social community (*appetitus societalis*); I discuss how one can broaden the Grotian conception of sociality beyond its dominant (liberal) interpretations as the right to self-preservation and non-infringement of individual bodily and proprietary entitlements in society. Following Benjamin Straumann's interpretation of the Ciceronian philosophy of *oikeiosis* in *De Iure Belli ac Pacis* as indicative of a richer, 'positive' and virtue-centric conception of sociality (2003–4), I suggest that restitution is envisioned in Grotius' work not only as a corrective procedure in situations of individual wrongdoing modelled on the 'justice of contracts', but also as a political act with broader curative and reparative social effects. Finally, I consider Grotius' connection between restitution and the Roman law of post-liminium (*ius postlimini*), according to which persons made captive under conditions of war were restored to their previous status when they re-entered the territorial jurisdiction of their homeland. The logic connecting restitution and postliminium is that they are both encompassed by the act of returning to 'the former condition of things' (Alexandrowicz [1969] 2017). This elucidates different, though overlapping, meanings of return at play in the modern restitutive discourse, including the return of expropriated objects to their previous owner; the subject's return as home-coming and repatriation; and the subject's return to a previously occupied position or condition.

The next restitutive scene is staged as an interlocution between Mary Shelley's *Frankenstein* and moral sentiment philosophers of the eighteenth century, and it regards the connection between the modern restitutive trope and reparation as premised on shared humanity. The problem that the Creature from *Frankenstein* illuminates is the conditional logic of restitution, which is open only to those who are already included in human society; animals, monsters and other non-humans do not partake in restitution. Joseph Butler and David Hume both argued that benevolence, understood as a human response to the suffering of others in ways that remedy and benefit them, was 'natural', instinctive, affective and congruent with the pursuits of self-interest. Asad (2015: 402) summarises this proposition as a gesture of '[r]eaching out compassionately to another's pain'. I argue that the concept of benevolence has a central place in the construction of prelapsarian desires in Shelley's novel. For Victor Frankenstein social benevolence is the organising ethical principle of his childhood both in terms of the direct experiens of his parents' modern model of parenting, and in being a child-witness to their public charity and philanthropy. It is the ideal of benevolent society that Victor betrays through his obsession with scientific knowledge, which becomes isolated from the question of its social effects and moral implications, and which he undermines by making the Creature. The Creature represents for the other protagonists humanity's 'radical outside'; he is both excluded from the benevolent society and divested of restitutive possibilities. While the Creature passionately desires to be the recipient of his creator's and Da Laceys' benevolent and compassionate affects, his monstrous condition prevents him from ever entering the 'benevolent relation' – not only does the Creature come to stand for a monstrous distortion of humanity, but he also never figures as a suffering being, and incites disgust and fear, not pity.

I depict the Creature as a 'figure of unrestitutability' because the possibilities of return, undoing and repair are barred for him by virtue of his constitutive exclusion from humanity. The Creature has nowhere to return and no prelapsarian state to recover; he is a necro-assemblage, a patchwork-like composition of cadaveric fragments, without a unified past and without the status of personhood. But he also cannot serve as a restitutive object for Victor, who desires to undo his 'act of inhumanity' (a phrase that I borrow from Joseph Butler) and return to the state *from before* his betrayal of society and abandonment of benevolence. The only kind of undoing that Victor comes up with is the killing of the Creature, but it is an act entirely devoid of sacrificial productivity, or, for that matter, of criminal responsibility (as such, the Creature is perhaps a good illustration of Giorgio Agamben's figure of the *homo sacer* (see 1998)). The Creature as a figure of unrestitutability leads to questions about who/what the contemporary 'unrestitutables' are; what exactly remains forbidden to them, and how these blocked or barred restitutions relate to prior exclusions from the category of humanity and from the 'natural' relations of benevolence.

The next restitutive scene is reconstructed in Émile Durkheim's 1893 *The Division of Labor in Society*, as well as in his later anthropological studies on punitive institutions and laws, which offers an exposition of the logic of restitution, both in terms of its differentiation from 'repressive norms' and in the context of the production of modern sociality. Durkheim theorises restitution in terms of the social effects of intensified division of labour in industrial societies, which is identifiable within the domain of law, and which consists of corrective and remedial response to wrongdoing that aims to do justice for, and to repair, the consequences of wrongdoing for the social fabric. Durkheim's key restitutive image is a clock that is turned back, as if expressing the underlying desires of the restitutive law to 'restore the past' to 'its normal state' ([1984] 2014: 88). Durkheim conceptualises restitution as a binary opposite of the categories of 'repressive law' or 'punitive law', which are said to characterise traditional societies, and which aim at making the wrongdoer suffer (either by imposing bodily pain on them, or by some kind of divestiture). This close nexus of repressive law, past wrongdoing and suffering has its origins in human passions, which Durkheim calls 'collective anger', that arise in response to the violation of the common systems of beliefs and values. It also means that political and juridical enactments of restitution, in opposition to the passion-infused repressive norms, become synonymous to a corrective and remedial response to wrongdoing, and are imbued with assumptions of non-violence and the absence of injurious desires. What Durkheim's binary taxonomy of remedial legal norms obscures – and this happens not coincidentally, as it were, but is due to the fact that restitutive law stands in a synecdochic relation to Durkheim's philosophy of modernity and modern sociality – are the political, and perhaps also ethical, stakes in reparative undertakings.

I then turn to two texts from Durkheim's later oeuvre in order to suggest that there are productive possibilities residing in reading Durkheim's work as internally heterogeneous, perhaps even as inconsistent, and in not taking too seriously the traditional sociological distinction between his 'late' and 'early' writings. 'Individualism and the Intellectuals' – an essay that Durkheim wrote in an attempt to highlight the political and moral stakes of the Dreyfus Affair, and which made him into a prominent *Dreyfusard* figure among the French public of the late nineteenth century – illuminates the ideological and affective link between restitution and the humanitarian idiom of 'suffering humanity'. The imperative of generating a remedial response to the suffering of others to whom one is not bound by kinship, but solely by the virtue of belonging to shared category of humanity, became for Durkheim the core element of the modern collective consciousness. This conceptual and philosophic link between restitution and humanitarianism suggests that the corrective and remedial workings of modern law – the undoing of wrongs – operates upon, and is enabled by, activation of humanitarian affects; what sets restitution in motion, is the extent to which such wrongs coincide with sites of suffering. The second text is Durkheim's work on the origins of property, which complicates the view of material objects and things from *The Division of Labor in Society* as incapable of forming generative social bonds. By proposing that the Western conception of private property erases its original relation to acts of consecration of objects for religious social functions, and that it renders material things incapable of investing persons with socially meaningful properties and characteristics, Durkheim potentially helps to re-imagine restitution of cultural objects. From this perspective, reintroduction of things into their provenance communities is not only about their return or re-homing, but also constitutes a political event of 'setting apart' and dedication, investing objects with capacity and affordance of participating in post-conflict sociality.

Finally, a selection of texts by psychoanalytic authors, including Sigmund Freud and Melanie Klein, on undoing, restitution and reparation, forms the fourth restitutive scene in this book. This chapter includes elaboration of the insights from psychoanalysis into theory of restitution alongside two non-identical, though overlapping, trajectories – the concept of retroactive annulment, or undoing (*Undgeschehenmachen*) and Klein's theory of reparative action – as well as into the discussion of *status quo ante*, which has been closely connected to the history of the concept of restitution. The first of these trajectories, restitution-as-undoing, concerns the temporal aspect of restitution as making 'unhappen' past actions or thoughts, with Freud's study of the Rat Man as a paradigmatic case of the dynamics of *Undgeschehenmachen*. I argue that these restitutive pursuits lie beyond reparative possibilities, because while the object's return or re-acquisition might be achievable, the psychic investments and desires attached to these returns are not. Contrasted with restitution-as-undoing is restitution-as-repair, which I align with the Kleinian conceptualisation of restitution: a reparative and curative undertaking, which follows the subject's destructive impulse towards the love-object. Instructive here is Klein's analysis of Maurice Ravel's 1925 opera *The Child and the Spells: a Lyric Fantasy in Two Parts* (with libretto written by Colette), where, after an initial explosion of injurious desires towards a range of animate and inanimate love-objects – all associated with the Kleinian 'nasty mother', the true target of infantile aggressiveness – the child embraces a reparative position by showing pity at the sight of a suffering animal. Through his remedial action, the child not only signifies the victory of restitution over the desire to destroy his others, but also affirms beyond doubt his belonging to the category of humanity, or as Klein puts it, is 'restored to the human world of helping' and '"being good"' ([1929] 2011: loc. 4942). In her discussion with Ella Freeman Sharpe about the psychic category of *status quo ante* that took place within the forum of the British 'Controversial Discussions' in the 1940s, Klein spoke about the subject's imaginary retrocession to a situation *prior to* frustration and destructive fantasies, and to the idealised state where the subject 'only loved'. I also bring into the discussion an earlier work by Joan Riviere, who presents *status quo ante* as an expression of the subject's refusal to submit to the psychoanalytic process; her theoretical–analytical intervention presents the psychoanalytic 'unrestitutable subject' as one that refuses 'to get better', and obstinately clings to the neurotic state.

I

IN DOMINUM PRISTINUM STATUERE: HUGO GROTIUS' THEORY OF RESTITUTION AND THE RETURN OF THE FORMER CONDITION OF THINGS

One of the earliest modern elaborations of the restitutive principle is found in the writings of Hugo Grotius (1583–1645). While Grotius drew strongly on the Thomistic notion of reparative response to sin in conceptualising restitution as correction of wrongs,[1] he articulated the restitutive norm not within a moral or theological framework per se, but as an international legal principle regarding the conduct of warfare and relations between sovereign states. In this chapter I focus on Grotius' theory of restitution in his 1625 magnum opus, *De Iure Belli ac Pacis* ([1738] 2005), which Grotius composed during his imprisonment and exile from the Netherlands, following his trial for his anti-clerical politics (Israel 1995: 447–9).[2] *De Iure Belli* elaborated the principles of just war, which he derived from natural law (*ius naturale*) and from the customary law of nations (*ius gentium*) (Tuck 1993; 1999). I also consider Grotius' theoretical discourse on restitution, *De Indies*, which was composed in 1604, and published in 1868 as *De Iure Praedae* (*Commentary on the Laws of Prize and Booty* ([1901] 2001)). Upon its belated publication, that work was interpreted largely in the context of nineteenth-century civilisational and humanitarian discourses, which underpinned the early attempts at developing internationally binding norms of 'humane warfare' (Blom 2014).[3] The context of *De Iure Praedae* was the need to develop a legal–theoretical justification for the capturing of a Portuguese merchant ship by the Dutch East India Company's fleet in 1603. It included Grotius' famous formulations of the doctrine of *mare liberum* (Dumbauld 1970; Tuck 1993; 1999; van Ittersum 2006).[4]

Putting for now aside the significant differences between *De Iure Belli* and *De Iure Praedae*,[5] both texts start with an elaboration of foundational principles of justice from which Grotius derives a distinctively subjective theory of rights and freedoms.[6] The Grotian conception of rights as inviolable entitlements and liberties of a person – rather than as a descriptor of conduct concurrent with measures of justice – became, in the words of Knud Haakonssen (1985: 240), 'one of the cornerstones of modern individualism in political theory'. By arguing that nations, not unlike individual persons, 'are motivated by [the principles of] survival and self-interest', Grotius extended the conception of right-holders from persons to sovereign states (Fitzmaurice 2014: 88; see also Tuck 1993; 1999). The 'natural liberty' was expressed through the dual freedom to act and to acquire, to use and retain property according to one's will. Grotius also confirmed the unrestrained action and possession as a prerogative when he wrote in *De Iure Praedae* ([1901] 2001: 28): 'God created man *autexousious* [αυτεξούσιος] "free and *sui iuris*", so that the actions of each individual and the use of his possessions were made subject not to another's will but to his own', and, further, 'liberty in regard to actions is equivalent to ownership in regard to property'.

The shared premise of *De Iure Belli* and *De Iure Praedae* is not only that sovereign states, just like individual citizens, have legal rights and duties, but also that armed conflict is a 'law-enforcement procedure' (Dumbauld 1970: 31). As such, Grotius occupies an intermediary position between the belief that 'everything was allowable [in war]' and the belief that 'nothing was' (Dumbauld 1970: 75). Grotius argued that wartime acquisition of enemy property (spoils and booty) was a justified act when it was part of a compensatory and corrective mechanism in response to an *earlier* injustice – in the case of the Dutch capture of the Portuguese ship in 1603, Grotius argued that it was a corrective response to a prior wrongdoing, namely, the Spanish and Portuguese attempts to monopolise the commercial colonial relations in the East Indies and their claim to territorial sovereignty over coastal waters ([1901] 2001: 240–2). The consequence of the Grotian logic was that *war was considered to be continuous with law*, and that it was invested with redressive and punitive authority (cf. Bull, Kingsbury and Roberts 1992). Acts of aggression could be legitimately waged in pursuit of compensation for endured losses.

Grotius characterises restitution as a form of compensatory justice, following in this regard the late Scholastic thinkers and their adaptation of the Aristotelian taxonomy of justice.[7] Another important term used to describe the Grotian conception of restitution is 'expletive justice' (Geddert 2014; Koskenniemi 2019). The adjective 'expletive' invokes an image of completing something that is lacking, or levelling something that is out of balance; it is a 'completive' or 'rebalancing' act of justice-making (from the Latin *explativus*, 'serving to fill out'). Within the tradition of compensatory and expletive justice, restitution became a matter of rectification of past wrongs, rather than of allocation, and it pertained not to 'communal affairs', but was 'peculiar to the individual' (Grotius [1901] 2001: 26). Grotian restitution has remained indebted to the depictions of society as an equilibrium, whereby wrongdoing produces social and ethical instability or imbalance. The return of misappropriated things to their original owners also brings about the subject's return to the moral and legal equilibrium *from before* the wrongdoing. For Grotius, the recovery of dispossessed objects was synonymous with the reinstatement of ownership (cf. Nichols 2018).

Furthermore, the notion of spoils of war is important in considering the category of restitutive objects in the Grotian theory of legitimate warfare because it illuminates the exceptions to the workings of post-conflict restitutive logic. For Grotius, the practice of booty-taking during warfare that meets standards of just conduct *does not* give rise to post-conflict restitutive demands (cf. May 2012a; 2012b; 2014). Rather, as in the case of the acquisition of the Portuguese ship and cargo by the Dutch fleet, such expropriative acts can be legitimate, honourable and expedient, and can themselves be measures of corrective justice, that is, a form of restitution. Grotius follows the restitutive logic of Francisco de Vitoria outlined in the 1532 *De Indies et De Iure Belli*, who distinguished between 'immovables' (land), subject to post-war restitution, and 'immovables', which were not necessarily subject to restitutive or compensatory demands (Pagden 2012: 44–5; May and Edenberg 2013: 5). In his contribution to the just war debates on the legitimacy of colonial conquest, Vitoria argued that '[a]ll movables vest in the seizor by the law of nations, even if in amount they exceed what will compensate for damages sustained' (cited in Meron 1998: 50). Grotius' discussion of the law of postliminium – the restoration of rights upon return – in Book III of *De Iure Belli* is premised on a strong distinction between recoverable and non-recoverable things, as well as between those individual and state subjects who can claim postliminium and those who cannot.[8]

The Grotian construction of the restitutive subject as part of his theory of legitimate warfare rests on an exclusion. In post-medieval Europe infidels, pirates and barbarians were barred from the possibility of claiming restitution (Tuck 1993). They could be *expropriated with impunity*; for instance, in regard to infidels, Henry of Segusio wrote that they were 'by definition sinners' who 'forfeited any right to hold property or political office' (cited in Tuck 2003: 150; see also Blom 2014). Grotius was a critic of the Spanish and Portuguese conquest of the native populations of the East Indies – and an advocate of the commercial imperialism practiced by the Netherlands, which he saw as reciprocally beneficial for the colonising nations and the colonised groups alike. At the same time, especially in his later writings, Grotius adopted the language of 'barbarism' and the theological narratives of the early modern era that equated 'barbarism' with 'sins against natural law', namely, cannibalism and incest. Grotius also advocated for the right of states 'to inflict violence on barbaric people' (Tuck 1999: 89). These 'non-recoverable things' and 'unrestitutable subjects' were exempt from the logic of proprietary return; their expropriation did not count as dispossession and did not cause an injury that was in need of diorthotic response. Importantly, just as infidels, pirates and barbarians were excluded from making restitutive demands, so were those subjects whose belonging to civilised humanity was compromised – be it through their non-participation in the community of Christian faith, or their banishment from law or their inhuman acts. As such inhuman, or not-fully-human, subjects they affirmed the link between restitutive justice and humanity, or human-ness, be it from its outside.

In what follows, I analyse Grotius' theory of restitution in natural and positive law from three angles: (1) the location of restitution within the tradition of compensatory justice; (2) the link between restitution and sociality, which in turn leads to the question of whether the norm of restitution is primarily a function of the law of inoffensiveness and the principle of self-preservation, or whether it invokes a more substantial and positive articulation of post-conflict sociality; and (3) the discussion of post-war recovery of things as a kind of 'revival' of the ancient Roman law of postliminium. As such, I suggest that Grotius' theory of restitution contributes three elements, or three motifs, to the modern restitutive imaginary: (1) that the work of restitution is to correct and compensate for the injustice of expropriation; (2) that restitution invokes the effect of re-balancing the sociality put out of balance by violence and wrongdoing, and (3) that restitution operates upon a reversal to a state prior to the conflict, which symbolically 'makes-unhappen' the wrongdoing. These prelapsarian and retrocessive tropes are loosely interwoven within the broader preoccupation with restitution as a political fantasy of undoing and renewal, whereby the return of property (*res privatis*, the privately ownable things) allows the subject to return to the original state.

THE CORRECTIVE AND COMPENSATORY JUSTICE OF RESTITUTION

In the 'Prolegomena' of *De Iure Praedae* Grotius calls restitution a 'task' of compensatory justice, which has as its goal 'preservation [of] good' and 'correction [of] evil' ([1901] 2001: 26). That twofold goal of restitution derives from two natural law axioms (*leges*), namely, that '[e]vil deeds must be corrected [*malefacta corrigenda*]' and that '[g]ood deeds must be recompensed' ([1901] 2001: 26). This dual articulation of restitution in natural law invokes a link between the Scholastic theorising of *restitutio* for wrongdoing and the Greek word for 'retaliation' or 'reprisal', ντιπεπονθός, which invokes 'counterweight' or 'reciprocity', the Latin root *talio* meaning 'exaction of payment in kind', and should be considered in Grotius' framework of just war philosophy (cf. Winkel

2005). 'In accordance with this form of justice', Grotius argues ([1901] 2001: 29–30), 'he who has derived gain from another's good deed repays that exact amount to the benefactor whose possessions have been diminished', while at the same time 'he who has suffered loss through the evil deed of another received the exact equivalent of that loss from the malefactor whose possessions have been increased'.

The Scholastic theological notion of restitution is commutative: it framed justice as mutuality and interchangeability of obligations, emphasised the exactness of reparations, and saw the just as the mean between loss and gain. It draws on the corrective, or arithmetic, model in the Aristotelian philosophy of justice, where 'position[s] of the parties [are] not established by reference to their particular role as members of society' (Giglio 2004: 150), or, as Grotius puts it ([1901] 2001: 27) in *De Iure Praedae*, considered as 'parts of the whole'. Rather, commutative justice corrects the *'excess of gain* on the agent's part and an *excess of pain* on the victim's part . . .' (Giglio 2004: 150; emphasis mine). Two sixteenth-century thinkers of late scholasticism, Francisco de Vitoria (1483–1546) and Dominicus Soto (1494–1560), contributed to this moral theological formulation of restitution. Francisco de Vitoria argued in *De Iustitia* that '[to] make restitution is *to reinstate the previous owner [to] his position* [*restituere est in dominum pristinum statuere*]' and that restitution aims 'to achieve equality, which is what pertains to commutative justice' (cited in Giglio 2004: 158; emphasis mine). Dominicus Soto wrote in *De Iustitia et Iure* that '[r]estitution implies the giving back of the very thing which is unjustly subtracted or detailed: giving back is necessary because it is indeed an act of commutative justice' (quoted in Giglio 2004: 160).

In *De Iure Praedae* Grotius follows the commutative logic of restitution as a simultaneous act of the nullification of unjust profit *and* correction of the injurious consequences of wrongdoing. Insofar as 'unjust gain' and 'suffered loss' are correlative categories, pivotal in restitutive justice is the image of re-establishing equilibrium by means of neutralising that gain and loss. In both the case of the 'obligation *ex contractu*', which arises from the breaking of the contract, and of the 'obligation *ex delicto*', which arises from wrongdoing, it becomes a matter of 'true justice', as Grotius puts it ([1901] 2001: 26, 27), that the expropriated thing is returned.[9] With this, Jeremy Seth Geddert (2014) argues, Grotius locates restitution within the tradition of strict, or expletive, justice, which is based on 'calculative reasoning and backward-looking orientation', as well as on 'reciprocal action'.[10] Expletive justice of restitution, which Geddert (2014: 576) contrasts to attributive, and more political, form of justice of punishment, operates upon the assumption of 'perfect rights and duties [which] can be fully . . . implemented'. The expletive justice articulation of restitution is conspicuous in *De Iure Belli ac Pacis* in Grotius' use of the Aristotelian notion of transactional justice (συναλλακτική), or the 'justice of contracts': 'if I have a Right to demand Restitution of my Goods, which are in the Possession of another, it is not by virtue of any Contract, and yet it is the Justice in question that gives me such a right' ([1738] 2005: 142–3, I.VIII.1). For Grotius, thus, restitution forms the basis of a legal and moral obligation, which derives from the institution of property (cf. Rutherforth [1754–6] 1832).

While in the 'Prolegomena' the commutative definition of restitution is strictly differentiated from matters of just allocation, Grotius also admits that sometimes 'things properly pertaining to the parts . . . affect the whole' ([1901] 2001: 27). It is thus a matter of a collective concern that the twofold function of restitution, that is, the preservation of good and the correction of evil, should result in 'proportionate satisfaction' because – and here Grotius resorts to bodily and medical metaphors to enforce his analogy between the individual human body and the collective political body – restitution ensures that the whole of society remains 'sound'. It guards the social body 'against contagion' ([1901] 2001: 27). While restitution is an act of corrective justice in a situation of 'individual injury', which Grotius contrasts to 'universal injury', Grotius also blurs somewhat that distinction when he writes that 'an injury inflicted upon one individual is the concern of all' ([1901] 2001: 30). The Grotian restitution includes also a punitive dimension in that it inevitably demanded that the perpetrators of wrongdoing should suffer a loss. Here again, Grotius uses a medical metaphor, comparing the system of restitutive justice with a physician who 'inflict[s] pain' upon the body, motivated by wider 'considerations of health', expressing a Thomistic sentiment whereby restitution both rectifies the injury suffered by the victim *and* offers a redeeming pathway for the wrongdoer.[11]

This implicit redemptive dimension of restitutive action, situated within the framework of just war philosophy, allows Grotius to connect restitution with a form of punishment for wrongdoing called 'chastisement [*castigatio*]'. Deriving 'chastisement' from the corrective interventions of 'admonition' (Taurus) and of 'setting straight' (Plato), Grotius defines it as a 'curative procedure', which operates through 'the application of opposites' ([1901] 2001: 27; see also Tuckness 2010: 722–3). It involves 'an attempt to correct the particular individual punished and also to render him more useful to humanity' ([1901] 2001: 27). The Grotian use of chastisement (*castigatio*) to designate punitive action undertaken for corrective purposes incorporates the notion of *castus*, making pure, or achieving purity through punishment, and the Middle English word *chastien*, which means 'to inflict pain'. The Grotian link between restitution and *castigation*, and the double etymology of 'chastisement' brings to the surface two meanings that largely disappear from the modern theory of restitution: the desire for a pure or pristine condition *and* the emphasis on bodily pain and proprietary loss as restitutive means. Among different acts of chastisement Grotius includes the wrongdoer's divestiture of property in order to 'remedy the effect of excessive [material] gain' and infliction of pain as a correction of the 'condition arising from an excess of pleasure' (1901] 2001: 27). The notion of 'excess' (of gain or of pleasure) as a marker of injustice in Grotius' elaboration of corrective procedures of justice is another Aristotelian trait in *De Iure Praedae*: justice is imagined as a arithmetical medium, and 'excesses' and 'defects' are deviation from the just medium.[12]

The two laws (*leges*) of compensatory justices in *De Iure Praedae* – the preservation of good and the correction of evil – are derived from rules (*regulae*), which are axiomatic sources of specific requirements of conduct, and the 'seemingly uncontentious primary principles [containing] propositions about the nature of law' (Tuck 1983: 51). The rules validate and authorise the laws. One such rule derives from the connection between natural law and the divine commandment to humanity. Grotius elaborates this through an etymological discussion of law, *ius*, or *iussa* – 'things commanded' and 'secret formula[e]' (1901] 2001: 21) – which is what he calls in *De Iure Praedae* the 'primary law of nature', and, in *De Iure Belli ac Pacis*, the 'divine volitional law'. In the natural law framework this 'commanded thing' is not revealed prophetically 'through oracles and supernatural portents', but it manifests 'in the very design of the Creator', that is, in the natural order of the world, including the human moral and rational faculties (1901] 2001: 21).

Natural law grounds the principle of self-preservation, which Grotius likens to self-love, and which he sees as operative among humans and non-humans: 'all things in nature are tenderly regardful of self, and seek their own happiness and security', Grotius writes in *De Iure Praedae* (1901] 2001: 21; see also van Gelderen 2011). For that reason, he argues that 'all duty . . . consists . . . in those things which in some way pertain to self', and he classifies such 'things' as either internal or external to the body, adopting in this respect Plato's distinction between two concerns of justice – 'the care of the body and the possession of property' (1901] 2001: 21).[13] The principle of self-preservation is the first precept of the law of nature listed in the 'Prolegomena', and it consists of the right to '. . . *defend [one's own] life*' and to shun that which threatens to prove injurious' ([1901] 2001: 23; emphasis in the original). Analogous to the law of self-preservation is the law of appropriation, which permits the subject to '*acquire for oneself, and to retain, those things which are useful for life*' ([1901] 2001: 23; emphasis in the original). As such, Grotius assumes that certain kinds of property have a direct bearing on the subject's capacity for self-preservation insofar as they consist of 'that which is important for the conduct of life', and makes the law of self-preservation and the law of appropriation as correlative and synergetic.

Grotius interprets the fact that humans are embodied beings ('corporeal entities') as a sign of the capacity to be affected by other (human and non-human) bodies, in ways that he classifies as either beneficial or injurious. That capacity to be affected translates the laws of self-preservation and appropriation into modes of being with others that can be gestured at through the reference to contemporary notions of inter-corporeality and inter-affectivity as the underpinning of human sociality. Grotius imagines the natural laws guaranteeing people protection from harm and the prospects for acquisition of goods as a relational movement of bodies: he argues that the law of self-preservation is put into practice as 'the repulsion of one body from another' – and the law of appropriation as 'the attachment of one body to another' ([1901] 2001: 23). This effectuates two aspects of sociality, and two modes of being in the world, whereby the subject exercises their rights to self-preservation and to appropriation through overlapping actions of warding off and acquisition, or attraction, of other bodies ([1901] 2001: 23). The seizure of things can be a legitimate execution of the right of appropriation in the circumstances when the institution of property imbricates with guarantees of security and life-sustenance, that is, in regard to things 'necessary to being', rather than things 'necessary only to well-being' (in other words, things that guarantee the safety of life, rather than comfort). The category of 'things' includes biological and zoological entities; animals and plants are for Grotius such first 'safety objects' that guarantee life and preservation because they are 'gifts [bestowed by God] upon the human race'. Their appropriation is the necessary condition for the application of self-preservation principle; Grotius writes that 'such gifts could be turned to use only through acquisition of possession by individuals' and that 'the act of taking possession [*possessio*], [is] the forerunner of use [*usus*], and subsequently of ownership [*dominium*]' ([1901] 2001: 23). While self-preservation and self-love are inferable principles of the natural world, what makes them distinctively and exclusively human is what Grotius terms the 'social impulse [*socialis motus*]', which gives rise to pact-making (τὰ συμβόλαια) and contracturalism, namely, '[the] reciprocal acts and sentiments' and 'the intermingling of one's own goods and ills with the goods and ills of others' ([1901] 2001: 23). The natural principle of sociality of human beings, *oikeiôsis* (οἰκέωοίν) means that the subjective rights to safety and to acquisition of things have corresponding prohibitions in *De Iure Praedae*: the law of inoffensiveness ('[l]et no one inflict injury upon his fellow') and the law of abstinence ('[l]et no one seize possession of that which has been taken into the possession of another') ([1901] 2001: 23). The result of the law of inoffensiveness is the achievement of peaceful coexistence ('life is rendered secure'). The effect of the law of abstinence is that 'distinctions of ownership arise, together with the . . . concept of Mine and Thine' ([1901] 2001: 25).

The compensatory and commutative justice of restitution arises at the interstices of these four laws. While restitution is a direct remedial action in response to the violation of the law of abstinence, it is also relevant for the law of inoffensiveness. Grotius elaborates at length in *De Iure Belli ac Pacis* that since (legitimate) warfare is an extension of peaceful practices of executing rights and redressing wrongs, restitutive demands can provide justifiable reasons for military hostility. Richard Tuck links the strategy of legitimising offensive warfare through appeal to restitutive claims to Augustine who in *Quaestiones in Pentateuchum* argued that the 'revenge of injuries caused when the nations or *civitas* with which war is envisaged has either neglected to make recompense for some illegitimate act committed by its members, or to return what has been injuriously taken' (cited in Tuck 1999: 55). In *De Iure Praedae* Grotius makes an argument that some acts of seizure, namely, *rem hostile*, or 'enemy property' (prize and booty taken during and the warfare), do not legitimise restitutive demands in situations when the expropriative acts derive justification from the other *leges*, including the laws of self-preservation and appropriation.[14] If state hostilities meet the criteria of 'just war', booty-taking is permitted; just as 'killing in war [was] not a murder, so the capture of enemy property [was] not robbery' (Dumbauld 1970: 43). 'Prize' or 'booty' are defined as 'the property of him who seizes it in just war, [and which is] taken not only from the goods of him who fights unjustly, but also from those of all his subjects (women and children not excepted) until complete satisfaction has been given to the just belligerent for that which is due him' (Grotius [1901] 2001: 103).

From this perspective, the Dutch confiscation of the Portuguese merchant ship was an act of legitimate appropriation, rather than an injurious act of dispossession in need of redress, because it undermined prior (illegitimate) claim by the Spanish and Portuguese colonial powers to trade monopoly with the East Indies. Grotius argued that such monopoly would be a violation of the law of appropriation, because it disrespected other's claims to acquisition, preservation and use of 'objects important to life', in regard to both other colonial nations and to the native populations. Grotius argued that since 'the Portuguese . . . prevented the Dutch from trading freely with whatsoever East Indian nations the latter might choose for their trade', they were obliged 'to make reparation for all of the profits lost to the Dutch' ([1901] 2001: 226). He also condemned the violence against the native East Indies populations perpetrated by the Portuguese ([1901] 2001: 154–6; see Tuck 1983; Ittersum 2010; van Gelderen 2011; Fitzmaurice 2014).[15] The confiscation of enemy property was not an act of wrongdoing, but a way of enforcing rights and correcting prior violations of the natural law tenets, and it constituted a rightful transfer of property. It was a form of restitution in accordance with the proposition that the goal of just war was the implementation of judicial remedies. For Grotius 'the greater the estimate of the loss [suffered by the enemy], . . . the further one may proceed in seizing spoils by way of reparation without resorting to additional judicial measures; for [the] very attempt to obtain reparations is . . . one of the consequences of war' ([1901] 2001: 105). The seized cargo was not a Dutch 'profit', but 'reparation[s] for [incurred] losses' ([1901] 2001: 271).[16] Such conceptualisation of prize and booty exempts some acts of appropriation within the normative framework of just war from restitutive demands for a return to a prior proprietary position; rather, these 'unrestitutable' losses were for Grotius acts of corrective justice.

Restitution, Sociality, *Oikeiôsis*

In *De Iure Belli ac Pacis* restitution features as one of the natural law principles derived from the uniquely human inclination towards social life (*appetitus societalis*), which Grotius describes as a 'care of maintaining society'. *Appetitus societalis* has five aspects, roughly corresponding to the contents of the *leges* in *De Iure Praedae*: '[a]bstaining from [that] which is another's; . . . the Restitution of what we have of another's, or the Profit we have made by it, the Obligation of fulfilling Promises, the Reparation of a Damage done through our own Default, and the Merit of Punishment among Men' ([1738] 2005: 86, VIII). The anthropological faculty of sociability, or what Grotius calls the 'Desire of Society', is a disposition to 'live with those of [our] own Kind, not in any Manner whatever, but peaceably, and in a Community regulated according to the best of [our] Understanding' ([1738] 2005: 79, 81, VI; cf. van Gelderen 2011).[17] By linking restitution to the law of peaceful coexistence – defined in *De Iure Belli* as a 'natural' and uniquely human (*homini proprium*) characteristic, which no other animate beings displayed – Grotius has assigned to the restitutive principle a role in the formation and preservation of non-violent sociability. For Grotius, all societies must respect norms of inviolability of a person and of property (cf. Tuck 1983: 59–60). In contrast, 'if every Man were to seize on the Good of another, and enrich himself by the Spoils of his Neighbour, human Society and Commerce would necessary be dissolved' ([1738] 2005: 184–5, II.I.3).

The claim of natural human sociability has been interpreted as a counterbalance to the other strong inclination that Grotius identifies as the pursuit of 'private Advantage'. As such, some scholars have also argued that the philosophic category of the Grotian *appetitus societalis* should be interpreted in minimalist terms that align with the political liberty paradigm of non-infringement. Making an argument for the recognition of the continuities between Grotius' and Hobbes' political philosophic projects, Richard Tuck (1983: 57) has stressed '[the] minimalist character of the [Grotian] principles of sociability'. In his reading, 'sociality' equals collective guarantees of 'protection and comfort', as well as prohibition against inflicting harm on others, but does not invalidate self-interest as 'the primary and over-riding principle' of human behaviour (Tuck 1983: 57; see also Tuck 1993: 197–9). Knud Haakonssen (1985: 241–2) has proposed that the exposition of Grotius' ostensibly Aristotelian position on natural human sociability in *De Iure Belli* should be read side-by-side with its starkly non-Aristotelian interpretation as non-infringement of others' subjective right to bodily and proprietary safety. Thus, Haakonssen concludes that 'living socially' meant for Grotius 'no more than living without injuring the rights of others' (1985: 241).[18] In this interpretation of *appetitus societalis*, restitution is a corrective response to the violation of the rule of proprietary inviolability, closely tied to the principle of personal and bodily inviolability, and the restitutive principle is relevant for the formation and preservation of sociability to the extent that it ensures social respect for the institution of private property.

In contrast, Benjamin Straumann (2003–4; 2015) suggests that Grotius' idea of sociability is more robust and more substantial than a statement of negative rights and the inviolability of property. Rather, Straumann draws attention to the importance of the concept of *oikeiôsis* (οἰκέωοίν), or the Latin terms *conciliato* and *commendatio*, in the Grotian elaboration of sociability, and, with it, to the hitherto insufficiently recognised influence of Cicero, and Stoicism more broadly, on the argumentation in *De Iure Belli* (see also Brooke 2012). The Stoic conception of *oikeiôsis* means making, or perceiving, something as one's own, or being at home in relation to other animate or inanimate beings. Gisela Streiker (1996: 281) defines it as 'recognition and appreciation of oneself as belonging to oneself' (see also Brennan 2005: 154–68; Frim 2019). In English, *oikeiôsis* has been translated as 'appropriation', or, somewhat less often, as 'familiarisation'; it has also been contrasted to the philosophic concept of *allotriôsis*, or 'alienation' (the root οἶκος means 'house' and οἰκιακός means 'habit') (Cassin et al. 2014: 727–8). Straumann (2003–4: 42) makes a distinction between *oikeiôsis* as, on the one hand, 'the recognition and appreciation of oneself as belonging to oneself . . . observed in all living creatures, and . . . reflected in the impulse for self-preservation', and, on the other hand, its anthropological interpretation as a 'human recognition and appreciation of the human race as belonging to the individual human being'. In the Ciceronian tradition *oikeiôsis* could mean the self-preservative impulse, as well as the virtue ethics of intrinsic good, whereby achieving harmonious relation with nature comes to mean acting in accordance with that good. Accordingly, Straumann (2003–4: 49–51) suggests that Grotius' use of *oikeiôsis* as the basis of human sociability is indicative of the expansion of his political conception of rights and liberties, and of his theory of restitution specifically, beyond the principle of self-preservation as love of the self and in the direction of the 'superior good' (*honestum*), which Barbeyrac translated as 'decent' or 'commendable' actions ([1738] 2005: 180–1, n.5). Straumann also notes a resonance between the way that Grotius conceptualised the commendable action (*honestum*) and the writings of the Stoic philosopher Hierocles, who had included *oikeiôsis* in his philosophy of 'appropriate acts' (καθήκοντα) and duties. Such 'appropriate acts', according to Hierocles, develop concentrically from self, the family, tribal groupings, to encompass the more abstract categories of humanity (cf. Haakonssen 1985: 244; Frim 2019).

In chapter II of *De Iure Belli* Grotius adopts Cicero's distinction between, on the one hand, the 'First Impressions of Nature' and 'Knowledge of the Conformity of Things with Reason'. The former means the 'Instinct whereby every Animal seeks its own Preservation, and loves its Condition, and whatever tends to maintain it, [and] avoids its Destruction, and every Thing that seems to threaten it' ([1738] 2005: 180–1, II.1.1). Grotius' phrase the 'First Impressions of Nature', as Straumann argues, draws on the Stoic notion of *honestum*. These two phrases reflect the different formulation the tradition of *oikeiôsis* – first, the making, or belonging to oneself through pursuit of self-love and self-interest, and, secondly, the practice of the rational faculties of anticipation, conclusion and comparison that enable the identification of the superior good, that is, what is just.[19] Grotius incorporated the meanings of *oikeiôsis* as both the impulse of self-preservation (including not only avoidance of bodily harm, but also the attainment and retention of things useful for life), and of *oikeiôsis* as acting in harmony with what is good (natural law). Related to his theory of just war, this meant that military conflict was to be considered legitimate not only when it follows the logic of *oikeiôsis* as self-preservation (for instance, in case of defensive wars, or wars motivated by the desire to reclaim unjustly seized possessions and land necessary for the sustenance of life),[20] but also when they were 'virtuous' in their modes of conduct (cf. Straumann 2003–4: 64–5).

Later in *De Iure Belli*, Grotius articulates the notion of *oikeiôsis* as appropriate, or rightful, action, that is, as acting in accordance with natural law, by invoking the concept of 'commendable action' of *decorum*. *Decorum* can either be expressed negatively, that is, as a negation or absence of vice, or through the naming of specific 'actions'. This in turn illuminates the relation between, on the one hand, the *involuntary right* in *De Iure Belli*, which was based on the universal law of nature, whereby one can speak of action that is commendable because it adheres to what is commanded,[21] and, on the other hand, the *voluntary right*, which is derived from the public will, and which includes the civil rights of citizens and the rights of nations. Grotius writes that *decorum* 'becomes the subject of [voluntary] Laws both Divine and Human, which by prescribing Things relating thereto, renders them obligatory, whereas before they were only commendable' ([1738] 2005: 82–183, II.1.3). The use of the concept of commendable action, *decorum*, in the dual context of the comportment of both individual citizens and sovereign states draws on a richer and 'positive' idea of sociality in *De Iure Belli* than self-preservation, which limits sociality to the norms of bodily and proprietary non-infringement. This also means that for Grotius acts of wrongdoing in inter-personal and inter-state relations are not reducible to the violation the principle of self-preservation; rather, Grotius clarifies that 'by unjust we mean that which has *a necessary Repugnance* to a reasonable and sociable Nature' ([1738] 2005: 182, II.1.3; emphasis mine). From the perspective of this richer and 'positive' notion of *oikeiôsis*, restitutive action is seen as more than the domestic and international norms of securing the non-infringement of persons and states, and the non-appropriation of personal and state properties. Rather, it draws on the conception of sociality based on the notion of a commendable action and virtuous comportment. An integral part of Natural Law, restitution provides the normative grounding for the 'negative' mechanisms for undoing past wrongs and injuries, as well as is a philosophic source of a 'positive' articulation of the universal standards of justice, *en pair* with oath-making, promise-keeping and gratitude to benefactors (cf. [1738] 2005: 182, II.1.3. In chapter I of *De Iure Belli* Grotius describes an act of expropriation both as a violation of the prohibition against the seizure of another person's property, *and* as a vice and deviation from the ideal of commendable conduct, *decorum*; Grotius calls expropriation 'a wicked Thing', an act 'Dishonest by Nature' and 'Hateful to God' ([1738] 2005: 154, I.IX.4). This emphasises further the broader remedial role assigned to restitution in *De Iure Belli*, beyond the narrow corrective function of the 'justice of contracts'. While Grotius does adopt the Aristotelian idea of restitution as a synallagmatic relation, and thus defines the restitutive subjects through referencing their contractual obligations towards other individuals, rather than, for instance, in regard to their social roles or the social allocation of goods, he also views expropriation through the prism of its broader societal effects, and draws on a moral conception of expropriation as wicked and socially injurious action. In *De Iure Belli* restitution is thus not only invested with the diorthotic, corrective capacity in regard to the isolated positions of a 'debtor' and a 'creditor', but also becomes inscribed with the possibilities of broader social and moral repair.

Finally, it needs to be noted in regard to Grotius' richer and 'positive' conception of sociality in *De Iure Belli* that restitution rests on an anthropological premise. Derived from the 'desire for society', unique to the human species, restitution figures as one of the trajectories for practicing the 'care of maintaining society'. As already mentioned, Grotius follows here a distinction taken from the Stoic philosophy of *oikeiôsis* between, on the one hand, a drive or an impulse towards species togetherness, identifiable among animals and humans alike, that derives from its guarantee of security and preservation, and, on the other hand, the capacity for a peaceful coexistence, neighbourliness and community grounded in the recognition and appreciation of humanity as such. For the Stoics, this primary disposition is identifiable in any animate subject that sustains and nourishes life, and Grotius follows the Stoic logic of self-preservation when he notes in *De Iure Belli* that even inanimate entities display an 'aptitude' to safeguard their existence. However, the specifically human dispositions towards peaceful coexistence and the reciprocity of care among humans derives, for Grotius, from the capacity of moral discernment and moral judgement. The faculty for moral judgement is absent in non-human animate beings for, while animals might be capable of inflicting injury, Grotius writes that '*they know not what it is to hurt with a View of hurting*, and with a Sense of the Evil that is in it' (([1738] 2005: 158, I.XI.3; emphasis mine). In other words, while non-human beings are capable of inflicting pain on others, depriving them of sources of nourishment or shelter, and of killing them, the *homini proprium* aspect of wrongdoing is doing harm with *the intention of harming*; it is a wrongdoing detached from the goals of self-preservation. The Grotian conception of restitution is thus closely related to the anthropological disposition of *appetitus societalis* in that it provides a corrective and remedial pathway for recuperating wrongdoing accomplished (to paraphrase Grotius) 'with a view to' inflicting suffering and divestiture on fellow human persons (and, in international relations, on other sovereign states). Animals, plants and minerals *cannot make restitution* – they cannot make good an injustice of dispossession, because they cannot dispossess (each other) in the first place. For Grotius, then, the restitutive *raison d'être* is to address and *repair* that uniquely human capacity for injurious action – dedicated to inflicting bodily harm or material deprivation on others *in and of itself* – which in turn rest on prior philosophic assumptions about moral life and the human faculties of action and judgement.

FURTHER RESTITUTIVE TROPES IN *DE IURE BELLI*: POSTLIMINIUM AND THE 'FORMER CONDITION OF THINGS'

In Book III of *De Iure Belli*, which elaborates the normative and philosophic framework of *ius post bellum*, Grotius focuses on return and recovery of things in positive and customary law from the perspective of postliminium (*ius postlimini*). Postliminium was an ancient Roman legal norm by which persons and things made captive or seized under conditions of war were restored to their previous status at the point of coming under the territorial jurisdiction of the Roman Empire, or of its allies. I suggest that in addition to the previously identified elements of Grotius' natural law conception of restitution – its corrective and diorthotic operations, its socially reparative effects and its Stoic philosophic grounding – Grotius' use of postliminium infuses the modern restitutive imaginary with retrocessive and prelapsarian meanings. In particular, it illuminates the philosophic and political stakes of the idea of restitution as a return of/to 'the former condition of things' (Alexandrowicz [1969] 2017). Through the 'revival' of the Roman law of postliminium, Grotius 'props'[22] his theory of restitution upon the image of a subject crossing a threshold to a site of prior belonging, who thereby undergoes a reversal to a former status, as well as the re-establishment of the original (pre-captive) relations to persons and things. Moreover, through the act of return, the subject is revived, reborn, *brought back to life*. This infusion of restitutive theory with the postliminal, prelapsarian and retrocessive imagery of subjective returns and revivals blurs the distinction between legal performatives and magical acts: at the heart of restitutive imagination is an annulment and undoing of the past through declaration of its invalidity or non-existence.

The origin of postliminium is the Roman legal tradition, postliminium applied to Roman citizens taken into enemy captivity during warfare; it declared the prisoners' post-conflict border-crossing into Roman territory (or into any of its allied territories) as a moment of the reinstatement of their pre-conflict civic status, relations and property (see Alexandrowicz [1969] 2017). While the origins of postliminium in Roman law are uncertain, Ireland (1944: 586) speculates that it sprang from an ancient legal doctrine that sanctioned the loss of citizenship of Roman soldiers upon their capture by an enemy. The loss of political personhood by the captives meant that from the perspective of Roman law they became slaves and, in the words of Esposito (2015: 6), were 'thrust into the realm of things'.[23]

By including postliminium among the rules of just warfare as the basis for the 'Right to Returning' in Book III of *De Iure Belli*, Grotius follows the direction of the Italian jurist Alberico Gentili, who in his 1585 *De Iure Belli Libri Tres* proposed postliminium as a principle of peace treaties (see Lesaffer 2010). Grotius invokes the Roman *ius postlimini* as a way of 'propping' the post-conflict norm of restitution within the normative framework of *ius post bellum*. In the course of his elaboration Grotius invokes three distinct meanings of 'restitutive returns'. First, 'return' implies the subject's action of crossing a state boundary as a threshold that demarcates enemies and friends. Next, Grotius writes about 'return' in the sense of the subject's political reappearance after a period during which the subject had been divested of free civic status and, in fact, of civic life. In this formulation 'return' is conceptually akin to 'resurrection' – legally, the subject resurges within the bounds of the polis *as if* returning from the dead. Finally, Grotius invokes the idea of 'return' as a temporal annulment of wrongs and as the *ius post belli* restoration of the pre-conflict status of things. These three interwoven, though different, post-conflict tropes of restitutive returns reflect postliminal logic, and, as I suggest in what follows, its foundations in the delineation of the boundary between sacred sites and common sites in Roman antiquity (see Burrill 1860; Alexandrowicz [1969] 2017).

The dominant interpretation of postliminium has referenced the principle of invalidity of illegitimate acts (*ex injuria jus non oritur*).[24] Grotius adopts the definition of postliminium provided by Q. Muncius Scaevola Pontifex, legal author and politician of the Roman republic from the period of the Social War (91–88 BC). According to Cicero, it was Scaevola who emphasised that the central part of postliminium was the subject's re-entering into, and repossession of, his prior place of residence after a period of absence (it was primarily the house, and only secondarily the state). What is interesting in the broader context of elaborating the norms of *ius post bellum*, is that Grotius notes in passing that the prefix 'post' in postliminium 'may signify a Return', citing an alternative etymology of the prefix 'post' from Roman mythology. Here the prefix 'post' in *postliminium* means not (being) 'after' (the event in question); rather, Grotius relates the prefix 'post' to the figure of a Roman goddess Postvorta, a female divinity of childbirth, who looked to the child's past ([1738]

2005: 1381–2, IX.I.2).[25] As such, it does not imply that the past event is no longer in existence; rather, it means something akin to an orientation of having a 'view on the past' or having a 'past outlook' or 'past orientation' *in the present*.

In regard to the term 'liminium', Grotius writes that it signifies a 'Frontier' (a boundary, or a threshold), and that it is derived from the words *'limen'* ('applied to the Entrance of private Dwellings') and *'limes'* ('the Lands of the State') ([1738] 2005: 1382, IX.I.2).[26] Burrill suggests (1860: 316) that '[as] the threshold of a house makes, as it were, a limit or boundary of it, so the ancients chose to call the boundary or border of the empire its threshold'. This becomes apparent in the semantic connection between the concept of postliminium and the word 'elimination' – while the meaning of the former is that of crossing over the threshold, the latter signifies (being) thrust out of/ over the threshold. Grotius writes that in ancient Athens '[the] banishing of a Person [was called] *Eliminare*, and Banishment [was] termed *Eliminium, thrusting out of [the] Bounds, or Limits'* ([1738] 2005: 1382, IX.I.2; emphasis in the original). Burrill (1860: 316) writes that 'the ancients chose to call the boundary or border of the empire its threshold' an analogy to 'the threshold of a house [that] makes . . . a limit or boundary of it'. Accordingly, *ius postlimini* was activated by, and imagined as, the *event of crossing over a line*; most likely, as I elaborate below, with a religious genealogy of traversing boundaries between consecrated sites, reserved for sacred practices and rituals, and common or profane places of residence.

Grotius explicitly states his preference for the interpretation of *ius postlimini* developed by the Roman scholar Scaevola to that of Servius Suloicius Rufus. While Rufus emphasised the temporal dimension of return, Scaevola drew attention to its spatial aspects ([1738] 2005: 1381–2, IX.I.2, n.1). For Servius Suloicius Rufus at the core of *jus postlimini* was the temporal dimension of return in that the law consisted in *declarations of invalidity*, or, even, of the *non-occurrence* of the past, namely, the subject's captivity and enslavement by the enemy army. The subject's former status and position, civil rights, legal relations and material possessions were restored to him, albeit, depending on the context, with important qualifications and often upon additional conditions (see Buckland [1908] 2010; Levy 1943; Watson 1987).[27]

Alexandrowicz ([1969] 2017) identifies a key resemblance between postliminium and post-conflict restitution, which is that both are illocutionary acts[28] that invalidate or annul past events by reviving 'the former condition of things'. Similarly, Burrill (1860: 316) defines postliminium as a 'return or restoration of a person to a former estate or right', and he also suggests that at the core of postliminium is a realisation of a 'fiction[al]' situation. This is because postliminium *does not* announce the recovery of lost status and rights, but, rather, declares that the captive *had never been in captivity* and that his divestiture of status, relations and possessions *had not taken place*. As Smith puts it, *ius postlimini* was 'founded on the fiction of the captive *having never been absent from home*' (1875; emphasis mine).

Drawing upon Scaevola's genealogical account of the restitutive return, Grotius describes postliminium as 'that which ariseth from a return to the Frontiers, that is, the Territories of the State', which includes '[the] Persons recovering their Rights, and the Things returning to their former Masters' ([1738] 2005: 1383, IX.II.1, n.1). Grotius follows closely Pomponius' distinction between two postliminal trajectories, 'one under which we return to our friends from the enemy, and the other by which we recover something' (cited in *The Digest of Justinian* ([1903] 2014: 49 tit.15. s.14), and which corresponds to the grammatical distinction I introduced earlier in the book – between transitive restitutive action (where the subject and object are different), and between intransitive restitutive action (where the subject and object coincide). Grotius distinguishes between two kinds of postliminium, 'when we either return, or recover something' (2005 [1631]: 1384, IX.II.2).

Through *ius postlimini* the war-captive subject of the Roman state 'become[s] Master of himself]' and 'of all Things, that he had in any Nation at Peace, whether corporeal, or incorporeal' (2005 [1631]: 1389, IX.II.6.1). According to Smith (1875), the material objects that can be returned to their prior owner need to fulfil the criteria or 'appropriability' and of 'returnability'. He includes in the category of restitutable, or recoverable things (*res postlimini*), the occupied land, as well as 'slaves, mules, saddles, [and] horses', but excludes from it weapons, because 'arms . . . could not be honourably lost [in battle]'. However, even the objects fulfilling the criterion of 'appropriability' might not be 'returnable', which is the basis for the distinction *res postlimini* and *praeda* – spoils of war and booty, and Smith (1875) writes that 'when a thing had become a *praeda*, it had lost its capacity to be *res postlimini*'. *Praeda* were '[all] movables belonging to an enemy, which were captured by a Roman army'; by becoming *praeda*, these objects lost their status of individual property, and became the property of the state.

Grotius classifies land as recoverable through *ius postlimini*, but various 'Movables', including ships, as un-recoverable. He writes that 'Movables' are 'Part of the Spoil' ([1738] 2005: 1401–05, IX.XIII.1–IX.XIV.1). Other objects, such arms and soldiers' clothing, are subject to post-conflict recovery, though not by the virtue of postliminium; rather, they are returned because 'it was an odious Thing, and was even accounted criminal, for a Man to suffer his Arms and Cloaths to be taken from him . . .' ([1738] 2005: 1405, IX.XIV.2). Also, any objects requisitioned by illegitimate subjects ('Pirates and Robbers') are not recoverable through *ius postlimini*, which rested on the premise of legitimate wartime acquisition; rather, these objects were considered to never 'have . . . changed their Owner by the Right of Nations' ([1738] 2005: 1406, IX.XVI.1). In other words, *res postlimini* rely on the assumption of ownership as a necessary, though not always sufficient, condition of recovery.

Finally, for Grotius the restitutive return was also conditional upon the concept of political enmity: postliminium concerned a specific type of recovering, or restoring to, 'a previous condition, of anyone or anything taken unjustly by an *extraneus*', namely, a 'foreigner, stranger, [one coming] from without' (*The Digest of Justinian* ([1903] 2014: 49 tit.15.s.19). The concept of political friendship is also key in this context because *ius postlimini* became operative 'as soon as a Person (or any Thing capable of this Right) should come safe to our Friends' (Grotius inserted here an important caveat that 'Friends, or Allies, are not to be taken simply for those with whom we are at Peace, but those who join with us in the same War', 2005 [1631]: 1383, IX.II.1).[29] The notion of *limen* as a household threshold *and* as a border of the state territory emphasises the importance of the distinction between friends and enemies in the legal articulation. This is highlighted in Burrill's discussion (1860: 316) of the dual meaning of *limen* as a limit (*finis*) of the territorial jurisdiction of the state *and* as a boundary line (*terminus*) separating adversarial and hostile spaces from allied and benevolent ones.

Taking a starting-point in the religious and spiritual meanings of *limen* in antiquity, the nineteenth-century German philologist and classicist Karl Wilhelm Göttling made a connection between restoration of former status, or the condition of persons and things within the frame of *ius postlimini*, on the one hand, and the religious practice and institution of *pomoerium*, on the other. Etruscan in origin, *pomoerium* was a Roman practice of demarcating boundaries of a sacred sites called *ager effatus*, which sometimes coincided with city walls (but were not identical with them),[30] for the purpose of creating sites of interaction and communication between humans and divinities.[31]

One interpretation of *ius postlimini* saw it as a response to a (fictional) declaration of death coinciding with the seizure of a Roman citizen by an enemy army. According to the logic of the so-called 'fiction of the Cornelian law' (*fictio legic Corneliae*), the moment of capture was identical with the pronouncement of death (see Berger [1953] 1991; Watson 1990). The purpose of the institutionalisation of the legal fiction of death was the preservation of the legal validity of the subject's will in the situation of enemy captivity, which meant the loss of the status of free citizen (*diminutio capitis maxima*).[32] From the perspective of the foundational distinction between persons and things in Roman law (Esposito 2015; 2016), *fictio legic Corneliae* was thus a paradoxical situation where the person's death was the necessary condition for preserving their status of personhood. The loss of freedom, civic status and material possessions, which *ius postlimini* set to rectify and nullify, is a moment of fluidity and shifting of the boundary separating the class of persons and the class of things. By declaring the captive's fictional death, from a legal perspective the living body becomes a corpse and, following Esposito's insight (2015: 105), comes to occupy a site of indistinction between *res* and *personae* as *res religiosae*, and acquires the status of un-appropriable things. The law of postliminium reclaims that divested status of a person by *undoing* the thanatic effect of turning a living person into the *res religiosae* of a corpse. By nullifying the pronouncement of death, postliminium restored the former condition of things and brought the subject back to life.

The conceptual and genealogical link between the law of postliminium and recovery of status and possessions in Grotius' writings on *ius post bellum* needs to be considered in the context of his theory of restitution because of the striking suggestion that declaratory legal and political procedures that invalidate or undo past wrongdoing are not unlike magical procedures: they conjure and make appear what is presently not in existence. The Grotian outline of the genealogy of restitution propped upon the law of postliminium helps to identify the phantasmatic core of modern restitutive imaginary: the return to a prior condition of things, and the subject's return to life from a condition of their civil death. The restitutive subject is returned not only to the condition of biological aliveness, but that of legal persons, as they depart the condition of *res religiosae* that they occupied as a (fictional) corpse (which was a strategy preventing him from slipping into a category of privately appropriable things, *res corporales*, an enslaved war captive). By 'propping' his restitution theory upon the imagery from the law of postliminium, Grotius interwove the different meanings of return – return of expropriated things to a person; the person's homecoming and repatriation; the return to a previously occupied status or condition – to explain the objectives, justification and significance of restitution within the *ius post bellum* framework.

2

THE CREATURE AS A FIGURE OF UNRESTITUTABILITY, OR MONSTERS IN PARADISE NOT ALLOWED: BENEVOLENCE AND RESTITUTION IN MARY SHELLEY'S *FRANKENSTEIN*

'A monster's paradise!'
Derek Payne, *The Whisper of Dreams*, 2014

In Mary Shelley's *Frankenstein* ([1818] 2009) two recurring themes intersperse: the motif of universal benevolence and the motif of restitution and reparation. In regard to universal benevolence, *Frankenstein*, alongside Marquis de Sade's *Justine*, offers a prescient commentary on the powers of dissociation at work in the production of cultural beliefs in a natural human disposition to do good in the world, or what Nietzsche in *Twilight of the Idols* calls the moderns' 'softening of manners' ([1889] 2009: 56). Charles Taylor Charles Taylor (1992) identifies in *Sources of the Self* the provision of remedy in response to others' suffering as a pillar of modernity identity.[1] For Taylor a distinct 'moral intuition' characterises modern societies, and it includes an instinctual disinclination to impose pain on others and the desire to alleviate their suffering (Taylor 1992: 4–5). The distribution of sympathy and other benevolent affects in modern societies ostensibly happens regardless of the ties of class and kinship, and concerns *the suffering of strangers*, or what Luc Boltanski (1999) has called 'distant suffering', by virtue of a shared belonging to humanity.

The significance of the idea of benevolence as one of Taylor's 'sources of the self' in modernity is illustrated by some of the foundational literature of contemporary humanitarianism, perhaps most evidently by Henry Dunant's *A Memory of Solferino* ([1962] 2013). While read primarily as an attempt at mobilising international support for the formation of a battlefield emergency response system,[2] the book is also a clear expression of Dunant's awe at the outpouring of spontaneous altruism towards the wounded soldiers, regardless of their nationality or class.[3] Importantly, Dunant's key intention was not to generate *more* relief efforts, but to increase their overall productivity and efficiency by organising control structures for the already existing spontaneous outbursts of altruistic energy, which he interpreted as manifestations of natural human compassion.

The key term in understanding the political and philosophic stakes of the belief that humans instinctively act in ways that benefit and remedy others – and that, in Taylor's words (1992: 3), this belief has become an important part of the 'modern notion of what it is to be a human agent, a person, or a self' – is universal benevolence (cf. Frim 2019). In Mary Shelley's novel, benevolence functions as a trait characterising all the *properly human* protagonists. It is also formative of Victor Frankenstein's own childhood experience and education. As such, the novel could be read as a critical reflection on the philosophical and cultural significance of the idea of universal benevolence, and of the philosophy of sentiments more broadly, in eighteenth- and early nineteenth-century Europe.[4] Meaning an attitude of 'good-wishing', or 'good-willing', towards others (*bene*, 'well', and *volantem, volens*, 'to wish' or 'to will'),[5] the concept of universal social benevolence, often associated, though non-identical, with beneficence,[6] has been associated with the moral sentiment tradition and utilitarianism.[7] As Margaret Abruzzo (2011) has shown in the North American context, situating the idea of a charitable impulse towards unfortunate others as the basis of modern sociability had a formative impact on the development of the nineteenth-century humanitarian ideology and social movements (see also Barnett 2011; Asad 2015).

In Shelley's *Frankenstein*, the concept of universal social benevolence encounters its limits, or its threshold – its *limen* – in the figure of the Creature, who, while desiring to become the beneficiary of humanity's 'moral intuition', is categorically excluded from it. In spite of (or, perhaps, because of)[8] the utter 'misery' and 'wretchedness' of his appearance, the Creature does not 'excite . . . sympathy', as Victor puts it, when he declares himself void of any kindness or compassion towards his creation ([1818] 2009: 178). In fact, what is remarkably consistent about the way that the Creature presents himself to the world in the novel is his failure to arouse benevolent affects. The Creature's inability to kindle pity in others explains Victor's aggression towards his creation, which puts into motion a series of his morally dubious actions: the Creature's abandonment, the withdrawal of a promise to create the Creature's companion, and, finally, the revengeful homicidal pursuit.

In a posthumously published review of the novel, Percy Shelley expressed his belief in the 'essential humanity' of the Creature (quoted in Schoene-Harwood 2000: 21). Admiring the novel's psychological insight, Percy Shelley proposed that the reader becomes a witness to the Creature's transformation from a naturally kind, compassionate and sociable subject (basically, Rousseau's child) into its dark other, a malevolent subject. Shelley wrote: '[t]reat a person ill and he will become wicked . . . you have imposed on him malevolence' (quoted in Schoene-Harwood 2000: 21). In contrast to Percy Shelley's interpretation of *Frankenstein* as a portrayal and affirmation of the moral psychology of benevolence, I suggest that the Creature's inability to excite sympathetic affects in others can be read productively as a sign of his threshold status – not of his 'essential humanity', but of an irreducible and categorical *in*humanity – which illuminates the limits, and the ethical and political stakes, of the idea of benevolence.

In reading *Frankenstein* as a critique of the moral philosophy of universal benevolence and of the belief in moral progressivism, I also sketch the Creature as a figure of *unrestitutability*. Using Esposito's categories, one could perhaps say that the Creature is neither fully a person nor a thing. For that reason, he is not only excluded from humanity's benevolence, but also unable to undergo restitution, or to serve as a proper restitutive object that enables others' prelapsarian returns. We can read the figure of the Creature as the exemplification of the genealogical connection between restitution and revival, or resurrection, which I outlined in the introductory chapter, in regard to, for instance, the Dionysian *Bouphonia*. The Creature's galvanisation into life is not, properly speaking, a *creative* act, a distorted representation of the *ex nihilo* creation at the heart of the Judeo-Christian origin story, but, rather, a restorative or revivifying act. Its constitutive dynamic is not that of bringing into being, but of *bringing back to life*, or, in Victor's words, of 'bestowing animation upon lifeless matter' by undoing the 'corruptive' working of death upon the body; the undoing of death's transformation of the body into 'putrid matter ([1818] 2009: 53, 55). Just as the Creature illuminates the operations of 'constitutive exclusion' from the category of humanity upon which the idea of universal and natural benevolence of humanity pivots as the exclusion of the *in*human from human relations so does he also shed light on the restitutive desire for the retrieval of the former condition of things, for substitution and re-appropriation, given that the Creature remains barred from the prelapsarian state.

There are multiple acts of return, undoing and repair in *Frankenstein*. Victor's circular peregrinations within, and on the peripheries of, Europe almost always end with a *nostos* to his native Geneva. The exception is when, with the death of Victor's fiancée, Elisabeth, as well as of Victor's father, it becomes apparent that the undoing of the dire consequences of his 'unearthly occupation' ([1818] 2009: 188) cannot be achieved, other than as an act of vengeance on the Creature that claims Victor's life. Victor's revengeful pursuit of the Creature to the Arctic, a region virtually unknown to Shelley's contemporaries,[9] is in this context not just another departure from home, but, rather, a sign of barred return, a failed *nostos*. With the departure to the Arctic, Victor withdraws from the human world and 'quit[s] the neighbourhood of man' ([1818] 2009: 206) in a gesture of self-damnation. His killing of the Creature originates from a sense of obligation towards his 'fellow-creatures' ([1818] 2009: 265), but without any redemptive effects. Victor's sense of obligation to eliminate his creation from the world can thus be read in connection with Goldberg's suggestion (1959) that Victor transgresses not against God, but against his fellow humans; at the heart of his crime is the elevation of science and knowledge over and above social morality and its isolation from any productive endeavours aimed at increasing the social well-being. In other words, Victor disconnects the pursuits of knowledge from the principle of benevolence and universal fraternity. While he begins '[his] [scientific] pursuit[s] with benevolent intentions', as Goldberg puts it (1959: 33), Victor erroneously elevates the position of scientific knowledge to being independent from 'the fellow-feeling afforded by a compassionate society', and thus 'evade[s] the fulfilment of higher duties toward the social community, the brotherhood of man which forms the highest good'.

The Creature's assemblage and animation introjects a foreign element within modern society in that his presence is radically at odds with its organising ethics of benevolence and fraternity. While the primary desire of the Creature, which precedes even his desire for a female companion, is to be the recipient of human charity, companionship and compassion, he proves endemically incompatible with it. Every time the Creature appears among the humans, he is met with a refusal of sympathetic identification: no one *feels with* the monster.

The restitutive motif in *Frankenstein* consolidates around the Creature's making as the undoing of the work of death, as well as around Victor's aporetic desire to make the fact of the Creature's animation *to not have occurred*: the Creature's attempted killing is itself a kind of undoing of the past and of the workings of retroactive annulment. The reasons for the attempted undoing is not only (or, for that matter, not primarily) a pursuit of personal revenge on Victor's part; rather, it is linked to Victor's recognition that by introducing the Creature into the world, he had undermined the benevolent ethical foundations of social life. Not only has Victor not produced anything useful; he has made a something *male*volent.

My first step is to read *Frankenstein* as a critical engagement with the philosophic beliefs in the benevolent and sympathetic foundations of society. I look more closely at two contributions to the modern philosophy of benevolence, by Joseph Butler and by David Hume; their work is important for explicating the claim that benevolence is natural and universal (Butler), as well as for specifying the connection between universal benevolence and social utility (Hume), which provide some of the central elements for the history of Western humanitarianism. In a parallel reading of *Frankenstein* and of the modern philosophers of benevolence, I propose that Shelley's novel offers key insights into the concealed exclusionary logic upon which the discourse of universal humanity is based. The refusal of the Creature's earnest plea to be part of the benevolent relationship of shared humanity, or as he puts it, the 'desire to claim [humanity's] protection of kindness', is a poignant illustration of what Talal Asad has called a 'complex genealogy' of humanitarianism, which interlaces 'compassion and benevolence [with] violence and cruelty, an intertwining that is not merely a co-existence of the two, but a mutual dependence of each on the other' (2015: 393).[10] In *Frankenstein*, benevolence is the organising principle of society that Victor both seeks to recover and restore in the wake of his monstrous creation, and that ostensibly enables the passage to a prelapsarian state.

My next step is to trace the restitutive motifs of undoing, return and repair in the novel. Frankenstein transgresses against society by revealing the fiction of universal benevolence; he seeks to undo his deed by neutralising and retroactively annulling the Creature's existence, and by expelling him beyond the bounds of human society (and when that proves unsuccessful, by annihilating him). However, the Creature's making is a kind of undoing in itself, rather than a creative act, insofar as the Creature comes into existance not through a genuine making-appear, but, rather, as a return to life after death. The virtue of benevolence as a foundation of sociability is both the universal condition that channels restitution and a kind of prelapsarian state from which Victor departs by making the Creature. In Victor's eyes, restitution demands the Creature's annihilation from the face of the earth. It is not quite murder, nor sacrifice; rather, the annihilation has at its heart the 'making un-happen'. It is also a sign that the restitutive logic of prelapsarian returns has an important condition attached to it – it is open only to those who are included in the human community, and remains closed to Frankenstein's monstrous prodigy. By virtue of his exclusion from the benevolent relation, the Creature becomes both a figure of inhumanity *and* of unrestitutability; being barred from restitutive possibilities, the Creature illustrates the philosophic and political connection between restitution, reparation and universal humanity.

Modern Philosophy of Benevolence

Charles Taylor (1992: 4) describes the belief in social benevolence as one of three 'moral intuitions' that have come to determine the meaning of modern identity (the other two being individual autonomy and attention to quotidian life). In this context, one distinct aspect of the modern theory of benevolence is its instinctual character. This is what Taylor (1992: 5) means by 'natural benevolence' when he argues that a sympathetic remedial response in the face of the others' misfortune have become 'comparable to our love of sweet things . . . or our fear of falling'. Another distinct aspect is a disconnect between benevolence and the bonds of kinship, social class or religion; instead, benevolence is defined through the idiom of universal humanity. As such, the ethics of neighbourliness outlined by modern philosophy of the sentimental tradition, including Anthony Shaftesbury, Francis Hutcheson, Joseph Butler, David Hume and others, are closely imbricated with the question of what it means to be human. Insofar as the idea of kindness beyond the ties of kindship was grounded in the conviction that life was to be respected as an abstractly defined *human* life, it became 'our mode of access to the world' (Taylor 1992: 8). The crux of Taylor's argument is that the principle of benevolence has formed the implicit background of modern belief systems and ethical judgements, even when without being overtly and directly acknowledged. As such, benevolence belongs to the category of 'hypergoods', which 'not only are incomparably more important than others but provide standpoint from which these must be weighted, judged, decided about' (1992: 63).

The emphasis on practical and quotidian manifestations of benevolence also underwrites its complex relationship to Christianity (Taylor 1992: 84). The Enlightenment philosophy veers away from the Christian ethos of charity in the direction of the ethos of social utility, altruism and compassion, but in other ways also *intensifies* it by making charity into 'one of the central beliefs of modern Western culture', meaning that 'we all should work to improve the human condition, relieve suffering, overcome poverty, increase prosperity, augment human welfare. We should strive to leave the world a more prosperous place than we found it' (Taylor 1992: 85).

Critical post-colonial readings of *Sources of the Self* have surveyed the relation between the 'Enlightenment imperative' of benevolence and moral progressivist interpretations of Western history (see, for example, Mulhall 2004; Asad 2015).[11] What is not being seen through the moral progressivist lens, they argue, is the consistent co-presence of 'compassion and benevolence [with] violence and cruelty' in Western modernity. 'Modern humanitarianism . . . uses violence to subdue violence'; military humanitarianism is not a '"perversion" of genuine humanitarianism, but . . . another articulation of impulses and contradictions' evident in the history of interventions, protectionism and defences 'undertaken by and for [and in the name of] human beings' (Asad 2015: 394). What is suspicious about the postulate of universal benevolence is the extent to which it historically coincides with the concealment and justification of colonial violence.

The background to the eighteenth-century philosophy of benevolence in the work of Joseph Butler (1692–1752) and David Hume (1711–76), among others, is the refutation of 'selfish philosophy' and the rejection of psychological egoism, associated with Hobbes and espoused explicitly by Bernard Mandeville.[12] In a series of sermons on the topic of human nature, Joseph Butler ([1726; 1729] 2006), an English bishop, theologian and a known critic of deistic philosophy, outlined the difference between self-love and the love of the other, which he addressed in theological defined *philanthropia* (φιλανθρωπία), or charity, with the view of breaking down their Mandevillean binary opposition between the social and political impulses of egoism and altruism (see also Roberts 1973; Frey 1992). Butler argued that most social expressions of self-love did not manifest as a moral principle, or as explicit motivation, where the subject took their own happiness as the object of their actions. Rather, it manifested as a passion and affection, whereby the subject derived pleasure or gratification from their actions, while taking somebody or something else as its object. While benevo-lence – the love of the neighbour – was a public affection and self-love a private one, Butler argued that they were parallel and mutually reinforcing.

By arguing for the recognition of the primacy of benevolent motivations in social relations, Butler articulated (what he believed was) an anti-Hobbesian position: altruistic and compassionate behaviour was irreducible to the desire for physical reward or emotional gratification. The motivations of self-love and neighbour-love were not only capable of coexisting, but could be mutually reinforcing, because virtuous behaviour brought about a sense of happiness (derived from satisfaction of appetites and desires) and a sense of enjoyment. Importantly, benevolence was not a source of a virtuous behaviour, but also a gesture affirming the virtue of the other and the recognition of the other as virtuous. Benevolent disposition was derived from the theologically understood conception of 'common humanity'. Butler called benevolent deeds 'action(s) of humanity' and contrasted them to 'action(s) of cruelty' and 'action(s) of inhu-manity' ([1726; 1729] 2006: 12). Such 'action(s) of cruelty' and 'action(s) of inhumanity' were not necessarily descriptors of atrocities, but, rather, of deeds and comportment that were seen as devoid of concerns for fellow humans and showed no sign of benevolent orientation towards others. In my analysis of Shelley's novel I suggest that Victor's making of the Creature acquires the status of such an 'action of inhumanity', in that it destabilises and undermines rela-tions of benevolence, and shows the limit of virtue, of the virtuous disposition towards others, and of its allegedly universal scope in particular.

Butler described benevolence as 'natural'. He argued that just as self-love operated as a guarantee of self-preservation of individual organisms, so did benevolence ensure the well-being of society: '[f]rom [the] comparison of benevolence and self-love, of our public and private affections, of the courses of life they lead to . . . it is manifest that *we were made for society, and to pro-mote the happiness of it, as that we were intended to take care of our own life and health and private good*' ([1726; 1729] 2006: 10; emphasis in the original).

Butler's preoccupation with the idea of 'human nature' in this context helps to grapple with the question of the political stakes of asserting the 'naturalness' and universality of benevolence. In the first, most general, sense, Butler defines 'human nature' as 'no more than some principle in man, without regard either to the kind or degree of it', which was taken to motivate human actions in general, be they of a virtuous or vicious kind ([1726; 1729] 2006: 19). Butler's second meaning of 'human nature' concerned specifically 'those passions which are strongest [in us]', and that 'most influence the [vicious] actions'; or, in Butler's Christianic interpretation, the original transgression of the first man had left a mark on all of humanity. This sense of 'human nature' was synonymous with an inclination to commit iniquity ([1726; 1729] 2006: 19). In other words, Butler's first conception of 'human nature' was a name for human instincts and dispositions generally, and the second conception pertained specifically to the human tendency to undertake vicious actions, seen as a moral echo of the 'original sin'.

There was, however, also a third conception of 'nature' in Butler's work, which resonated closely with how he theorized benevolence; it was a norm descriptor of being 'naturally supreme' to other social norms or conventions. In other words, it was a provision of constituting a 'law, guide, or authority to other principles or passions' (Garrett 2018). It is with a view to this third conception of 'human nature' that Butler articulated his famous proposition about benevolence that 'the common virtues and the common vices of mankind may be traced up to benevolence or the want of it . . .'; as such, Butler did not consider benevolence to be a virtue, but, rather 'that part of the nature of man . . . which . . . leads him to society . . . a superior principle of reflection or conscience' ([1726; 1729] 2006: 123, 20).[13] There is an interesting resonance, then, between Butler's conception of benevolence as a kind of innate disposition to social life and what Hugo Grotius in De Iure Belli called appetitus societalis, 'desire for society', within the normative and political framework exceeding the negative liberty model. For Butler, it was through exerting an attitude of benevolence that one became an autonomous 'moral agent', constituting 'a law to [oneself]', as 'a faculty . . . supreme of all others, and which bears its own authority of being so' ([1726; 1729] 2006: 21). Benevolence was described as 'natural' not in the sense of a general characteristic of men, but as a universal impulse towards sociability, governance and social order – a source of virtuous behaviour, rather than a virtue in itself.

The Scottish Enlightenment philosopher and essayist David Hume argued for the coexistence, and potential compatibility, of benevolence and self-interest in his moral philosophy, and, with some similarity to Butler, also described benevolence as 'natural' (see Roberts 1973; Whelan 1980; Broiles 2012). However, Hume's moral philosophy differed from Butler's in its epistemological orientation;

rather than locate the source of ethics in a theological reflection on natural human drives and impulses, Hume was closely aligned with empiricism, and with a moral sentiment tradition that linked ethics to inner sensations of approval and disapproval (cf. Harrison 1976; Mackie 1981; Norton and Taylor 2008). In *An Enquiry Concerning the Principles of Morals* ([1751] 1998), Hume described benevolence as a social virtue, in that, like justice, benevolence could be 'exercised only in reference to other human beings' (Merrill 2011).[14]

By emphasising the practical consequences of benevolent action, Hume expressed a similar view to the one Francis Bacon espoused over a century earlier, when he wrote in *Novum Organum* that scientific knowledge production should 'relieve the condition of mankind' (cited in Taylor 1992: 85). In the context of Shelley's novel, this is illustrated negatively by Victor Frankenstein; Victor violates the Baconian principle that production of knowledge must make a contribution to social well-being by the virtue of the moral alignment between individual pursuits and ambitions, on the one hand, and the 'desire for society', on the other. Hume ([1751] 1998) writes about the 'spreading [of] kindly influence' through 'meritorious act[s]', and, paraphrasing Zarathustra, exemplifies them as creative deeds: '[t]o plant a tree, to cultivate a field, to beget children'; and with a remedial or reparative effect: '[f]rom him the hungry receive food, the naked clothing, the ignorant and slothful skill and industry'; '[g]iving alms to common beggars [carries] relief to the distressed and indigent'. The representation of modern European society in Shelley's *Frankenstein* illustrates this point, as the protagonists are motivated by the pursuits of 'practical benevolence' as a way of realising their roles in, and contributions to, modern sociality. Chastising Victor for 'excessive' despondence and sorrow after the death of Victor's youngest brother, the father warns him that strong affects can thwart personal 'improvement and enjoyment', and even prevent 'the *discharge of daily usefulness*, without which no man is fit for society' ([1818] 2009: 106; emphasis mine).[15]

While Hume sometimes uses the term 'benevolence' synonymously to 'humanity' in *An Enquiry concerning the Principles of Morals* (cf. Taylor 2013), in his texts the term most often signifies either a class of specific virtues and affections characterised by their socially salutary effects, such as generosity, kindness and charity, or it stands for a general principle of sociability and an ethical orientation towards the enhancement of the well-being others. It is thus interesting that Hume, after having seemingly equated social benevolence with an individual's usefulness in society, problematises the identification of benevolence with utility. In his reading of Plutarch's description of Pericles' death, Hume defines benevolence by what it is not, rather than what it is. When praised for his life accomplishments, including his statesmanship, military conquests and patronage of arts, the dying Pericles replies: '[y]ou forget the most eminent of my praises . . . [which is that] *no citizen has even yet worne mourning on my account*' (cited in Hume [1751] 1998: s. 2, pt 2; emphasis mine). The fact that what Pericles counts as his key life achievement is not his contribution to social well-being, but that *he has spared others grief* directs Hume's philosophy of benevolence away from altruism and social utility. Rather, Hume articulates benevolence as something that exceeds postulates of usefulness and expediency – in Frankenstein this position is represented by Victor's father – and which bridges modern moral philosophy and Shelley's novel. Victor's 'problem' is not that his creation has been socially 'useless' (that is, that it is *outside* the principle of social benevolence), but, rather, that Victor has actively brought about grief and suffering. The ambivalence of Shelley's representation of benevolence suggests that it is not only the grief of Victor's fellow humans that is at hand; perhaps a graver misdeed has been the grief brought to the Creature himself. Victor is the maker of an afflicted and suffering life. Ironically, on his own deathbed, Victor appears very much as a figure of anti-Pericles when he says to Capitan Walton: '[w]hen younger . . . I believed myself destined for some great enterprise . . . But this thought . . . now serves only to plunge me lower in the dust. All my speculations and hopes are as nothing; and, like the archangel who aspired to omnipotence, I am chained in an eternal hell . . . [H]ow am I sunk!' ([1818] 2009: 264).

Central to Hume's notion of benevolence, and to the philosophy of moral sentiments and moral epistemology more broadly, is the concept of sympathy – a descriptor of the psychological mechanism of social representation, communication and transfer of feelings and affective states (see Roberts 1973: 91–7). In *A Treatise of Human Nature* ([1739] 1973: 427, 365) Hume argues that sympathy involves 'the conversion of an idea into an impression by the force of imagination', and that 'the minds of men are mirrors to one another, not only because they reflect each other's emotions, but also because those rays of passions, sentiments and opinions may be often reverberated and decay away by insensible degrees'. As such, the mechanism of sympathy unfolds over three consecutive stages: the identification of the somatic and verbal expressions of emotions; formulation of an idea about specific passions; and the conversion of the idea into impression, which requires a resemblance or associative links between the self and the other (contiguity or causation). While factors such as kinship, language, culture or the frequency of social interactions, can facilitate affective communication and identification, or what Hume refers to as our 'partial' concern for family and friends, which is when benevolence is 'naturally' strongest, the lowest common denominator for the mechanism of sympathy to operate is the category humanity ('impartial sympathy'). He writes in *An Enquiry* ([1751] 1998: s. 2, pt 2) that 'nothing can bestow more merit on any human creature than the sentiment of benevolence in an eminent degree', and that this merit arises in particular 'from its tendency to promote the interest of our species, and bestow happiness on human society'.[16] It is the mechanism of sympathy – the capacity to 'receive' the affects of other 'fellow humans' not simply as abstract ideas, but as bodily impressions and experiences – or what Hume has called 'the sentiment of humanity' – that in Shelley's novel breaks down and proves inoperative, with the appearance of the Creature. Hume's juxtaposition of benevolence and justice maps onto his distinction between 'natural virtues' and 'artificial virtues' (Roberts 1973: 99–100). While the former correspond to 'original inclinations' and 'natural impulses', which 'arouse spontaneous approval in spectators without regard to anything but the immediate context', the latter 'consist in conduct in accordance with . . . general moral rules and conventions' (Whelan 1980: 107, 105). The 'artificial virtues' demand of the subject a formal observance, rather than depend on the sympathetic mechanism, which is the strongest in the partial contexts of contiguity and causation, and substantially weaker (though still operative) in regard to the impartial and inclusive category of 'universal humanity'.[17]

'MY DESIRE TO CLAIM THEIR KINDNESS': THE LIMITS OF BENEVOLENCE

The events of *Frankenstein* unfold against the backdrop of Shelley's depiction of a European society in 1790s, which reflects Butler and Hume's characterisation of social benevolence, both more broadly as a kindly disposition and charitable feelings towards others, and in the more specific sense of philanthropic activities. Benevolence is the formative element of the friendship between Captain Walton and Victor Frankenstein, as well as between Victor and Henry Clerval. Walton's listening to Victor's story includes a strong sympathetic component; put in Hume's language, Walton 'receives by communication' Victor's 'inclinations and sentiments' ([1739] 1973: 316). The practice of listening produces an affective response of fondness, empathy and even veneration for who in Walton's eyes is an admirable person in need of repair. He writes to his sister Margaret about Victor: '[m]y affection for my guest increases every day. He excites at once my admiration and my pity to an astonishing degree. How can I see so noble a creature destroyed by misery, without feeling the most poignant grief?' ([1818] 2009: 20).

Even more striking is the benevolent component in Henry Clerval's affection. Victor's childhood friend, Clerval, is reunited with him shortly after Victor's making of the Creature, and Clerval cares for Victor in illness (care for an ailing human is a reversal-figure of Victor's hubristic act of infusing dead tissue with life). Through the 'unbounded and unremitting attentions of [a] friend', Victor undergoes a kind of reparative return, though only temporarily, and is *restored to life* ([1818] 2009: 74; emphasis mine). Clerval's practice of benevolence is restorative in contrast to the insalubrious effects of Victor's scientific pursuits and their detrimental impact on sociability. Victor admits that Clerval's friendship 'called forth the better feelings of my heart; he again taught me to love the aspects of nature, and the cheerful faces of children' ([1818] 2009: 76). What is restored, then, is not only physical health, but also certain quality of innocence, and Victor's capacity for an aesthetic experience and appreciation of happiness in the world. While Victor's pursuits of forbidden scientific knowledge have had a negative effect on his own benevolent disposition – it dims his own 'natural' impulse to remedy the world – it is that capacity that, thanks to Clerval, undergoes repair. Victor's address to Clerval signals achievement of a restitutive return: 'Excellent friend! . . . your gentleness and affection warmed and opened my senses; I became the same happy creature who, a few years ago, loved and beloved by all, had no sorrow and care' ([1818] 2009: 76).

In addition to the benevolent grounding of friendship, equally significant is Shelley's characterisation of family life, and of childhood in particular, in terms of moral sentiment and social benevolence. In terms strikingly reminiscent of Hume's characterisation of a benevolent patriarch whose 'children never feel his authority, but when employed for their advantage' ([1751] 1998: s. 2, pt 2), Victor's parents are described as 'not the tyrants to rule our lot according to their caprice, but the agents and creators of all the many delights which we enjoyed' ([1818] 2009: 24). Victor's parents are also bona fide humanitarians. They personify Hume's 'human, beneficent man' (and woman) from whom 'the hungry receive food, the naked clothing, the ignorant and slothful skill and industry' ([1751] 1998: s. 2, pt 2). These efforts in poverty relief are not part of any formal obligations, but, rather, an ethical imperative: '[t]heir benevolent disposition often made them enter the cottages of the poor', Victor says ([1818] 2009: 24), '[it] was more than a duty; it was a necessity, a passion . . .' What is apparent in these characterisations of Victor's friendship and of his childhood and upbringing, is that the ideal of benevolence functions as a source of ethical behaviour and the organising principle of social life that Victor comes to recognise as the world before his *lapsus*, his fall, and which he subsequently tries to repair and restore, but with no success.

The Frankensteins' sense of ethical necessity also motivates their adoption of Elizabeth, an orphaned and dispossessed child of noble background ([1818] 2009: 29–30). Her adoption narrative is a kind of *retrieval* of a 'child fairer than a garden rose among dark-leaved brambles', with hair like 'brightest living gold' and 'a crown of distinction on her head', from the 'rude abode' of her plebeian carers. Here, the parents' benevolent attitudes coexist with, and incorporate, a class obligation to a rescue one of their own from the potential corruption by the ignoble classes. Elizabeth's adoption fulfils a dual desire of the Frankenstein family the desire for a female child and for gifting Victor with a female companion, a future wife: '[my mother] presented Elizabeth to me as *her promised gift* [and] I, with childish seriousness, interpreted her words literally and looked upon Elizabeth as mine – mine to protect, love, and cherish . . . my more than sister, since till death she was to be mine only' ([1818] 2009: 30–1; emphasis mine). Elizabeth's objectification as Victor's gift illuminates the ethical stakes of the benevolent relation: according to Butler, the benevolent subject must take other than oneself as the object of his or her remedial actions. The fact that Elizabeth's adoption by the Frankenstein family becomes synonymous with Victor's bequest blurs the distinction between serving as an object of others' benevolence and appropriation, and suggests that the Frankensteins as 'subjects of sympathy' depend on the existence of a vulnerable 'subject of suffering' (Asad 2015), like Elizabeth, to sustain their identity.

Important to social manifestations of benevolence in the novel is the figure of the face. This is another Humean motif: in the sympathetic theory inner orientations and inclinations of the subject always manifest on the body, in particular, they are perceptible and discernible through facial expressions. The human protagonists are often described as having a *benevolent countenance*, and looking at their faces produces pleasurable feelings. This contrasts starkly with the experience of looking at the Creature's face, which is a 'sight tremendous and abhorrent' ([1818] 2009: 116). The Creature's response to others' benevolent countenance differs from his pleasures of viewing inanimate or natural objects. The face of the other engenders in the Creature reverence, and is interpreted as a kind of ethical guarantee of kind intentions (see [1818] 2009: 128). This universal reliance on opticality for detecting benevolent intentions poses a problem for a blind protagonist, the old Da Lacey, when he encounters but cannot see the Creature.

It is with the view of recognising the importance of the idea of benevolence in the characterisation of modern European society in *Frankenstein* that Victor's failure to live up to the ideal of social utility and beneficence acquires its significance (see Goldberg 1959; Ziolkowski 1981).[18] Victor describes the effects of his upbringing: '. . . my heart overflowed with kindness, and the love of virtue. I had begun life with benevolent intentions, and thirsted for the moment when I should put them in practice and make myself useful to my fellow beings' ([1818] 2009: 105). He develops a passion for natural philosophy and for exploring the 'secrets of nature', derived from occult and alchemist texts ([1818] 2009: 35–9). During his studies at the University of Ingolstadt, while already committed to the pursuit of vivification of dead matter in his 'workshop of filthy creation', Victor draws indirectly on the theory of moral sentiment, and on the ethical guideposts of feelings, to undertake moral assessment of his work ([1818] 2009: 56). He notes the adverse effects of his work on his ability to appreciate and be affected and enchanted by nature, and on his sociability. There occurs a rupture between his scientific ambitions and the desire to augment society's well-being, as Victor withdraws from the social world ([1818] 2009: 76, 57):

> Study had . . . secluded me from the intercourse of my fellow-creatures, and rendered me unsocial . . . [a] selfish pursuit had cramped and narrowed me . . .
> [and]
> [i]f the study to which you apply yourself has a tendency to weaken your affections, and to destroy your taste for those simple pleasures . . . than that study is certainly unlawful, that is to say, not befitting the human mind.

The making of the Creature is a result of that rift between scientific knowledge production and the contribution to societal well-being. The Creature magnifies his maker's hubristic disregard for charitable sociability in being perceived as *male*volent, that is, actively ill-disposed towards others. Victor says: 'I had unchained an enemy among them, whose joy it was to shed their blood, and to revel in their groans' ([1818] 2009: 231).

The Creature's primary desire, which precedes even his desire for a female companion, is to join the human community and to become the receiver and beneficiary of human benevolence – in the words of the Creature, to be 'one among my fellows' ([1818] 2009: 145). Confronting Victor in the surrounding of the Alps, the Creature demands that he 'does [his] duty' towards the Creature, postulating his duty to complete the act of creation by providing the Creature with a species companion, and also, perhaps less obviously, an obligation to listen to the Creature's story.[19] The Creature's audacious gesture of declaring himself a subject of rights – the rights to companionship, sociability and to self-preservation – and thus a fellow human being, are a demand for inclusion in the benevolent relation. He says: '[to me are] thy justice, and even thy clemency and affection . . . most due' ([1818] 2009: 118).

However, the Creature seems constitutively unable to engender benevolent feelings in others. 'How can I move thee?' he asks Victor ([1818] 2009: 118), '[w]ill no intreaties cause thee to turn a favourable eye upon thy creature, who implores thy goodness and compassion?'. Victor describes himself as utterly devoid of any compassionate sentiment towards his progeny, and refuses to recognise him as a fellow human and a person, but, rather, something akin to a thing, a 'filthy mass that moved and talked' ([1818] 2009: 179). The Creature's exclusion from humanity and from personhood is not presented as a volitional act on Victor's part, but, rather, as a result of a more fundamental impediment or bar in operation. 'I *could not* sympathise with him', says Victor ([1818] 2009: 179; emphasis mine).

Finally, the Creature also gives account of his own loss of benevolence. The thesis of the 'original goodness of the monster' reflects Rousseau's characterisation of compassion as a pre-civilisational disposition.[20] The Creature's benevolent disposition is responsive: it develops sympathetically and is augmented through his observations of the 'micro-society' of the Da Lacey family. He has an 'ardent desire' to 'relieve the sufferings of every human creature' ([1818] 2009: 193). The Creature's words are an apt illustration of Hume's notion of sympathy: '[t]he gentle manners and beauty desire to claim their protection and kindness; my heart yearned to be known and loved by these amiable creatures; to see the sweet looks of the cottagers greatly endeared them to me: when they were unhappy, I felt depressed; when they rejoiced, I sympathised in their joys' ([1818] 2009: 134). And, later, 'I dared not think that they would turn them from me with disdain and horror. The poor that stopped at their door were never driven away. I asked, it is true, for greater treasures than a little food or rest: I required kindness and sympathy; but I did not believe myself unworthy of it' (2009 [1818]: 160).

The Creature's desire to be included in the human community of benevolence remains unfulfilled. Instead of being accommodated within it, he is violently expelled. Denise Gigante (2000) argues that what makes the Creature's inclusion in humanity impossible is the ugliness and repulsiveness of his appearance insofar as it indicates not simply the absence of beauty, but something far more substantive.[21] The Creature turns a misanthropic gaze at humanity as a whole, rather than his individual malefactors, because he considers his rejection to be an exclusion from the universal human community of equals. His status of a threshold being manifests as the inability to become either the subject or the object of benevolence. Roberto Esposito writes (2015: 101), citing the work of French psychoanalyst Pierre Legendre on the legal status of the body in *Code civil*, that 'death forces the body into the category of thing'. With the Creature, we have then a curious case of an entity (or, rather, enti*ties*, given his conglomerate nature) that seems to pass from the regime of a person into that of a thing, and then back again, from the regime of a thing into that of a person. *Frankenstein* presents a case of a life-form permanently suspended between these two modes of epistemic and social organisation, which threatens to reveal that social benevolence rests on the logic of othering and exclusion, and that it generates and legitimizes violence against those who have been barred from it. The Creature's threshold position between a 'person' and a 'thing' becomes the source of his *in*humanity.

'MY LITTLE BABY CAME TO LIFE AGAIN':
DREAMS OF RESTITUTION IN *FRANKENSTEIN*

The tropes of undoing, return and reversal abound in *Frankenstein*. In what follows, I propose to organise them in a way that will help to uncover their relation to the idea of benevolent foundations of sociality, to present restitution as a process and procedure of return to a prelapsarian condition of the subject. In *Frankenstein* restitution is not only bound with the question of the binary epistemology of 'persons' and 'things', but is also granted to those who are recognised as belonging to humanity and included in the benevolent relation. The restitutive tropes in *Frankenstein* take the forms of undoing, substitution and repair, but none of them are ever realised; instead, restitutive endeavours in the novel fail, prove to be insufficient, incomplete and futile. We should, then, perhaps speak more appropriately about restitutive 'traces' or 'attempts' (cf. Sebald 2004) in the novel, rather than restitution as anything definitive or accomplished. This also shows more clearly what is at stake in the proposition that the Creature is a figure of unrestitutability; because of his ejection from the human community, he is also denied any possibility of return, undoing and repair. This is not only because there is no prelapsarian condition for the Creature to return to – he is, after all, an animated composition of fragments, a 'necro-assemblage' – but also because the elimination of the Creature's monstrous presence creates the possibility of restitution for Victor. In other words, the Creature as a figure of unrestitutability is the 'constitutive outside' of the restitutive and reparative possibilities of those 'properly human' characters in the novel, partaking in the ethics of universal benevolence.

Victor's achievement of composing an organic whole from dead tissue fragments and their subsequent animation situates *Frankenstein* within the narrative and mythological context of the motif of overcoming death, and has stipulated rich speculative genealogy of the novel, including the European medieval alchemy and experimental anatomy (most famously, perhaps, in Victor's real-life predecessor, Johann Conrad Dippel (see Florescu 1999)). The motif of overcoming death in Shelley's novel hinges upon a double reversal: by stitching together and galvanising fragments of corpses into an organic whole, Victor *undoes* death's *undoing* of living person into an inanimate 'thing', or what he calls the body's transformation into a 'putrid matter' ([1818] 2009: 55). This part of the narrative unfolds as if (in) a reverie, and Victor refers to his necropolitan montage of the Creature as a nightmare. Also, Victor's desire for the undoing or unmaking of irreversible past is consistent with the dream structure of the novel (see Glance 1996; Rieder 2003; Benford 2010).[22]

Then, there is also other 'dreaming' of the Creature. There is the famous dream that Mary Shelley had in a cottage at Lake Geneva in 1816; a dream of an irreverent scientist who animated a corpse that, as Shelley reported, 'haunted her midnight pillow'. But there is also Shelley's earlier and less known eerie dream that occurred in the aftermath of the death of her infant daughter, Clara (Rieder 2003).[23] In a diary-entry from 19 March 1815, Mary Shelley noted her recurring night vision of the dead child's return: '[d]ream that my little baby came to life again – that it had only been cold & and that we rubbed it by the fire & it lived' (cited in Bronfen 1994; see also Schoene-Harwood 2000: 57).[24]

The uncanny apparition of the infant has the form of a wish fulfilment of undoing death of the love-object, and for the retroactive annulment of the fact that the child died, sheds light on Victor's narrativisation of the Creature's montage and animation as a dream occurrence. As such, it shows the dream-like narrative to be expressive of a suppressed desire for making-unhappen an irreversible event of loss. A terrain of psychic operations that Freud described as a defence mechanism of *Ungeschehenmachen*, or 'undoing-what-has-been-done' ([1949] 1959), the two narratives of Shelley's dream about her dead child 'living again' and Victor's composition and animation of dead matter into an organic whole, pivot on an enactment of 'magical procedures'. In the first, the mother applies manual friction to bring a child back to life – a procedure that reveals the child not to have died in the first place – and, in the second, the scientist applies an electric current to animate the assembled lifeless body. Victor gives insight into these underpinning operations of making-unhappen in his confession to Captain Walton: '. . . I thought . . . that if I could bestow animation upon lifeless matter, I might in the process of time . . . *renew life where death had apparently devoted the body to corruption*' ([1818] 2009: 55; emphasis mine).

An influential interpretation of *Frankenstein* casts it as a retelling of the Miltonian creation story (cf. Schoene-Harwood 2000). However, it is a highly distorted act of creating in that Victor's work is not bringing into being anything new, but, rather, it reshapes and reassembles the Creature from pre-existing material of fragments of dead tissue. At the heart of Victor's achievement is thus a return of a former (and irreversibly altered) condition of things. In the previous chapter, I outlined the idea of restitutive imaginary as a legal–political construct in the thought of Hugo Grotius that operates upon a fantasy of undoing and reversal to a previous status or situation (*postliminium*) through acts of object relocation and re-acquisition. If the restitutive objects seem to be missing in *Frankenstein* (though there are, of course, the dead fragments and the galvanising force of electricity that serve as kinds of objects promising to enable the subject's return), this is because a clear restitutive subject position in the novel also fails to emerge. The Creature occupies an indeterminate place between the subject undergoing life-renewal and the object facilitating it, but proving to be incapable of either. Restitution in *Frankenstein* is the act of life restoration, which fails to achieve its desired effects; the re-animated parts of the Creature's stitched body – 'black lips', 'watery eyes', 'shrivelled complexion'[25] – appear somewhat alive, but also somewhat dead, attributes of both a person *and* a thing.

In response to Victor's refusal to make him a female companion, the Creature kills Victor's beloved in what is perceived to be an act of retributive and retaliatory justice. Elizabeth's killing constitutes not only the Creature's more obvious attempt to punish Victor and to inflict suffering on him, but also to equalise their status: now both the Creature and Victor are solitary, companionless and childless. As I mentioned earlier, Elizabeth's adoption into the Frankenstein family pivoted on her objectification as a gift for young Victor to first play with and care for, and later to marry; an objectification that helps him to solidify the position of a patriarchal benevolent subject. Just as Elizabeth becomes the recipient of Victor's affection and generosity – a position forever denied to his monstrous progeny – so does she come to stand for a restitutive and redemptive promise in the face of Victor's guilt and despair. Elizabeth becomes the desired restitutive object as their marital union comes to signify for Victor an absolution from his 'unhallowed' deeds ([1818] 2009: 231); an imaginary return to their adolescent relationship, and a possibility of undoing, through forgetting of the unbearable and irreversible truth of ever having made the Creature. Victor says: 'one consolation for my unparalleled suffering . . . the prospect of that day when, enfranchised from my miserable slavery, I might claim Elizabeth, and *forget the past in union with her*' (2009 [1818]: 189; my emphasis). The despair felt by Victor at the realisation of the irreversibility of his act of 'birthing' the Creature into the world reverberates throughout the novel with each death, including Elizabeth's killing, as well as the deaths of William, Justine, Clerval, and Victor's father. These deaths are narrated by the main protagonist as the gradual elimination of the possibility for Victor to ever return to human communion, love and friendship. Victor says to Walton: '. . . when you speak of new ties, and fresh affections, [do you think] that any can replace those who are gone? Can any man be to me as Clerval was; or any woman another Elizabeth?' ([1818] 2009: 265). These perhaps surprising words (given that they are coming from a scientist who has just successfully galvanised dead matter into existence) emphasise the differential status of death in the novel; the anonymous corpses whose pieces are assembled into the Creature are clearly no more than 'things' to Victor, but dead friends and companions retain the status of 'persons'. The possibility of their re-animation does not arise; their deaths are final and irrevocable.

Similarly, unrestitutability and irreversibility are invoked in the context of the Creature's death, which Shelley narrates as not only an end of singular life, but as kind of 'extinction' in that on his deathbed the Creature laments not just his own individual disappearance, but that of his kind. The fact that the Creature self-identifies as monstrous and unsightly has been frequently remarked upon (see Sterrenburg 1979; Bewell 1988);[26] it has been less frequently noted, however, that by pondering his monstrosity, the Creature also affirms himself as representative of a distinct kind, or species; '[w]hen I looked around', he says, 'I saw and heard of none like me' ([1818] 2009: 144). As such, the Creature at the same time identifies and *dis*-identifies as the Miltonian Adam. The Creature's statement '[l]ike Adam, I was apparently united by no link to any other being in existence', is thus immediately followed with the words: 'his state was far different from mine in every other respect. He had come forth from the hands of God a perfect creature . . . but I was wretched, helpless, and alone' ([1818] 2009: 124). While Adam remains a singular representative of his kind for a limited time only, the Creature dies companionless, species-less and childless. When he addresses Walton with words of farewell, 'I leave you, and in you the last of humankind whom these eyes will ever behold . . . soon . . . I shall die, and what I now feel be no longer felt' ([1818] 2009: 128), the Creature announces his death as the disappearance of a unique witness of the human condition, looking at humanity from the position of its exclusion. The Creature's final words, '[s]oon these burning miseries will be extinct' ([1818] 2009: 129), suggest that what is coming to an end exceeds his individual existence; rather, the Creature announces the soon-to-come end of humanity's inhuman witness. Keenly observing the Da Lacey family from the secrecy of his hiding place, the Creature expresses the wish to join their community: '[t]he more I saw of them, the greater became my desire to claim their protection and kindness', and 'my heart yearned to be known and loved by these amiable creatures; to see their sweet looks directed towards me with affection was the utmost limit of my ambition' ([1818] 2009: 101). Ironically, given that the Creature remains forever barred from the human community, even he partakes in the depictions of the benevolent society as one unsullied by violence.

Reading *Frankenstein* through the prism of the motifs of benevolence and restitutability reveals ways in which the Creature's ejection from humanity intersects with the restitutive tropes in the novel, and results in the consolidation of the Creature's unrestitutability. The Creature can be neither the subject nor the object of restitution; he has nowhere to return and nothing to restore. He is also unable to facilitate Victor's restitutive pursuits – in contrast to Elizabeth who signifies for Victor the promise of the return of the childhood world of generosity and compassion, and of the erasure and forgetting of his crimes, he remains trapped between the epistemological categories of persons and things. The interweaving of the benevolent and restitutive motifs in *Frankenstein* supports the observation that modern restitutive imaginaries rest on the assumptions of human community. Humanity as a construct that is at risk of being compromised and sullied by violence, remains in need of restoration and restitution; through 'reaching out compassionately to another's pain' (Asad 2015: 402), humanity returns to its prelapsarian self.

3

ÉMILE DURKHEIM'S RESTITUTIVE HUMANITARIANISM: FROM ORGANIC SOLIDARITY TO THE 'SOLIDARITY OF THINGS'

In eighteenth- and nineteenth-century continental Europe the law of restitution was included in the reformed legal codes as the key mechanism for gain-based recovery: the 1794 Prussian Code, the 1811 Austrian Civil Code, the 1896 German Civil Code and the 1907 Swiss Civil Code asserted the legitimacy of possessory and proprietary actions in the situations classified as wrongful interference with the rights of ownership (Giglio 2004; Sabahi 2011). David argues (1972: 71) that these codes were deeply influenced by the natural law philosophy conception of restitution, and that they affirmed restitution to be 'the ideal form of indemnification' due to its corrective and remedial effects. By re-establishing the status quo, restitution was thought to 'eliminate the harm as completely as [it was] . . . possible' (David 1972: 71).

In this chapter I look at Émile Durkheim's socio-legal theory of restitution, focusing in the first instance on his 1893 *De la division du travail social* ([1893] 2007; [1984] 2014), and situating the Durkheimian conception of restitutive law in the context of his philosophy of modern sociality. Commenting on what he saw as a decreasing severity of European penal law in the modern period, Durkheim argued that there was a causal relation between the emergence of restitutive legal norms and the socio-economic transformation of European societies. By sketching out a conceptual and sociological nexus of the restitutive orientation of modern European law, the increased division of labour in industrialised societies, and the socio-cultural transformations of penal institutions, Durkheim sets up another 'restitutive scene' in the focus of this book. At hand is namely an imaginary depiction of a subject who repossesses a lost object, and who, by the virtue of that act of re-acquisition, returns to the former condition of things – to their legal status and relations from *before* the occurrence of crime. In the dominant rights-based interpretations of restitution, this has meant the return to the proprietary status quo and a reversal to the position that the victim would have occupied, had no violations of their property rights occurred.

In *The Division of Labor in Society* ([1984]) 2014: 88–104), Durkheim also elaborates the relationship between law and the emergence of different types of social bonds; in modern European societies restitutive law produces modes of communal unity of action and sentiment, which Durkheim called 'organic solidarity [*la solidarité organique*]'. The distinctive sociological feature of 'organic solidarity' was that, rather than building on feudal, religious or kinship bonds, characteristic of traditional societies, it was a function of interdependence and complementarity of labour among the increasingly more individualised members of industrial acquisitive societies. In analysing Durkheim's theory of restitution, I use the idea of 'restitutive scene' because I want to suggest that Durkheim, committed as he is to the task of structural sociological analysis, also unfolds and relies on a kind of *imaginary* of restitution. This means, in the narrow sense, that Durkheim inserts into his exposition imaginal constructs of, for example, a clock that is being turned back, ostensibly for illustrative and explanatory purposes, but which also become sites where tensions in his theory manifest. This also means, in a broader sense, that through his analysis Durkheim is engaged in a task of *imaginal politics*; he envisions modern law, modern sociality and solidarity with illocutionary force that exceeds the goals of sociological analysis, and the analysis reflects and reinforces specific normative, epistemological and philosophic orientations. By identifying restitution as a corrective and remedial response to wrongdoing, and by situating it in a binary opposition to punitive and repressive law, Durkheim unfolds imaginary that associates restitution with non-violent interventions of the law (cf. [1984] 2014: 55).

Durkheim's socio-legal theory, including his depiction of the restitutive function of modern law, has been subject to post-colonial, critical anthropological and feminist discussions, not least because of the binary opposition of modern and traditional sociality, and because of the beliefs in the assumptions about 'primitivism' on his sociological analysis (see, for example, Barnes 1966; Giddens 1978; Wityak and Wallace 1981; Lehmann 1994; Gane 2002; Cristi 2012). I focus on how the ostensibly binary opposite categories of modern and traditional law, and society and solidarity in *The Division of Labor* become less stable and less certain when interpreted through the prism of Durkheim's later work. That concerns, in particular, his writings on the ethos of humanitarianism, individualism, and the 'origins' and transformations of crime. Drawing on Roland Barthes' constructs of '*scriptable*' and '*lisible*', Smith and Alexander (2008: 2) suggest that there is a need for 'unauthorised' interpretations of Durkheim, which depart from regarding his texts as 'closed, definitive and "writerly"', and that view them instead as 'open, suggestive, and "readerly"'.[1] Following this suggestion, I draw on selected Durkheimian writings to both elucidate *and* complicate the restitutive imaginary from *The Division of Labor*.

REPRESSIVE SANCTIONS AND MECHANICAL SOLIDARITY

The context of Durkheim's theorising of restitutive law in *The Division of Labor* are his sociological observations of the changing character of bonds and connections in modern industrialised societies. Durkheim asks whether the socio-economic, industrial and technological developments in nineteenth-century Europe, which accelerated professional specialisation and the division of labour in society, produced social atomisation and alienation. Durkheim's views on the socio-economic changes in the modern period are often described as falling between the 'optimist' and 'pessimist' positions. Coser argues ([1984] 2014: xii–xiii) that, on the one hand, Durkheim rejected the 'optimist' view associated with the work of Adam Smith that the '[v]astly increased productive capacities would raise the level of human happiness to previously undreamed of degrees', but that, on the other hand, Durkheim also disagreed with the views of the romantics for whom 'society as an engine for the production and multiplication of goods was inherently hostile to society as the moral foundation of personality' (Pocock, cited in Coser ([1984] 2014: xiii).[2] Instead, Durkheim, 'a dispassionate student of society' and a committed social reform-ist, focused on the question of the conditions for reconciling the value of individual autonomy with 'the necessary regulation and discipline that were required to maintain social order in modern differentiated types of society' (Coser [1984] 2014: xiv). His theory of restitutive sanctions developed from this goal of bringing together the concerns about social individualisation and atomisation with the question of the nature of collective bonds in modernity.[3] Contrary to his conservative contemporaries who equated individualism with alienation, and contrary to Auguste Comte, Ferdinand Tönnies and others, for whom the end of feudalism and of the traditional system of shared values and norms heralded a decline in social cohesion, Durkheim postulated that the rise of individualism in industrial Europe meant transformation, rather than elimi-nation, of social solidarity.[4]

In the preface to the first edition of *De la division du travail social* ([1893] 2007: 46; [1984]) 2014: 7), Durkheim presents the question concerning the tightening new social bonds and the preponderance of individualist and humanist ideals as a paradox:

> How does it come about that the individual, whilst becoming more auton-omous [*plus autonome*], depends ever more closely upon society? How

can he become at the same time more of an individual [*plus personnel*] and yet more linked to society [*plus solidaire*]? For it is indisputable that these two movements, however contradictory they appear to be, are carried on in tandem . . . It has seemed to us that what resolved this apparent antinomy was the transformation of social solidarity which arises from the ever-increasing division of labour.

Durkheim uses the terminology of solidarity in the sense of 'social connection [*le lien social*]', that is, as a relationship between the individual and society. According to Jones (2001: 90), Durkheim's use of the term 'solidarity' in his early oeuvre reflects his 'associational and relational' approach, as well as suggests psychological, representational and communicative connotations. Durkheim sought to explain the apparent paradox of concurring individualism and solidarity in modern societies through his analysis and taxonomy of the social effects of the division of labour. Using Darwinian metaphors and adopting a social evolutionary view, Durkheim assumed that increasing structural differentiation and functional specialisation are key factors in the emergence of modern sociality. *De la division du travail social* drew from the scholarship of nineteenth-century colonial anthropology,[5] which assumed the existence of 'organic' and 'morphological' likeness among members of the same grouping. The idea of societal change was situated in the evolutionary epistemological framework, and was based on the assumption that human societies exist on a 'morphological and historical continuum' (Barnes 1966: 166). Durkheim's assumptions about 'primitivism' and intra-group resemblance played a crucial role in his taxonomy of modern and traditional law and solidarity, including his characterisation of restitutive sanctions.[6] Not unlike other oppositional sociological categories developed by Durkheim's contemporaries – Spencer's 'military societies' and 'industrial societies'; Maine's 'status societies' and 'contract societies'; and Tönnies' '*Gemeinschaft*' and '*Gesellschaft*' – the binary conceptions of law and solidarity in *The Division of Labor in Society* have no intermediary phases (Barnes 1966: 161; Lukes and Scull 1983: 10; Coser [1984] 2014: xv).

Durkheim ([1984]) 2014: 106–7) relates these assumptions to outline an explanatory framework of the low degrees of labour division and of professional specialisation in traditional (or what he calls 'primitive') societies. He emphasises in particular the public role of religion as a sociological factor that eliminates the possibility of 'originality' and that produces homogeneity of ideas, beliefs and moral attitudes:

[O]riginality [in traditional societies] is not only rare; there is, so to speak, no room for it. Everybody then accepts and practices without argument the same religion; different sects and quarrels are unknown:

they would not be tolerated. At this time religion includes everything, extends to everything. It embraces, although in a very confused state, besides religious beliefs proper, ethics, law, the principles of political organization, and even science, or at least what passes for it. It regulates even the minutiae of private life. Thus to state that religious consciousnesses are then identical, and that this identity is absolute, is implicitly to assert that . . . every individual consciousness is roughly made up of the same elements.

Durkheim's well-known term of 'common' or 'collective' consciousness [*la conscience commune*] captures the idea that beliefs, attitudes and sentiments in society as irreducible to the sum total of its individual parts ([1893] 2007: 81; [1984] 2014: 63). Jones argues (2001: 85) that the Durkheimian 'common consciousness' postulates the existence of a belief and value system that 'identifies and constitutes relationships within a determinate portion of reality', and 'symbolizes and postulates a realm of significations'.[7] In the first instance, Durkheim associates the existence of such 'collective consciousness' with traditional societies, and he ponders the possibility of the decline of shared moral sensibilities in industrial acquisitive societies. He argues that in traditional societies, characterised by highly concentrated and centripetal collective belief systems, punitive functions of the law, or what Durkheim calls 'repressive law [*droit répressif*]' prevail over restorative and remedial operations of the law, or 'restitutive law [*droit restitutif*]'. This proposition rests on the assumption that the domain of law constitutes an accessible and measurable manifestation of the changes in the nature of societal bonds and in collective value systems. Law constitutes a kind of 'external index [*un fait extérieur*]' that enables the study of 'changes in the nature of social solidarity' – of the 'internal datum [*un fait interne*]' of collective moral transformations (Giddens 1977: 76). Criminalisation of social behaviour was for Durkheim a key element in tracking the 'external index' of social change.

Durkheim defined 'crime' as an 'act that offends the collective consciousness', and argued that 'crime disturbs those feelings that in any one type of society are to be found in every healthy consciousness [*le crime froisse des sentiments qui, pour un même type social, se retrouvent dans toutes les consciences saines*]'. Hence, 'it is always to the collective consciousness that we must return [because] from it . . . all criminality flows' ([1893] 2007: 76; [1984] 2014: 52, 59). In societies characterised by a density of collective morality systems the primary response to crime are repressive sanctions. Their severity corresponds to the perceptions of the damage caused by the wrongdoer to the body social ([1984] 2014: 58). Durkheim's sociology of crime relied on the assumption that primary social function of punishment was not to 'control crime, but to sustain and enhance solidarity' (Lukes [1984] 2014: xxxi). Or, in Durkheim's words ([1984] 2014: 83), the 'real function [of punishment] is to maintain inviolate the cohesion of society by sustaining the common consciousness in all its vigour'. The evocative language used by Durkheim to describe punitive legal action in traditional societies, including terms such as 'passionate reaction', 'an act of vengeance', 'an expiation for the past', coheres with the epistemological framework of colonial anthropology, centred around the figure of a 'primitive society'. What is important for my attempt at elucidating the Durkheimian restitutive imaginary is the striking absence of any note of reparative or restorative legal mechanisms or any shared ethos of restitution-making in the description of non-Western indigenous cultures (cf. Johnstone 2002; Acorn 2004). Further, Durkheim postulates a close nexus between repressive law and the collective desire to inflict bodily pain on the wrongdoer, or to make them suffer a loss. Repressive sanctions, Durkheim argues ([1893] 2007: 71; [1984] 2014: 55), consist 'in some injury [*une douleur*], or at least some disadvantage [*une diminution*] imposed upon the perpetrator of a crime', and their purpose is 'to do harm to [the wrongdoer] through his fortune, his honour, his life, or his liberty, or to deprive him of some object he enjoys.' Arguing that this injurious punitive action takes suffering as a goal in itself, Durkheim ([1984] 2014: 67) further writes that 'primitive peoples punish for the sake of punishing, causing the guilty person to suffer solely for the sake of suffering and without expecting any advantage for themselves from the suffering they inflict upon him'. As a result, they do not punish 'fairly' or 'usefully'. The spectacle of the suffering wrongdoer serves as a collective reminder that, in spite (or perhaps because) of the criminal occurrence, '*the sentiments of the collectivity are still collective*, that *the communion of minds sharing the same faith remains absolute*' ([1984] 2014: 83; emphasis mine).

While the historical accuracy of the Durkheimian representation of non-Western, traditional and indigenous law has been widely questioned,[8] what needs further consideration is the importance of this depiction of legal norms and punitive passions in 'repressive societies' for conceptualising restitution as their opposite – a non-violent and non-retaliatory response to wrongdoing and a sign of modern law's distance from 'collective anger' and revengeful passions. Durkheim's characterisation of restitution as the operations of law that are *exempt from injurious desires* coincides with his later reflections, such as his 1898 essay on 'moral individualism', on the impact of modern humanitarian ideology, including sacralisation of human life and the moral imperative to remedy and prevent suffering (cf. Cladis 2012; Paoletti 2012). Contrasted with the dynamics of repressive law, restitution is a product of what Lukes and Scull (1983: 27) aptly call the 'progressive humanization of punishment'; it is oriented not at the imposition of injury upon the offenders, but at the restoration of harmony of social relations, which is assumed to have existed prior to the crime. While Durkheim envisions the possibility of modern expiatory rituals as part of restitutive law, he does explicitly state that such rituals require alternative iconographies to those of a suffering wrongdoer, including remorseful speech and compunctious gestures (cf. Giddens 1977: 76).

The alleged homogeneity of collective morality and the prevalence of repressive norms in traditional societies coincide with a formation of social bonding ('*le lien social*') that Durkheim calls 'mechanical'. This 'mechanical solidarity [*la solidarité mécanique*]', also sometimes called a 'solidarity by similarities [*la solidarite par similitudes*]', emerges on the basis of resemblances and proximities within groups characterised by a highly 'elevated [*élevée*]' collective consciousness.[9] It is opposed to modern types of social: 'organic solidarity [*la solidarité organique*]'. The vernacular of 'mechanical' and 'organic' social bonds (which Durkheim did not use again after the publication of *The Division of Labor in Society*)[10] suggests a distinction between a condition or processes that are 'machinic', and those that are imbued with life (cf. Giddens 1978; Smith and Alexander 2008). What is machinic about the formation of social bonds in traditional societies is that they form an 'an aggregate', rather than, like in a living organism, consisting of mutually corresponding and interdependent elements and reciprocal connections (Giddens 1978: 26). Whereas repressive productions of solidarity are perceived to be akin to the working of inanimate and inorganic systems, Durkheim's use of the metaphors of 'life' and 'organicity' to capture the process of modern solidarity formation defines them as units of both functional differentiation and integration. Durkheim ([1984] 2014: 101) argues that in the case of *la solidarité mécanique* '[t]he social molecules cohere . . . as a unit in so far as they lack any movement of their own, as do the molecules of inorganic bodies'. Durkheim ([1984] 2014: 101) further compares the 'mechanical' social bonds to 'the cohesion that links together the elements of mineral bodies, in contrast to that which encompasses the animal bodies'. While molecules in mineral bodies are depicted as replicas of one another, the constitutive elements of animal bodies are functionally and morphologically distinct and interdependent. While mechanical solidarity assumes individuals' resemblance, and organic solidarity implies that:

> . . . they are different from one another. The former type is possible only in so far as the individual personality is absorbed into the collective personality; the latter is possible only if each one of us has a sphere of action that is peculiarly our own [*une sphère d'action qui lui est propre*], and consequently a personality [*une personnalité*] . . . Modern law plays a part analogous in society to that of the nervous system in the organism [and] [t]hat system . . . has the task of regulating the various bodily functions in such a way that they work harmoniously together [*concourir harmoniquement*]. ([1893] 2007: 122, 120; [1984] 2014: 102)

Building on the imaginary of mechanicity and inorganicity, Durkheim also proposes that the traditional type of social bonding is comparable with property relations. Specifically, the connection between individuals and their group formations *corresponds to* the relationship of inanimate things as property to persons as owners: 'the bond that . . . unites individual with [traditional] society is *completely analogous* to [the bond] which links a thing to a person' (Durkheim [1984] 2014: 102; emphasis mine). The repressive logic of the legal norms, and in particular their foundation upon vengeful wishes and the demands of 'collective anger', sheds light on Durkheim's reliance on the machinic language in the production of sociality; he considered this process to be 'unthinking [*irréfléchis*]', because of the public significance of passions and sentiments ([1893] 2007: 104; [1984]) 2014: 83, 98). Repressive norms produced social responses akin to 'involuntary movements' or 'instinctive reflexes', as Jones puts it (1986: 28), rather than to deliberate, purposeful and reflective action. '[W]hatever the origin of these sentiments', Durkheim writes ([1984]) 2014: 82), 'once they constitute a part of the collective type . . . everything that serves to undermine them at the same time undermines social cohesion and is prejudicial to society'. The formation of 'mechanical' social bonds is not only depicted as unreflective and devoid of spontaneity and originality, which only living beings are capable of, but also – due to the conceptual link between the idea of spontaneous action and individual freedom – as a social framework that precludes the possibility of liberty.

Restitutive Law and Organic Solidarity

The historical and sociological context of Durkheim's theory of restitution was the question concerning the social impact of the division of labour in industrial Europe in the eighteenth and nineteenth centuries, as well as the about role in the individualist idea, and the weakening and diffusion of shared norms and values. At stake in the socio-economic processes that Durkheim analysed was a 'replacement of an artisan mode of production' by 'a mode of production based on a much finer differentiation of tasks and . . . coordinated activities of a large number of persons', whereby the 'final product was the result of the integration of the work of a greater number of workers who were submitted to overall discipline and coordination' (Coser [1984] 2014: xii). Rather than characterise it primarily as an economic phenomenon, Durkheim depicted the division of labour in Europe as activation of mechanisms of societal transformation and as the emergence of a new collective ethos, centred around individual life. Akin to functionally specialised and internally coordinated elements of a living organism, participation in modern society was viewed in the light of Durkheim's philosophic outlook on modern sociality as the reality of interdependence and its effects on action, whilst attempting to preserve the autonomy and specificity of the parts.

As mentioned earlier, the key 'external index [*fait extérieur*]' for measuring and analysing social change was restitutive law. By 'restitution' Durkheim meant not a domain of law, even though it manifested most conspicuously in 'civil law, procedural law, administrative law, and constitutional law' ([1984]) 2014: 55), but, rather, the distinctive modality and operations of law in modern society at large. In contrast to repressive law, which had at its core the wrong-doer's bodily pain and/or their loss, restitutive law had the effect of 'restoring the previous state of affairs [*la remise des choses en état*]', and 're-establishing relationships that have been disturbed from their normal form [*le rétablissement des rapports troublés sous leur forme normale*]' (Durkheim ([1893] 2007: 72; [1984]) 2014: 55). This restitutive logic manifested either 'by forcibly redressing the action impugned, restoring it to the type from which it has deviated [*au type dont il a dévié*], or by annulling it, that is, depriving it of all social value [*privé de toute valeur sociale*]' ([1893] 2007: 72; [1984]) 2014: 55).

Important in this dual trajectory of restitution as either a restoration or as a value annulment is the goal of returning to the status quo as 'a simple repair of thing [*une simple remise en état*]' ([1893] 2007: 106; [1984]) 2014: 88). This is illustrated by Durkheim's image of a clock that is turned back; restitutive sanctions are a 'means of putting back the clock so as to restore the past [*un moyen de revenir sur le passé pour le restituer*], so far as possible, to its normal state [*sa forme normale*]' ([1893] 2007: 106; [1984] 2014: 88). Durkheim's restitutive imaginary blurs the distinction between the previously outlined transitive and intransitive grammatical aspects of restitution; first, as a reversal of an unjust gain whereby the object is returned to its previous owner; and, secondly, as the subject's return to a previous place, position or condition – their 'normal form [*forme normale*]'. The two meanings of restitution as a return of a thing to a person and a return of a person or a thing to a previous state imbricate with one another. The turning-back of a clock as a metaphor for restitutive action is not only a figure of temporal undoing, but it also illuminates Durkheim's idea of the corrective function of law. Durkheim's language of 'normalcy' and 'pathology' of forms ('*les forms anormales*') connects the question of criminal wrongdoing and social discord or disharmony.[11] The incongruities and unrests within the body social are metaphorised as a cellular failure or as organic pathology within a bodily organism. This in turn presents restitution as a remedial response to the illness of/in society. The articulation of restitution as a legal power to 'make un-happen' rests on the image of society as an organic body – a living unit of differentiated and interdependent parts – to whom norm violation causes a malfunctioning or an ailment.[12] For that reason, by reinstating the *status quo ante*, restitutive law cures wounded body social.

Restitution, posited as the binary opposite to the punitive and repressive responses to wrongdoing, is the action of 'righting . . . balance [that has been] upset by the violations' (Coser [1984] 2014: xvii). In restitution, the figures of the law are said to '*pronounce . . . the law*', but not to 'talk of punishment'; the offender is thus not condemned to suffer, but '*merely . . . to submit to [the law]*', Durkheim writes ([1984] 2014: 88). This highlights an interesting asymmetry between the social functions of modern and traditional laws: while the repressive speech act consists of the punitive declaration that the wrongdoer should suffer (on their body and/or through acts of material divestiture), the restitutive speech act does *not* address the wrongdoer in its capacity of imposing on them pain or loss, but 'only' asks of them, in a self-referential gesture, *to obey and submit to the law*. In other words, in the case of restitution, the law takes itself as an object of its declaration, and affirms itself.

In regard to the transformation of the 'collective consciousness' in modern societies, restitutive law is located in 'the furthest zones of consciousness and [to] extend . . . well beyond [it]. *The more [the restitutive law] becomes truly itself, the more it takes its distance [plus il devient vraiment, lui-même, plus il s'en éloigne]*' ([1893] 2007: 107; [1984] 2014: 89). While repressive sanctions respond to prohibitions against acts that offend the societal value system, restitutive sanctions have an indirect relationship to the 'collective consciousness' – the more restitution crystallises as a distinctive socio-legal response to wrongdoing, the weaker its reflection of specific societal norms, values and precepts. Durkheim's striking formulation that '[t]he more [restitution] becomes truly itself, the more it takes its distance' from a shared system of beliefs and norms has been interpreted as a statement about diffusion, pluralisation and weakening of the impact of collective beliefs on individual lives under the conditions of advanced labour division (cf. Lukes and Skull 1983). It also signifies a gap, or a disjunction, between the domains of ethics and the study of law in Durkheim's work, which in turn makes Lukes and Skull (1983: 3) propose that Durkheim's focus is not 'on the law per se, but on the linkages, analogies and parallels between legal and moral roles'.

'RESTITUTIVE HUMANITARIANISM'

I have proposed that Durkheim's theory of repressive and restitutive legal sanctions, and of their corresponding types of social bonding, 'mechanical solidarity' and 'organic solidarity' presented in *The Division of Labor*, fits within an epistemic framework that maps sociological inquiry onto biological propositions about an organism's health and well-being. Wrongdoing disturbs the healthy operation of the body social, and restitution is a way of introducing remedial measures to cure it – the terminology of 'repair' and 'reparation' in the context of the Durkheimian 'organic solidarity' is thus potentially misleading to the extent that it invokes an inanimate and unfeeling object that has been 'broken' rather than 'wounded'. In this section I turn to Durkheim's later writings in order to focus more closely on his conceptual connection between restitutive operations of law and humanitarian ideology. I use the phrase 'restitutive humanitarianism' to characterise Durkheim's philosophic position that links 'moral individualism' and the claims of the sacrality of human life in modern societies, with his elaboration of the idea of restitution. When viewed through the optic of Durkheim's humanitarian ethics, restitution does not (any more) appear diametrically opposed to repressive law, but, rather, retains a historical and anthropological connection to it. Restitution retains, if also obscures, a relation to the figure of human suffering of loss, which, in *The Division of Labor*, Durkheim had strictly restricted to repressive law and to traditional 'collective consciousness'.

When reading together *The Division of Labor* with Durkheim's 'Individualism and the Intellectuals' (1898; 1969), it becomes apparent that the category of modern ('organic') social bonds cannot be reduced to an analytical function, and be subsumed under the 'external index' of law, but that it is also a repository of normative and ideological contents, specifically in relation to the idea of universal humanity. Durkheim (1898; 1969) connects restitution with an abstractly defined 'human person [*personne humaine*]', which in 'Individualism and the Intellectuals' is, partly, a figure of societal responsibility to ameliorate the suffering of others. However, to the extent that Durkheim is interested in grounding social obligations in a de-personified and generalised notions of shared humanity, he also, inadvertently, comes to articulate the idea of humanity's obscured complementary element, namely *in*humanity. Through the gesture of separating modern law from the collective desire to see the perpetrator suffer and endure loss, restitution situates them *within* universal humanity. In 'Individualism and the Intellectuals', however, Durkheim sketches yet another link between restitution and the figure of suffering humanity, whereby restitution is imagined as *a remedial response to* suffering. What renders restitution operational within the nexus of modern law and humanitarian ideology is the activation of sympathetic affects in response to the *personne humaine* and the sentiment of horror ('*un sentiment d'horreur*') at the site of 'inhuman acts'.

While in *The Division of Labor in Society* Durkheim initially suggests that in industrial societies the collective consciousness gradually diffuses and potentially reaches the point of disappearance, elsewhere, including in 'Individualism and the Intellectuals', he envisions the emergence of a distinctly modern system of shared ethical beliefs. While the dichotomous conceptualisation of the repressive law, linked to punishment, and the restitutive law, linked to the correction of the misdeed and the 'reparation' of the wounded social body, dominates the earlier narrative of the collective consciousness, Durkheim's subsequent texts on the sociology of law recognise the continuity of repressive and punitive operations of law. In his review of Gaston Richard's monograph on the origins of the law (1893; 1983c), Durkheim argues that crime forms a bridge between modern and traditional laws. He expands his definition of crime as an infringement of society's moral coherence to also include 'debt' that requires re-payment. Instead of situating contract law in opposition to repressive law, in the essay on 'The Origins of Law' Durkheim presents the former as, at least initially, continuous with punitive orientations of law. The restitutive logic of '[making] amends for the harm [one] has done' is a result of 'a debt contracted by the criminal, *simply by virtue of his offence*' (1983c: 169; emphasis mine). Since repressive law also originates in 'a debt of security which society owes its members' (1983c: 170), restitution and repression appear to have shared origins and logic.

In 'Individualism and the Intellectuals' (1969), Durkheim considers the position of 'moral individualism', which he contrasts with utilitarian philosophy, and which he sees as centred around calculated transactions and the maximisation of personal returns. The position of moral individualism means a shared respect for the inviolability of human life, which, Durkheim proposes, constitutes the content of the modern *conscience collective*.[13] Viewing restitution through the conceptual and ideological prism of moral individualism, rather than, as in *The Division of Labor*, equating it with the ostensible absence of punitive and vindictive affects within the domain of the law, Durkheim reflects on the link between restitutive law and human suffering. On the one hand, by virtue of its overlaps with repressive law restitution no longer appears to be entirely devoid of the collective punitive passions or purged of the desires to make the wrongdoer undergo a loss (1983b: 80). On the other hand, restitution relates to the ideology of moral individualism at the level of what Giddens (1978: 28) calls 'moral impulsion'; it is practiced within the dominant system of beliefs and values founded upon the ideals of moral significance of individuals and the wrongness of suffering.[14] Restitution both expresses and consolidates the modern 'collective consciousness' around 'sympathy for all that is human', and around the 'wider pity for all sufferings, for all human miseries, [and] a more ardent desire to combat and alleviate them' (Durkheim 1969: 24).

Durkheim wrote that essay in response to the social and political crisis of the Third French Republic brought about by the 'Dreyfus Affair'. It was a reply to the intervention made by a prominent anti-Dreyfusard, Ferdinand Brunetière, who defended the strong position of the army in the French society, claimed that Jews were partly responsible for the rise of anti-Semitism, and objurgated the liberal individualistic stance of the *Dreyfusard* intellectuals for their alleged anarchism (see Lukes 1969: 16–18). Durkheim argued that the near-sacred signification of 'suffering humanity' was in modern societies the 'functional equivalent' to the role played by religion in traditional societies (Lukes 1969: 18). In Western modernity individualism had acquired the status of a quasi-religious dogma because it had elevated the dignity and worth of an abstract 'human person [*la personne humaine*]' onto the level of a moral guideline for behaviour (Durkheim 1969: 20–1). However, moral individualism needed to be distinguished from the 'egoistic cult of the self', and, even more so, from the uncurbed pursuits to maximise the private interests of laissez faire economics. For Durkheim moral individualism had the potential to counter the effects of social alienation and atomisation because it 'avert[ed] our attention from what concerns us personally [and] from all that relates to our empirical individuality', towards seeking 'that which our human condition demands [*que réclame notre condition d'homme*]' and 'that which we hold in common with all our fellow men [*qu'elle nous est commune avec tous nos semblables*]' (1898: 6; 1969: 21):

> [In moral individualism] human person, whose definition serves as the touchstone according to which good must be distinguished from evil, is considered as sacred, in what one might call the ritual sense of the word . . . It is conceived as being invested with that mysterious property which creates an empty space around holy objects [*le vide autour des choses saintes*], which keeps them away from profane contacts and which draws them away from ordinary life. And it is exactly this feature which induces the respect of which it is an object. Whoever makes an attempt on a man's life, on a man's liberty, [or] on a man's honour inspires us with a feeling of horror [*un sentiment d'horreur*], in every way analogous to that which the believer experiences when he sees his idol profaned. Such a morality . . . is *a religion of which man is, at the same time, both believer and God* . . . [Moral individualism] has penetrated our institutions and our customs, it has become part of our whole life, and, if we really must rid ourselves of it, it is our entire moral organization that must be rebuilt at the same time (1898: 6; 1969: 21–2; emphasis mine).

The restitutive operation of law – the return to the way things were before the crime – historically prevailed over law's punitive functions, but that did not mean that modern law lost the tight connection to *conscience collective*. Rather, as public moral attitudes became organised around the sacrality of life, and the imperative of remedial response to suffering, law has incorporated, and evolved around, humanitarian sensitivity. Durkheim thus credits 'moral individualism' with providing modern societies with social cohesion and with 'collective effervescence' (a term from Durkheim's sociology of religion): the group's coming together to communicate and to engage in action. Durkheim borrows Charles Renouvier's phrase 'the cult of the individual' as a name for the humanitarian dogma (see 1969: 22–3; [1984] 2014: 312–17), in order to juxtapose it with Christianity; on the one hand, humanitarianism displaces the Christian religion from its formative role in the Western collective conscience, on the other hand, it preserves Christianity by integrating and reworking some its motifs (1969: 26; see also 1983b: 93).[15]

Central to this distinction between 'man in general and the man whom we are' is Durkheim's interpretation of the Kantian notion of moral action rooted in a deliberate disconnection from one's 'particular circumstances . . . [including] social condition . . . class or caste interests', and grounded instead in the abstraction and universalisation of the human condition (1969: 21; see also 1983b: 100). Thus, the extraction of the concept of humanity from the particularities of race, gender and class preconditions its status as an object of collective dedication and devotion. Moral individualism is 'glorification not of the self, but of the individual in general' (1969: 24). This is because the axiom of universal dignity and the inviolability of a person's life does not derive from 'individual qualities [and] particular characteristics [that] distinguish him from others', but, on the contrary, 'from a higher source, one which he shares with all men' (1969: 23). Universalisation of the concept of humanity is for Durkheim a sign that it plays a religious role as the belief that 'humanity that is sacred and worthy of respect' solidifies into the conscience collective (1969: 23). As such, 'moral individualism' must remain *disinterested [in] the concrete and diverse forms under which [humanity] presents itself* (1969: 23: emphasis mine). It is universal in the sense of being 'distributed among all [of the subject's] fellows', and a source of both collective obligations *and* a way of traversing atomism and solipsism of modern individuality: '[the subject] cannot take [humanity] as a goal for his conduct without being obliged to go beyond himself [*sortir de soi-même*, get out of, or exit, oneself] and turn towards others [*se répandre au-dehors*, spread, diffuse or permeate outside (of oneself)]' (1898: 8–9; 1969: 23). For the Dreyfusards, Alfred Dreyfus was a paradigmatic embodiment of such 'suffering humanity'; he was a pietà-like figuration, who, at the level of the affirmation of life's sacredness, transcended the particularity of his class, race and life circumstances (Jones 2001: 56). Dreyfus' perception as a suffering 'man in general [*l'homme en général*]' made him the recipient of 'sentiments of sympathy' and 'fellow-feeling' (1983b: 100), and formed the basis for solidarity politics among the progressive sections of the French *fin de siècle* society. The idiom of *l'humanité souffrante* marks the moral and political terrain of *what is intolerable* and what demands remedial response.

These moral figurations of 'a man *in abstracto*' and 'humanity in general' are important for understanding how in Durkheim's work the corrective and remedial workings of modern law intersect with the elevation of the humanitarian affects to the status of a collective belief system – I call this intersection of restitution and the moral conception of suffering 'restitutive humanitarianism'. The notion of abstract humanity as a quality that is shared and irreducible to the particularity of social circumstances, becomes in Durkheim's account a moral and political gesture through which the social bond (*lien social*) of 'organic solidarity' emerge and consolidate. 'Individualism and the Intellectuals' adds a layer of complexity to Durkheim's theory of solidarity in that, rather than solely conceptualised as the effect of the changing socio-economic conditions of labour, it imbues solidarity with an affective component. In societies characterised by Durkheim as the 'constantly changing circumstances' and a 'state of plasticity and instability,' collectives no longer have 'anything in common *other than their humanity*' as 'there remains nothing that men may love and honour in common, apart from man himself' (1969: 26; emphasis mine).

In the Durkheimian 'restitutive scene' the corrective and remedial workings of the law – the undoing of wrongs – operate upon, and are enabled by, the activation of humanitarian affects, which Durkheim organises on a scale from 'positive' to 'negative': pity and empathy, as well as outrage, repugnance and horror. In the essay 'The Evolution of Punishment', published in 1901, Durkheim describes the humanitarian sensitivity in (paradoxically Nietzschean) terms of the 'softening of mores [*l'adoucissement des mœurs*]' and as a 'more developed altruism' (1901, 19; 1983b: 97, 100). The strongly emotive terms used by Durkheim to describe suffering – 'repugnant', 'odious', 'abominable' – suggest that events designated as 'inhuman acts [*les actes inhumains*]' or 'acts which lack humanity [*actes qui manquent d'humanité*]' carry with them the implication of *intolerable events* that are in need of remedial action (1901, 19; 1983b: 97, 100).[16] Suffering produces in the moderns a 'feeling of horror [*un sentiment d'horreur*]' (1901, 19; 1983b: 100).[17] Rather than a binary opposition between repressive law and restitutive law, Durkheim's conception of the evolution of law accounts for a plurality of factors, including the 'progressive softening' of norms and the diminishing moral 'distance' between the victim (*l'offenseur*) and the wrongdoer (*l'offensé*) – their sharing in the category of universal humanity. The collective moral sensitivity to suffering provides the grounds upon which restitutive law ascertains its dominance, and overcomes, if never fully, its attachment to injurious desires by recognising the perpetrator's humanity. Durkheim writes that '[the] sympathy we feel for every man who suffers, the horror which all destructive violence causes us; it is the same sympathy and the same horror which inflames this anger' (1983b: 99). But also, as the changing character of law incorporates the ethical construct of the 'suffering humanity [*l'humanité souffrante*]', the restitutive return comes to signify *undoing suffering*: restoring the subject to a condition *prior to* suffering as their 'normal state'.[18]

THE RESTITUTION OF THINGS

In presenting Durkheim's theory of restitution as the subject's restoration to their 'normal state' I have focused primarily on the transitive grammar of restitution, that is, the return of the subject to an earlier condition, rather than on the intransitive grammar of restitution as a return of an object to a person in an attempt at making good a loss. In the final section of this chapter, I turn to the question of things in Durkheim's work, and to his insights into the role that inanimate objects, primarily as property, play in his restitutive humanitarianism. Underlying Durkheim's ideas about moral individualism and restitutive law is an unarticulated assumption about a stable and fixed boundary between persons and things: by the virtue of not being things, human persons are included in universal humanity, and are granted respect, worth and dignity. The motifs of things in Durkheim's work include mentions of things' lack of spontaneous appearance in the world; they are incapable of impacting social relations or of initiating action without external force; and they do not generate solidarity (cf. Durkheim 1983b; [1984] 2014). Not only is restitution a uniquely human operation, but there is also a connection between being recognised as a restitutive subject *and* the status of personhood, assigned to those who assume a proprietary relationship to things. Within the conceptual matrix of restitutive humanitarianism, restitution's response to, and correction of, the specific types of wrongdoing that consist of confiscation and dispossession of things, is premised on the notion of property as the primary framework for the relationship between humans and inanimate objects (material things are synonymous to property, and for the restitution to take place they need to be 'appropriable' and 'ownable').

In *The Division of Labor in Society* Durkheim writes that while 'things are a part of society' and 'there exists a solidarity of things [*une solidarité des choses*] whose nature is special enough to be outwardly revealed in legal consequences', as illustrated by property law, such solidarity does not take 'shape from the elements drawn together [in] an entity capable of acting in unison [and] it contributes nothing to the unity of the body social' ([1893] 2007: 111; [1984] 2014: 91, 92). This 'solidarity of things' does not generate or produce social bonds. Restitution in the sense of the return of objects (and without implying its intended reparative social effects) does not 'cause the persons whom [the returned things] bring into contact to cooperate', but, it 'merely restore[s] or maintain[s] . . . that negative solidarity which has been disturbed in its functioning' ([1984] 2014: 93). Rather, it 'unravel[s] more efficiently what has been united by force of circumstance: to re-establish boundaries that have been violated and to reinstate each individual in his own domain' ([1984] 2014: 93).

In his discussion of the sacrosanct origins of property rights in one of the chapters of *Professional Ethics and Civic Morals*, Durkheim rethinks his earlier view on the social role of objects, including their place in restitution. Durkheim's ideas about the origins of the institution of property are perhaps best understood in contrast to Locke's theory; instead of locating the beginnings of property in human labour, Durkheim derives it from the objects' investment with sacral qualities by declaring them untouchable or inaccessible to society at large. Things' ownability is thus defined negatively as their withdrawal from communal access ([1890–1900] 1950; [1957] 1983; 1957; 1983c). In this view, property relations are continuous with the religious consecration of objects, and with their removal from broad social circulation. In 'The Nature and Origins of the Right of Property' ([1957] 1983: 158) Durkheim argues that '[t]he idea of property first invokes the idea of a thing. There seems to be a close connection between these two notions: that one can only possess things, and that all things can be possessed.' Durkheim's analysis differs from those interpretations of property rights that locate their origins in the tripartite principles of the Roman laws of *ius utendi* ('the right to make use of the thing as it is'), *ius frutendi* ('the right to the yield of the thing'), or *ius abutendi* ('the [right] of transforming the thing or even of destroying it'), (1957: 160–1). Instead, in Durkheim's negative definition of property as a 'thing withdrawn from common use for its use by a given object',[19] the originary act of appropriation invokes the removal of objects from the class of the commons, *res communes*, that is, those things that 'belong to no one because they belong to all and by their nature elude any appropriation' (1957: 163, 159). Just as in the case of religiously consecrated objects, crucial in the right of property is that '[all] other individuals [are] prohibited from enjoying the use of the object in question', and that 'the others [are prevented] from using it and even from approaching it' (1957: 164).

While locating the origins of individual property in the acts of removal of objects from the class of *res communes*, Durkheim reflects on the sacrosanct character of things, which results from 'setting [them] apart as something . . . belonging to the sphere of the divine . . . [whereby] those alone can have access to it who are taboo themselves or in the same degree as the object' (1957: 165). The characteristic trait of taboos is their *contagiousness*; the object's sacrosanct nature can transfer onto those in its proximity, often through haptic contact. In contrast to his depiction of things in *The Division of Labor in Society*, which are said to be lacking spontaneity and are incapable of social bonding, in *Professional Ethics and Civic Morals* Durkheim recognises the existence of a 'kind of moral community between the thing and the person which makes the one have a share in the social life and the social status of the other' (1957: 168).

This speculative theory of the origins of property rights complicates the thing–person binary in that, as Durkheim puts it (1957: 168), it can be 'the person who gives his name to the thing' *or* it can be 'the thing that gives its name to the person . . .', and 'which – if it has privileges deriving from its origin – transmits them to the person'. Durkheim's language suggests almost a *communal* connection between humans and inanimate object as part of the sacrosanct origins of property, whereby it bears a relation of resemblance to 'the sacred thing', and also displays certain agential properties, including the capacity for contagiousness (1957: 168–9). Departing from Durkheim's position, one could ask at this point whether this status reversal – when it is the material things that act on and call into being specific subject positions – hosts possibilities for critiquing appropriation and the belief that individual ownership is the dominant form of relation between humans and things. The sacred things display a capacity for conferring onto 'their' persons characteristics of, for instance, respect or honour. These for Durkheim (1957: 180) originate *from within the things* themselves: '[the] kind of sacredness that kept at a distance from the thing appropriated all individuals except the owner, does not derive from the owner; it resides initially in the thing itself', and '[the things] were inhabited by potencies [powers], rather than obscurely represented, and these were supposed to be their true owners, making the things untouchable to the profane'.[20] When viewed from the perspective of this sacrosanct genealogy, objects can invoke a sense of sociality, connecting human and non-human participants, which assumes objects' capacity to 'spontaneous[ly]' appear in the world.

Object consecration – an act of rendering them proper to the divine – and ownership are linked by the logic of removal or withdrawal from the common domain; accordingly, for Durkheim, the 'insulation or setting apart [of a thing is] more complete and more radical than that involved in the exclusive right of usage' (1957: 171). Durkheim's example of this genealogical convergence between property and *res sacrae* is the historical sanctification of landed property – he is referring to ancient laws whereby whoever violated land property could be killed with impunity (1957: 177–8). The 'setting apart' of things from the site of the commons has a spatial dimension, whereby the objects are encircled by a material boundary (a threshold or an enclosure) signifying prohibition of access: for instance, in ancient Greece and Rome such boundaries were the gates and walls of houses, or an 'uncultivated and untouched by a plough . . . strip of land' (1957: 172).

In setting up this peculiar genealogy of property,[21] Durkheim undermines his earlier distinction between 'negative' restitution of a return of objects to their owners, which does not generate social connections, and 'positive' restitution of the subject's return to their pre-conflict positions, which produces 'organic' solidarity. In the essay on the nature and origins of ownership, Durkheim reflects on the activity and appearance of material objects in the social world, and on the thingly capacity for forming 'bonds' that are of social significance and consequence (cf. 1957: 172). He also links the institution of private property to the gradual erasure of its genealogical connection to *res sacrae*, and speaks of the objects' concealed capacity to generate socially meaningful contents by downplaying the inanimate capacity for 'contagion' (1957: 185–6). Interestingly, this de-mystification of objects is for Durkheim closely linked to the history of the emergence of patrimonial family structure. When a single male person was invested with authority over the household consisting of women, other men, animals and things, he became the source of 'all [the] sacred virtues' – also those previously belonging to sacrosanct objects (1957: 186). From then onwards 'man [stood] above things, and it is a certain individual in particular who occupies this position, that is, who owns or possesses' (1957: 186). In an argument that, rather unexpectedly, could be read as a critique of patriarchy *and* of property, Durkheim speculates that the patrimonial subject, the head of the household and a proprietor of things, *absorbs* the sacrosanct and generative qualities previously assigned to things.

In Durkheim's later theory of restitution the distinction between 'positive' and 'negative' restitution from *The Division of Labor in Society* is unsustainable in the light of his writings on sacrosanct genealogy of property. Against the restitutive imaginary of re-appropriation and re-establishment of the proprietary status quo, Durkheim suggests an alternative avenue for conceptualising restitution: as the re-creation of thingly capacities for social bonds and thingly appearance in the world. In such alternative restitutive imaginary, restitution as a political moment of the re-introduction of things into their provenance communities is not unlike what Durkheim meant by 'consecration' – the 'setting apart', rather than simply 'return', that re-shapes and rearranges the restitutive sociality, the Durkheimian 'entity capable of acting in unison', into a solidarity of people and things.

4

'I ONLY LOVED': RESTITUTION IN PSYCHOANALYSIS

The theory of psychoanalysis presents restitution as a psychic situation marked by ambivalence of feelings, and, at the level of reparative and undoing endeavours, as an internally conflicted project. Thus, more than has been the case with some of the other texts examined in this book so far, the theory of psychoanalysis enables us to see in restitution concurrence of the subject's reparative impulse *and* violent desire, of love *and* hostility towards the object. And yet the insights of psychoanalysis into the process of restitution-making are not only that its subject hosts conflicting affects and impulses, but also, and perhaps more importantly, that the subject is actively involved in hiding and erasing that ambivalence. As such, restitution involves the 'cleaning up' of the psychic life so that the resultant position of the restitutive subject is freed of the traces of the violent and injurious desires. As this chapter's titular citation from Melanie Klein suggests, the subject of restitution has 'only loved'. This is, too, what the restitutive subject and the humanitarian subject, sketched out in my reading of *Frankenstein*, have in common: they are both ideologically and politically invested in connecting their positions to reparative and benevolent affects, and in actively erasing any traces of aggression or hostility.

My reading of restitutive writings of Sigmund Freud and Melanie Klein, the chief protagonists of this chapter, as well as of Karl Abraham, Otto Fenichel, Joan Riviere and Ella Freeman Sharpe, focuses on two restitutive tropes in psychoanalysis: undoing and reparation. These two different trajectories of psychoanalytic thinking about restitution – at times discordant, at times overlapping – are differentiated here as 'restitution-as-undoing' and as 'restitution-as-reparation'. This reading underscores the complexity of the language of restitution in psychoanalysis, as it sometimes features synonymously with the reparation of object representations (as instantiated in the earlier writings by Melanie Klein), and on other occasions signifies more narrowly defined actions of attempted recuperation of traumatic loss. At other times, the term restitution is invested with a distinctive temporal aspect of the subject's making-unhappen of past actions or thoughts, and still on other occasions, it features as part of critical discussions of the ethical implications of reparation, or, as Laubender aptly puts it (2019a: 51), 'the ethical stakes of all reparative endeavours' (see also Cox 1999; Kaufman 2007; Frosh 2013; Figlio 2017).

Within the rubric of the theoretical psychoanalytic notion of restitution-as-undoing, I highlight in particular the temporal aspect of restitution, namely, the neurotic subject's desired 'engineering' of past events by seeking to change *the very fact that they happened*. Freud's 1909 study of the Rat Man provides a paradigmatic case of such dynamics of undoing as making-unhappen ([1909] 1955; see also Lukacher 1988: 330–6; Wertz 2003). The aporetic modality of this case of restitution rests in the subject's phantasmatic pursuit of what lies beyond the retrocessive and reparative possibility – not simply the re-appropriation and/or rehoming of dispossessed love-objects, but the desire for erasing the historical truth of their seizure, and of the subsequent severance of their past relations and meanings. In turn, through the category of restitution-as-repair, I examine restitution as a reparative and curative undertaking, focusing primarily on Klein's important proposition that the restitutive impulse follows a destructive one in the subject's relation to the object (Rose 1993a; Laubender 2019a).

In the encyclopaedic entry on restitution in their *Psychoanalysis: the Major Concepts* (1990: 169), Moore and Fine refer to 'Psychoanalytic Comments on an Autobiographical Account of a Case of Paranoia' ([1958] 2001), published in 1911, where Freud conceptualises the schizophrenic's attempt at recovering lost libidinal investments in object representations. In 'Psychoanalytic Comments' Freud interprets the apocalyptic dreams and visions of Daniel Paul Schreber, a German jurist and politician who famously documented his subjective experience of dementia praecox in the 1903 autobiography, *Memoirs of My Nervous Illness*. Moore and Fine's decision to name this process of re-cathecting object representation 'restitution' is curious, given that Freud himself uses different terms – 'reconstruction [*die Reconstruktion*]' and 'process of recovery [*der Heilungvorgang*]' – to narrate the schizophrenic's strive to recover lost connection to the external world ([1911] 1955: 308; [1958] 2001: 71). Importantly, this recuperative process of 'recaptur[ing]' the lost 'relation . . . to the people and things in the world' does not seek to deny the shuttering impact of that loss (earlier Freud calls it '[a] world-catastrophe [*eine Weltkatastrophe*]'),[1] nor does it ever promise a complete and whole repair ([1911] 1955: 307; [1955] 2001: 71). Restitution as the re-cathexis of lost or abandoned object representations 'succeeds', Freud writes ([1955] 2001: 72), but 'never completely'. It does, however, achieve the 'undo[ing] [of] the work of repression [*die Verdrängung rückgängig macht*] and brings back the libido again on to the people it had abandoned' ([1911] 1955: 308; [1955] 2001: 72). Undoing (*Rückgängigmachung*) is here imagined as a partial, imperfect, but nevertheless operative re-instatement of the subject's love for the world, *amor mundi*, which connotes a process akin to a struggle or a battle (*sträuben, kämpfen*) ([1911] 1955: 265, 268).

Commenting on Freud's interest in Schreber's linguistic expressions, Otto Fenichel ([1946] 2014: 437) observes that the subject's language becomes the key platform upon which this restitutive striving unfolds. Schreber's testimony combined carefully orchestrated, and often excessively refined, verbal expressions with utterances that Freud described as 'disorganiz[ed]', 'incomprehensible' and 'nonsensical' (in Fenichel [1946] 2014: 437). Freud suggests that in the situation of dementia praecox language becomes 'subject to the same process as that which makes dream images out of dream thoughts' ([1946] 2014: 437). Both language and dreams are governed by 'the primary process' – just as Schreber's dreams are interpreted as sites of constantly sliding meanings (rather than as the absence of meaning), so are the seemingly nonsensical words suggestive of *displacement* (detachment of affect and psychic intensity from one idea and their location in another) and of *condensation* (the compression of affect and psychic intensity into one idea from multiple associative chains). It is precisely the situation where language is so manifestly governed by the unconscious processes that most clearly reveals for Freud, Fenichel argues ([1946] 2014: 437), the subject's 'restitutional striving towards the lost objective world'. Consequently, the restitutive subject '*regains something*, but *not all he wants*', as Fenichel puts it ([1946] 2014: 437; emphasis mine). Rather, 'instead of the lost object representations, he succeeds in *recapturing only their "shadows"*'. Here Fenichel's reading of 'Psychoanalytic Comments' moves from the interpretation of restitution as an incomplete recovery of libidinal attachment of objects to a reaffirmation of the subject's irreparable shuttering of the world. The emphasis on the trace or remnant ('shadows') of lost love-objects resonates with what Max Pensky (2003) has called, in a different context, *Nichtwiedergutzumachende*, 'that which can never be made good again'. The subject's 'restitutive strive' to recover lost and de-cathected object representations is a reparative endeavour that affirms the impossibility of restitution in any definite or final sense. The image of a restitutive subject painstakingly attempting to grasp and reconnect with the elusive and forever-sliding representations of lost objects emphasises the importance of psychoanalytic perspectives onto restitution theory. Here the failure of restitution to be fully and finally realised becomes a productive element, perhaps even something that conditions its possibility. Viewing restitution as a site of unconscious invest-ments and operations that underpin the liberal commitments to 'making good' after loss and dispossession through facilitated acts of re-appropriation, the psychoanalytic thinkers in this chapter feature as critical, and at times ironic, commentators of restitution.

RESTITUTION-AS-UNDOING: *RÜCKGÄNGIGMACHEN* AND

UNGESCHEHENMACHEN

In his theory of retroactive annulment of undesirable acts and psychic contents, called 'making-unhappen', Freud outlines a defensive mechanism of *ex post facto* cancellation that bears strong resemblance to the cluster of restitutive concepts analysed in this book. Laplanche and Pontalis define it as the 'mechanism whereby the subject makes an attempt to cause past thoughts, words, gestures or actions not to have occurred; to this end [the subject] makes use of thought or behaviour having *the opposite meaning*' ([1967] 1973: 477; emphasis mine). The aim is not simply the counter-cathecting of past occurrences, or neutralising them at the level of affect, or revising their meaning as the 'original event' through differential signification; rather, the goal is a more radical one: 'the [. . .] undoing of the past event (*Geschehen*) as such' ([1967] 1973: 478). Drawing on the framework of Vladimir Jankélévitch's moral philosophy and virtue ethics ([1967] 2019; 2005), one could relate the Freudian conception of undoing to Jankélévitch's distinction between '*quiddity*' (*what* something has been) and '*quoddity*' (*that* something has been). At the heart of undoing is a phantasmatic attempt at 'tinkering' with the quoddity of the first acts, deeds or thoughts; undoing seeks to cancel out – to actively disremember or erase – *the very fact of its occurrence*, rather than to 'only' engineer its affects or interpose counter-significations. Interpreting the Freudian (and post-Freudian) conception of undoing as a desire to erase *that* something happened, I want to consider undoing as a strand of the psychoana-lytic theory of restitution. This is because psychoanalysis allows us to peer 'under the skin' of the juridical rights-based discourse that equates restitution with the relocation and re-acquisition of things by illuminating restitution's complex subcutaneous imaginary of impossible returns, de-activations of the past and temporal reversal. The Holocaust survivor Jean Améry expresses that restitutive desire poignantly in his meditations on aging, when he describes the experience of being overtaken by 'the burning and just as hopeless wish . . . for the reversal of time. What has happened should unhappen, what has not happened should take place' (Améry 1994: 19; see also Zolkos 2010: 85–6).

The first direct mention of the undoing mechanism in Freud's oeuvre is found in the analysis of the Rat Man ([1909] 1955). In analysing the Rat Man's obsessions centred around the conflicting libidinal and aggressive impulses towards his father and his fiancée, Freud emphasises the proliferation of obsessive-compulsive behaviours that oscillated between affectionate and protective actions towards the fiancée, on the one hand, and, on the other, 'injurious desires' and the fantasies about endangering her safety and even her life. One act in particular appears significant to Freud: the Rat Man removes a stone from the road on which the carriage with his fiancée was coming, because he fears that the carriage might overturn and that she could come to harm. Subsequently, however, the Rat Man moves the stone back onto the road in a gesture of undoing the previous action. For Freud the importance of the second act is that it magically sought to annul or neutralise the first act. He writes that the 'true significance' of these two actions was that they represented '. . . a conflict between two opposing impulses of approximately equal strength', and he later identifies those impulses as 'love and hate' ([1909] 1955: 192). Suggesting that the impetus behind these compulsive acts was a 'battle between love and hate . . . raging in the lover's breast', Freud identifies a 'diphasic structure' of undoing, whereby the meaning of the second act becomes that of a 'critical repudiation' of the primary 'pathological action' ([1909] 1955: 193). The sequential and highly ritualised staging of actions seeking to cancel one another, or to render each other void, reflects the 'plastic form' of the subject's contradictory feelings towards the love-object, or what Freud in his later texts comes to term ambivalence (see Laplanche and Pontalis [1967] 1973: 27).

In the analysis of the Rat Man Freud uses the phrase '*rückgängig machen*' to describe the psychological mechanism of retroactive annulment, which James Stratchey then translates as 'undoing' (see also Freud [1911] 1955). However, in *Inhibitions, Symptoms and Anxiety* ([1926] 2010; [1949] 1959) Freud coins a new term for the annulment mechanism, *Ungeschehenmachen*, 'making-unhappen', or, literally, 'making [what has happened] not to take place'. While, according to Grimm's *Deutsches Wörterbuch*, the phrase *rückgängig machen* developed historically as a translation of Latin terms for preventing a certain course of action from occurring, or from re-occurring (*impedire, reprimere, repellere*), and thus conveyed the sense of rescindment in the mechanism at hand, the term *Ungeschehenmachen* captured the specific meaning of the temporal inscription of a psychic conflict, as well as of magical thinking activated by neurotics (Laplanche and Pontalis [1967] 1973: 478).[2] Discussing the connection between inhibition and anxiety, Freud suggests that the subject might try to 'undo' (*rückgängig machen*) the workings of a sexual function if they produce a tension or a feeling of unease. Later in that text, while analysing further the psychic operations of retroactive annulment, Freud uses the term *Ungeschehenmachen* to capture the psychic operations of 'negative magic' that is supposed to '"blow away" [*wegblasen*] not merely the consequence of some occurrence, experience or impression, but *those very events themselves*' ([1926] 2010: 20; [1949] 1959: 73–4; emphasis mine).

The interesting thing about *Ungeschehenmachen* is that it emerges at the interstices of human psychology, magic and ritual. This also renders unstable the boundary that Laplanche and Pontalis, following Freud, delineate between 'normal undoing' (aimed at annulling the affect accompanying the action) and 'pathological undoing' (aimed at annulling the action itself). Freud suggests that the effect of the 'undoing' act is to create a psychic fiction – a situation where neither of the actions is experienced as *ever having taken place*, 'whereas, in reality, both have' ([1949] 1959: 74). Operative in the retroactive annulment is thus a desire to 'abolish something' by consolidating the past as *'non arrivé'* ([1926] 2010: 20; [1949] 1959: 74; cf. 1996: 81 n.16). When Freud describes undoing as 'magical', he does not, I think, single it out as an act that is somehow 'unreal'; rather, Freud calls attention to the psyche's reliance on 'primitive thinking' in primary processes (cf. Steinmetz 2006), including symbolism and superstition: not unlike a magician making a rabbit disappear, the neurotic makes past actions, thoughts or events become non-existent.

Anna Freud included undoing (*Ungeschehenmachen*) within her register of defence techniques in obsessional neurosis ([1937] 1993: 43–4). Documenting the similarity between the mechanisms of isolation and undoing (first noted by Sigmund Freud), Anna Freud identifies the origins of undoing in the subject's capacity to separate the past event at hand and other actions, thoughts and relations ([1937] 1993: 34), or what Laplanche and Pontalis call 'the severing of associative connections' ([1967] 1973: 233). In *The Psychoanalytic Theory of Neurosis* ([1946] 2014) Otto Fenichel broadens the Freudian conceptualisation of undoing to include a variety of socio-psychological phenomena. For instance, in a figuration called '[the] Don Juan of Achievements' Fenichel describes uncurbed professional ambitions as an attempt at 'undoing' past failures and unconscious guilt ([1946] 2014: 502–3).

The importance of Fenichel's discussion for psychoanalytic theory of restitution is due to two innovative observations. First, Fenichel unpacks Freud's somewhat mechanic view of undoing as a biphasic reaction-formation, where the second event is imagined as a *reversion* of the first event. Fenichel suggests that at times undoing can be enacted through *repetition* or *intensification* of the first event.[3] In this case '"undoing" turns into "doing it again"', as the subject attempts to cancel the first deed by re-enacting it with a different mind-set, or with a different intention or affective content.[4] I have previously suggested that underlying the restitutive relocation and re-appropriation of confiscated objects is a political, as well as a psychic situation where a new subjective position emerges: the restitutive subject undergoes a return of/to the earlier condition of things. While Freud depicts undoing as a biphasic series of actions and thoughts, on the one hand, and counter-actions and counter-thoughts, on the other, Fenichel broadens (and complicates) the meaning of restitution-as-undoing by including within the theory of *Ungeschehenmachen* actions that repeat and intensify the first act. Fenichel's second innovative observation consists in making a direct connection between undoing and restitution as the '[s]trivings for reparation' ([1946] 2014: 155).[5] Fenichel argues that in traumatic neuroses undoing becomes the expression of the subject's spontaneous *restitutive efforts*, or what he calls 'the task of belated mastery', whereby the 'withdrawal towards a fresh start' offers a possibility of reconstructing 'the collapsed equilibrium' of affect. The restitutive aspect of undoing is particularly conspicuous in situation where the 'first acts' are 'imaginative destructions', that is, when the subject seeks to annul manifestations of aggressive impulses and sadistic drives towards the love-object (2014 [1946]: 155). Such reparative undoing often gives rise to creative sublimations and/or ritualistic compulsions and obsessions.[6] The fact that every act of restitution in Freud and Fenichel's case analyses ends in failure, and further frustrates the subject, contrasts with how creative, resourceful and optimistic their subjects appear in designing, plotting and implementing particular undoing strategies. In the case of restitution-as-undoing, the promise and the failure of *Ungeschehenmachen* are inextricable.

Status Quo in Psychoanalysis

An important link between the two restitutive registers in psychoanalysis – undoing and reparation – is the question of the status quo. I have described the *status quo ante* as the 'previously existing state of affairs', a situation of currency and prevalence, and an important element of the legal framework of contractual remedies, including restitution. For instance, Sabahi (2011: 61) provides a legal definition of restitution as the re-establishment of the *status quo ante*, or as re-introduction of 'the situation that had existed before the commission of [a] wrongful act'. In psychoanalysis, the *status quo ante* has been linked to homeostasis of psychic and social systems, and the subject's capacity to resist change (cf. Trotter 2019). It is in the context of discussing the subjective opposition to change that Melanie Klein distinguishes clearly between restitution as retroactive annulment and restitution as the subject's repair of/to the loved object (Likierman 2002: 107). Focusing on the question of the status quo will facilitate the dual task of, first, mapping the conceptual distinction between restitution-as-undoing and restitution-as-repair, and, next, of complicating this distinction by pointing to the seminal place of fantasy in both undoing and in reparation (see also Cox 1999: 16).

The use of the term 'status quo' in relation to the human psyche borrows from its definition in classical international law and international diplomacy as the post-conflict re-instatement of pre-conflict leadership, and the restoration of territorial and possessory losses incurred during the conflict.[7] Grewe suggests that the doctrine of *status quo ante* and the Roman *ius postliminus* have shared legal and philosophic origins ([1984] 2014: 438–40). In addition to 'its relationship with the effect of war, the notion of status quo also has a place in the sphere of the peaceful settlement of disputes as well as in diplomatic transactions concerning the maintenance and stability of local, regional or continental situations' (Grewe [1984] 2014: 439). Broadening its meaning beyond the narrow military and diplomatic context, Karl Marx has critically invoked the status quo as an expression of 'impotence' and as '[the] general conviction, that a certain state of facts, brought about by accident and any whatever circumstances, has stubbornly to be maintained, is a statement of bankruptcy, an admission of the leading powers, that they are incapable to further the sake of progress and civilization' (cited in Grewe [1984] 2014: 440). In a series of meetings and debates of the British Psychoanalytic Society called 'Controversial Discussions', which took place between 1941 and 1945, and comprised of presentations expounding and defending the Kleinian approach in the face of its criticism by Viennese émigrés,[8] the question of the status quo was addressed both by Ella Freeman Sharpe and by Melanie Klein (King and Steiner 1991; Rose 1993a; 1993b; 1993c).[9] It was understood in two ways: as the analysand's resistance to therapeutic change and as a desire for a return to a phantasmatic harmonious space prior to conflict – '"before the world was decomposed"'(King and Steiner 1991: 337). What is remarkable about the way that the problem of the status quo is constructed in the 'Controversial Discussions' is that it traverses the social and the psychic or phantasmatic domains, thereby suggesting, as Jacqueline Rose argues in a passage that quotes from Sharpe's intervention (1993a: 171), that at hand is the 'political provenance' of the psychoanalytic theory of restitution.[10]

Sharpe's comments on the subject's adherence to the status quo come as part of her exposition of the depressive position. In it Sharpe weaves tightly together the psychic longing for *the return of the same* with the politics of restoration of the pre-war social and economic situation in Britain, and undoubtedly also with the moment of crisis within psychoanalysis, which the 'Controversial Discussions' have come to signify (see Rose 1993a). Sharpe (1993a: 607) expresses this unwillingness to change metaphorically, as the subject's 'refusal to move' – stagnation and immobility. She asks (1993a: 606): '[h]ow many people still hope that the end of the war means a restoration of the pre-war conditions for which they are most homesick, although progressive minds . . . warn us that restoration of old conditions could only lead to renewed disaster'. What the thwarted analysis and the public advocacy of the antebellum social values and structures appear to have in common is that they both illuminate the psychic and political rewards of conservation.

While Sharpe describes the subject's desire for reverting to the former condition of things as an 'hallucination', she does not present it as an impossible task per se; the problem is not that the status quo is unachievable for the subject, but, rather, that it is disastrous in its effects. In her response to Sharpe, Melanie Klein (in King and Steiner 1992: 628) suggests that the desire for the status quo is underwritten by a dual idealisation of, first, the lost love-object and, secondly, of the subject's prior relationship to that object. Interestingly, Klein (ibid.: 628) also suggests that the subject's need to undertake these idealisations is premised on similar internal contents to those motivating reparation-making, namely, 'hatred, aggression, and guilt . . . in relation to loved objects'. However, while reparation aims to mend and alleviate the injurious effects of hostility towards the love-objects, the idealisation of the status quo enacts an imagined and fanta-sised reversal to a situation *prior* to the frustration and to the destructive fanta-sies. In a stark contrast to restitution-as-reparation, the return of the status quo is thus premised on 'the denial of the inherent aggression' of the subject, rather than on attempts at correcting and curing its consequences. The status quo con-stitutes an 'ideal situation' for the subject in that it represents a condition or an order *untainted by violence*; it is a state, Klein says, 'in which *aggression did not enter* into the patient's relationships to his love objects' (in King and Steiner 1992: 628; emphasis mine). The idealisation thus trails the following sequence of self-representation: 'I was not frustrated then – I did not hate then because I was not frustrated – I only loved – everything was perfect' (ibid.: 628).

The idealisation specific to the return of the status quo has to do, partly, with the subject's insufficient detachment from the object, namely, the infant's insufficient capacity to find substitution for the breast. Interesting in this con-text are also Klein and Sharpe's references to the Christian iconography of the 'original sin' and of prelapsarianism when describing the psychic appeal of the *return of the same*. Sharpe illustrates the status quo dynamic through the bibli-cal story of Adam and Eve's expulsion from paradise; she argues that the return to the Garden of Eden remains barred because the moment of expulsion is iden-tical with the emergence of sexual difference and with consolidation of libidinal desire. In the Garden of Eden, 'Adam and Eve were . . . like angels', and '[their] expulsion from [it], a depressed picture if ever there was one, synchronized with the discovery of the difference between the male and female genitals'. Klein's response to Sharpe also draws on a prelapsarian language. She says that, when viewed from the perspective of the status quo, the subject's capacity for destruc-tion towards the love-object is experienced 'as "original sin"'. The subject's aggression does not simply injure the internal 'good' object, but it also 'sullies' the (retrospectively idealised) object representations. The difference between restitution-as-reparation and return to the status quo is clearly delineated here: whereas reparation is a response to the *destruction or fragmentation of the 'good' object*, the return to the status quo is a reaction to the *defilement of 'pure' objects*. The subject's desire to 'recreate a situation in which no aggression against the loved object was aroused' as an operation of object-purification, and the denial that 'ambivalence and aggression are inherent' in object-relations, fol-lows the narrative trajectories of the Christian motifs of retrocession and return (Klein in King and Steiner 1992: 629).

What becomes apparent in the exchange between Sharpe and Klein is the importance of the narcissistic core of the status quo.[11] Here Sharpe's intervention exemplifies the intellectual entanglement of psychoanalytic critique and the feminist transvaluation of the sensorial 'feeling' body as a site of knowledge-production. In response to Glover's derogatory suggestion that the concept of narcissism has exhausted its psychoanalytic expediency, Sharpe says (in King and Steiner 1992: 608): '[for] me [narcissism] is slowly becoming not a term, intellectually apprehended, but a living understanding of a state and of experience. Perhaps one has got born a little more if one begins to feel what narcissism involves and what the enmeshment really means.' This striking formulation indirectly references Freud's statement that '[most] people are only half born', which Sharpe takes to mean the subject's stubborn adherence to the status quo (ibid.: 606).[12] When she argues that an 'overcoming' of the desire for the *return of the same* is possible within the analytic settings, Sharpe thus suggests that the repudiation of the concept of narcissism (and of the narcissistic core of the status quo in particular) among Klein's critics is a result of the intellectualisation of narcissism, and of blocking out its bodily, sensorial knowledge.[13]

Joan Riviere's 1936 essay on the negative therapeutic reaction articulates the psychoanalytic and political stakes in approaching the status quo as an aspect of restitution. The essay provides a conceptual backdrop to the aforementioned exchange between Sharpe and Klein during the 'Controversial Discussions'. Here the desire for the return of the same, or, in terms of restitution theory, for the 'original state', manifests as the subject's refusal 'to get well'. Riviere's essay consists of a close reading of a few passages from *The Ego and the Id* (a text that she translated into English in 1927), where Freud discusses so-called 'refractory cases', and where he poses the question of an 'unanalysable' subject. Freud ([1923] 2000: 298; [1927] 1961: 25–6) describes the negative therapeutic reaction as the analysand's inverse response 'to the progress of the treatment', which

> ... produces in them for the time being an exacerbation of their illness; they get worse during the treatment instead of getting better ... [there] is something in these people that sets itself against their recovery [*etwas der Genesung widersetzt*] ... the need for illness [*das Krankheitsbedürfnis*] has got the upper hand in them over the desire for recovery [*der Genesungswill*].

Combining Freud's reflections on the clinical effects of the unconscious sense of guilt and of the punitiveness of the super-ego with the conceptual insights from Karl Abraham's 1919 (1948) paper on neurotic resistance to analysis,[14] Riviere links the subject's resistance against the therapeutic process to the maniac and 'omnipotent denial of psychic reality'. This helps to identify her central question about the subjective stakes of the status quo: 'why does the need to control everything express itself so particularly in not getting well?' (1936: 142). She subsequently argues if '[there] is a kind of wish in the patient not to get well . . . [it] comes from the desire to preserve a status quo, *a condition of things which is proving bearable*' (1936: 142–3; emphasis mine). This formulation of the status quo as a state that the subject prefers to the risk of analysis, suggests that the prospect of psychic and social change has been associated with a condition that might prove *unendurable* for the subject. This articulates restitution alongside the desire for the return of the same as a state that the subject feels able to bear. As a political project of undoing, restitution in this perspective appears as not simply committed to conservation or preservation of the 'earlier' or 'primary' state, but also as underpinned by what, in that instance, acquires the status of the insufferable, or the intolerable; the kind of change that is bound to bring an end to the subject.

Further, Riviere explains that the attachment to the status quo and the resistance against 'getting well' are the subject's defences against coming to occupy the depressive position.[15] The subject sacrifices their own cure because they fear *something worse than ill-being*; the 'psychic truth behind his omnipotent denials is that the worst disasters have actually taken place', that the submission to the analysis would be tantamount to the psychic realisation of the disaster, and its inevitable outcome would be 'madness or suicide' (1936: 144). Underpinning the subject's desire for the status quo is a 'fear of being forced *to death himself* by the analysis', and the subject 'clings to analysis as *a forlorn hope*, in which at the same time he really has no faith' (1936: 145, 146; emphasis mine). Interestingly, Riviere directly contrasts status quo with a reparative or restorative action; she argues that the status quo becomes preferential to the subject when reparations come to signify the 'nightmare of desolation assuming shape' (1936: 145). The other status quo imaginaries in this book – the Durkheimian turning-back of a clock, or the Grotian captive subject crossing the border of the homeland as if returning from the land of the dead – have distinctly reparative undertones. Riviere's depiction of a *status quo ante* subject who refuses to get well, however, is haunted by the spectre of irreparability; by the 'inability to remedy matters' (1936: 146).

By arguing that the search for the omnipotent narcissistic enjoyment is merely a 'mask' worn by the refractory analysands concealing the depressive position, Riviere makes an additional conceptual step of reorienting the subject away from oneself and towards others, which allows her to articulate an insight that seems to elude both Freud and Abraham, namely, that at the heart of the refractory analysand's wish for the status quo lies not only fear against 'the impending death and disintegration' of the self, but also, and more deeply, the desire to 'cure and make well and happy all his loved and hated objects'

(1936: 147). While the subject perceives themselves as the originary force of the object's injury, which results from 'not [having] lov[ed] *them* enough', they unconsciously interpret the invitation to undertake a curative process as a betrayal of that injured other, and as a temptation (that must be refused) to attend to the self and to repair the self at the cost of de-prioritising the wounded other (1936: 147). Beneath the veneer of the paranoid and manifestly selfish subject position, the self-reparative orientation means actively forgetting 'his buried core of love and his need to think of others before himself at last' (1936: 147). The psychoanalytic speech act – an invitation to talk and disclose – is interpreted as a potential betrayal of the loved object. Rather, following a sense of obligation and indebtedness towards the other – an obligation that is both psychological *and* ethical – explains the preference for the 'uncured status quo [in] an unending analysis' (1936: 147). In Riviere's notion of the negative therapeutic reaction, the depressive orientation of the subject – where they face unyielding and irreparable loss – engenders ethics of restitutive commitment to the other, which becomes a pathway to self-reparation.[16]

RESTITUTION-AS-REPARATION: SUTURING AND WHOLE-MAKING, OR CHILD WITH SHARP SCISSORS

During the 'Controversial Discussions' Edward Glover raised the question of Klein's concept of restitution, suggesting that its origins lay in the Freudian writings on obsessional undoing and on reaction-formation;[17] a suggestion that Klein's supporters saw as a reductive reading of her theory of infantile restitutive tendencies by a 'Freudian purist' (in King and Steiner 1991: 337).[18] Without making any strict distinction between restitution and reparation, Susan Isaac argued that restitutive and reparative tendencies needed to be tied to the play of libidinal and aggressive inclinations of the subject; what the conceptual prism of undoing fails to recognise about reparation, she continued, was that the attacked object is also the infant's love-object (Isaac, in King and Steiner 1991: 343). While the Kleinian descriptions of the subject's attempt at mending the consequences of their destructive fantasies included mentions of undoing, Klein stated explicitly that the psyche's tendency 'to make reparations' was a 'wider concept' than Freudian *Ungeschehenmachen*, because an infant's repara-tive action went beyond the mechanisms of counter-cathecting and of reaction-formation (Klein [1935] 2011; 1948: 290, 48; see also Bibring 1943).[19]

The term 'restitution' subsequently became a place-holder for 'restor-ing [and] compensatory gestures' that the infant makes 'to address the destructive consequences of his own sadism through a lifelong activity of restoration', because of the feelings of guilt, depression and fear that such consequences evoke (see Likierman 2000: 127). The semantic and concep-tual overlap between the terms 'restitution', 'reparation' and 'restoration' in Klein's work has been a matter of controversy: while Susan Sherwin-White

(2018) has argued that Strachey's English translation of Klein's *The Psycho-analysis of Children* blurs Klein's differentiation between '*Wiederherstellung*' (restitution) and '*Wiedergutmachung*' (reparation), the authors of *The New Dictionary of Kleinian Thought* (Bott Spillius et al. 2011: 92) have insisted that, especially in her early work, Klein had used these terms largely inter-changeably, and only in her later writings showed a preference for the term 'reparation' (cf. Klein [1932] 1975). Laplanche and Pontalis suggest that Klein condensed two meanings in her theory of reparative action: *repairing something* and *making reparations to someone* ([1967] 1973: 389).[20] The latter was not identical to the Freudian *Undgeschehenmachen*, though it did contain an element of *undoing* of the object's destruction, in particular in the case of 'manic' reparation.[21]

Situating the origins of the Kleinian reparation predominantly in the framework of the Freudian undoing risks obfuscating the genealogical com-plexity of the idea of reparative action, which includes Karl Abraham's notion of the impulsive 'making-good after aggressions', elaborated in his 1924 text on libido development (Bott Spillius et al. 2011: 476).[22] Abraham ([1924] 1994: 75) pre-figures Melanie Klein's idea of reparation as an action that is inextricable from the subject's aggressive and destructive desires towards the love-object, by presenting the anal stage of libido development as the phase where ambivalence first manifests properly in the life of the subject. This happens through the concurrence of the subject's negative (eliminating and destructive) and positive (retaining) fantasy operations. Abraham articulates restitution as a result of a 'conserving set of tendencies', which spring directly from 'sadistic sources'. The conserving tendencies are linked to the infant's early experience of object loss (the anal elimination, or the 'clearing out'). The infant's coprophilic instinct to retain bodily contents forms the rudimen-tary expression of love-feelings ([1924] 1994: 76).[23] The objectification of the infantile faeces as the subject's early experience of private property brings about the subject's 'desire for domination' over objects by ordering them 'into a rigid and pedantic system' ([1924] 1994: 75, 77).[24] It thus exemplifies the mechanism of 'thingification' of bodily contents as the intermediate con-dition between a person and a thing.

The 'close alliance between conserving and destroying' discernible at the anal level of the libidinal development, is of particular relevance for under-standing melancholic states, which Abraham defines, in a close reading of Freud's essay on mourning and melancholia, as a 'radical disturbance of the subject's libidinal relation to his object' ([1924] 1994: 76). It is in the context of the melancholic loss that Abraham offers a description of restitution as the subject's loving desire to incorporate within the bounds of the self the previ-ously eliminated, or cast out, thing ([1924] 1994: 76, 85–6). Restitution as an attempt to re-acquire what has been lost models the action of introjection and of incorporation back (again) into the body. Rather than the Freudian imaginary of undoing as a temporal reversal, Abraham's restitutive imaginary is that of *an incorporating subject*; he argues that it is the 'expression of desire *to take back into [the] body* the [previously expelled] love-object', and thus 'a literal confirmation that the unconscious regards the loss of an object as an anal process, and its introjection as an oral one' ([1924] 1994: 86; emphasis mine). These two restitutive images make clear that the psychoanalytic theory of restitution has multiple vistas, including temporal reversal and incorporation and conservation of the previously ejected or expelled object. Abraham's key insight into the operation of undoing is that it signifies the overcoming of cruelty.

In her analysis of Klein's 1941 case study of Richard, Carolyn Laubender (2019a: 57) persuasively argues that the emphasis on the subject's oscillation between reparative and injurious impulses positions Klein as a thinker who offers important insights into 'curative endeavours' as 'projects geared towards reparation', which are not positioned 'outside of the circuits of violence and attack . . .' Rather, Laubender argues that 'the very imperative to repair can . . . be violent'. She also notes an important detail in Klein's departure from the Freudian orthodoxy, namely, that subject's non-verbal gestures and doings constitute analytic material that is equally as valid as verbal articulations – the ways in which Klein's juvenile analysands physically engaged (with) material things in a situation of play produced free associations and was an expression of unconscious fantasy lives. In Richard's case, for instance, his curative urge expressed itself haptically through inspection and repair of broken toys, and it illustrated the dynamics of the child's humanitarian affects (pity) emerging from the overcoming of cruelty, and of constructive tendencies developing from desires for destruction. Klein locates 'restitutive tendencies' in the infant's guilt feelings for having embarked upon the imaginative attacks on the mother's body/inside (the breast and the womb), and on the other fantasy figures that this body contained (the father's penis, brothers and sisters). This process coincided with the child's entry into the social and moral world, and was accompanied by the diminishing severity of the super-ego ([1932] 2011: loc. 5844).[25]

In her reading of Maurice Ravel's 1925 opera *The Child and the Spells: a Lyric Fantasy in Two Parts* (to which Colette wrote the libretto), Klein describes a child's destructive and reparative engagements with the world, manifesting primarily through haptic engagement with inanimate objects, as well as with the animal and plant world ([1929] 2011). The opera opens with a scene of a boy rebelling against his assigned task of studying. He is subsequently admonished by the mother and penalised with a withdrawal of a promise of oral pleasure: '[y]ou shall have dry bread and no sugar in your tea!', the mother says. She embodies the axiomatic figure of the 'nasty mother' who displays her 'power over the child' by withholding from him 'the desired thing' ([1929] 2011: loc. 5017; see also [1936] 2011: loc. 6747). In response, the child launches into a frenzied attack on the objects in the room, destroying toys and furniture with his hands and teeth, the 'weapons of the child's primary sadism', sullying them with spilled ink and ashes, 'the device of soiling with excrement' ([1929] 2011: loc. 4942). This is followed by an attempted stabbing of a squirrel that is perched on the windowsill. Klein interprets these destructive acts as the child's sadistic assault on the maternal body, and on 'the father's penis in it' ([1929] 2011: loc. 4942), with the intended effect of tearing them apart and sullying them with excrement. It is based on a persecutory projection, as for the child the 'united parents are extremely cruel and much dreaded assailants' ([1929] 2011: 4989).

Subsequently, the assaulted objects come to life and undertake a counter-attack in an apt illustration of the Kleinian dynamic of the 'vicious circle', whereby 'the child's anxiety impels it to destroy its object', resulting instead 'in an increases of ... anxiety' ([1933] 2011: loc. 5779) The hostile objects in Ravel's opera either obstinately refuse to perform their intended functions, spontaneously assign to themselves wholly different roles (the tea pot speaks Chinese), and threaten the petrified boy with acts of violence. Eventually they expel him outside the dwelling place of the household and into nature. The boy seeks refuge in the garden, but 'there again the air is full of terror', and Nature 'takes on the role of the mother whom he had assaulted' – the park animals and plants all attack the boy, a stranger in their midst ([1929] 2011: loc. 4989, 4942). As the hostile animals gather and argue 'who is to bite the child', the squirrel (a phallic-shaped animal representing the father's penis in the mother's assaulted body, whom the boy has previously attacked) becomes injured. Acting on an impulse, the boy reaches out with a curative gesture and binds the animal's wounded paw with his scarf, which represents for Klein a moment of over-coming of anal sadism and an 'advancement' into the phase of genital sexuality. Kneeling over the injured (and now cured) squirrel, the boy calls out 'Mama!' – the titular 'magic word' in the German translation of the opera – and accompanied by a procession of animals chanting 'This is a good child, a very well-behaved child' and 'Mama!', he marches off the stage ([1929] 2011: loc. 4942). The child's 'lust for destruction', which at first meets with a vindictive fantasy of gigantic persecutory maternal body, is subsequently overcome through what Klein emphasises is an intuitive and unpremeditated act of reparation of an injured animal body, whereby the boy becomes 'restored to *the human world of helping*, "being good"' ([1929] 2011: loc. 4942; emphasis mine). That inter-pretation underscores the ethics of empathic identification that Klein locates in reparative endeavours: 'responsibility ... manifests itself in *genuine sympathy with other people*, and in the ability to understand them, as they are and as they feel', which in turn underpins acts of reparation-making ([1937] 2011: loc.

7110; emphasis mine). In the case of the male protagonist of Ravel's *L'enfant et les sortilèges*, his attention to the wounded animal not only brings about the end of the persecutory projections as 'the hostile world changes into a friendly one', but it is also a moment of profound inner transformation as the child emerges, as a phoenix from the ashes of his own sadism, as a *subject capable of love* ([1929] 2011: loc. 4996).

Laubender discusses the ethical and political limits of the Kleinian conception of love in the overcoming of hostility, which is grounded in the 'parameters of one's own self' and which locates reparative motivation in the subject's capacity to identify (and diagnose) the other's injury '*as a means of to assuage* [the subject's] *guilt*' (2019a: 62; emphasis in the original). What is interesting in Klein's analysis of Ravel and Collette's opera is what I would call in line with my earlier analysis of the Creature in *Frankenstein*, its 'humanitarian language': the shift from aggressive to reparative impulses coincides with the boy's entry into the domain of common humanity defined as '[the] human world of helping' – a community of benevolent feelings and actions. The boy's passage into humanity is enabled through his embracement of sympathetic and benevolent affects, expressed spontaneously in response to suffering, and directed at their non-human recipient. The idiom of good humanity as a placeholder of compassionate affects and feelings towards suffering others is in Klein's text both the *platform* upon which the drama of restitution plays out, and is itself the lost-object that is being retrieved and to which the boy returns/is returned to. The wounded animal plays both the role of the 'restitutive object' and what Asad (2015) has called the 'subject of suffering': a necessary 'prop' in the child's overcoming of cruelty.

What kind of restitution is the child's curative act? It is partly an act of making-unhappen through temporal reversal, where the human subject undoes their previously attempted destruction of the animal, and partly a counter-act to the injurious desires that he had manifested earlier. Note that the child's acts of aggression manifested through an attempted *dismemberment* or *fragmentation* of the animal, and that the (counter-)act of restitution manifested through attempts at restoring the *wholeness* of the squirrel's body. Laplanche and Pontalis ([1967] 1973: 389, 20) list among different types of sadistic fantasies, including annihilation, devouring and elimination, that of shuttering the object into parts, or fragmentation. Referencing Daniel Lagache's distinction between 'activity' and 'aggressiveness', Laplanche and Pontalis aptly describe aggression as 'a radical force for disorganisation and fragmentation'. The English word 'fragmentation', from the Latin *fragmentum* meaning 'remnant' and a 'broken-off piece', has a far more concrete German equivalent: *ausschneiden* ('cutting out') and *zerschneiden* ('cutting up'). The German word imbues the action of the infant's onslaught onto the maternal body with an evocative violent image of piercing and slicing it with sharp implements. A curious reversal of Victor Frankenstein's attempts at stitching together and animating an assemblage of corporeal fragments, the boy in *L'enfant et les sortilèges* seeks to disintegrate the loved object's organic whole. This further emphasises the significance of the boy's reparative gesture: the tying of a scarf around the animal's paw is an act of undoing of the earlier action of piercing with a pen in an aggressive attempt at fragmenting and disorganising the object – the scarf is holding it together, preventing its 'falling apart', and working as an external tissue that binds the body.

The figure of the 'disintegrated object' is central to the Kleinian paranoid position. The infant's attempt at fragmenting the object into pieces in the hope of preventing their destructiveness proves futile: in the infant's aggressive fantasy, the severed parts turn into a 'multitude of persecutors', with 'each piece growing again into a persecutor. That in turn brings about the idea of a 'dangerous fragment': in *L'enfant et les sortilèges* the pierced squirrel is not only neutralised as an aggressor, but also 'proliferates' into a multitude of hostile animal beings ([1929] 2011: loc. 4941; [1935] 2011: loc. 6246). In contrast, in the depressive position, when the subject devotes themselves to reparative attempts, the object is united 'again into a whole' ([1935] 2011: loc. 6246).

The restitutive response to the injury of fragmentation is that of 'putting the dispersed bit . . . together again' (Laplanche and Pontalis [1967] 1973: 389). This needs further elaboration: it is not that the object is returned to a unified condition that they *had* prior to the violence of fragmentation, but, rather, that becoming-whole follows the fragmenting operation. Any prior 'object wholeness' in the infantile fantasy world is for Klein impossible without this prior shattering or fragmentation (cf. Rose 1993a). This is linked to the subject's sympathetic identification with the object, or what Klein calls the ego's introjection of the object, and to their subsequent surrender of persecutory fantasies ([1935] 2011: loc. 6167). The subject's recognition of the object's benevolent intentions and the confidence in their capacity to undertake a repair are connected, and both follow the desire to save the object from the destruction and suffering, which the subject had wished upon them ([1935] 2011: loc. 6093, 6193). In this way, I suggest, Klein's theory of restitution-as-reparation complicates the trope of a prelapsarian return; here restitution signifies the emergence of new relations, rather than the *re*-emergence of previous ones or the return to the status quo. In this case, the English prefix re- and the German prefix *wieder-* (in the words 'restitution' (*Wiedergutmachung*) and 'restoration' (*Wiederherstellung*)) should perhaps be read not as an indication that an earlier state is achieved, but, rather, as an attempt at suturing, or stitching, that follows the object's destruction and that *retains that destruction within itself*, both as a memory trace and as an always present possibility of re-occurrence.

Finally, the moment of '[putting] the object back together' coincides with the attempts of 'bringing it to life' or 'resuscitating' ([1935] 2011: loc. 6193, 6366).

In Klein's reading of *L'enfant et les sortilèges*, restitution as the desire to restore wholeness to the maternal body *after* it has been subjected to the fragmenting violence of cutting (*zerschnitten*) takes on a strikingly Frankensteinian aesthetic form – it consists of acts of *stitching the body together* and *imbuing it with life*. The paradox of this juxtaposition is, of course, that just as the repaired (sutured and revitalised) maternal body ceases to appear as a horrific persecutor, in Shelley's *Frankenstein* the Creature manifests his monstrous visual characteristics *after* he has been assembled and galvanised.

It is instructive to juxtapose how Melanie Klein and Mary Shelley invoke the idea of benevolence. In *Frankenstein*, as discussed in Chapter 2, benevolence is the organising principle of modern European society based on ethics of respect for universal humanity; the Creature demonstrates the limitations of the appeal to universal social goodness (and the possibility of violence that such appeal begets) by exemplifying the costs of abandonment and unworthiness of those placed outside the political parameters of humanity (the *in*humans). In Klein's writings on restitution, it is paramount that the child recognises and believes in the mother's benevolence; Klein writes, for instance, about the infant's early inability to recognise the object's benevolent intentions, or about benevolence being an 'extravagant belief' within the complex of the paranoid position ([1935] 2011: loc. 6112, 6582). Klein also uses the term 'benevolent circle' synonymously to her more common term 'virtuous circle' as a designation of the positive interplay of environmental and psychical elements in the infant's life, which brings about reparative desires ([1937] 2011: loc. 7712). And yet, precisely because the persecutory parental figure is never fully conjured away, but, as it were, lurks in the dark and can at any point make re-appearance, the Kleinian 'benevolence' is a precarious and uncertain state of affairs; not a steady foundation upon which restitution can perpetually rest, but a momentary affirmation.

EPILOGUE: RESTITUTION THAT
DOUBLES THE LOSS

Louise Erdrich's book *LaRose* (2016) tells the story of two families belonging to an Ojibwe tribe in North Dakota, whose lives are shattered by the accidental shooting of a child, Dusty, by the neighbour, Landreaux Iron, while hunting for deer.[1] The profound rift that the child's killing causes in the families' coexistence and in the local Ojibwe community at large can be repaired only through a compensatory ritual, whereby Landreaux's family performs an act of restitution to their neighbours by 'replacing' the killed child with their own son, LaRose. Adopted by Dusty's parents, Peter and Nola, LaRose becomes a substitutive presence in Ravich's family, filling the void caused by the killing; he stands in the place of another child, and, assuming a new name, personal objects and identity, *becomes* that other child. Upon his adoptive translocation pivots the novel's narrative of loss and restitution, which is situated beyond the juridical framework of rights and re-acquisitions, as well as beyond the Christian prelapsarian imaginary of returns. What remains unhealed, however, at least in the initial framing of the story, is the wound caused by LaRose's move into the Ravich family, even though his departure is not complete as he is permitted occasional visits to his birth parents and performs filial roles in both household settings. By the virtue of his dual filial presence, and developing a complex set of attachments to Dusty's mother, LaRose embarks on a task of reparation that cicatrises, even if not completely, the rift between the traumatised families.[2]

By presenting the fantasy of substituting a dead child with another as *an actual lived possibility*, and of suturing the communal fabric ruptured by the accidental killing through an old restitutive ritual, Erdrich's narrative provides a critical view onto the ways in which restitution has been imagined in literary and philosophic texts of Western modernity, and which I have located at a conjunction of the tropes of undoing, return and repair. The contrast between the Ojibwe adoptive rite described in *LaRose* and the prelapsarian and retrocessive imaginaries of restitution whereby the object's return to the subject coincides with, and enables, the subject's return to the original condition, asks for a reflection on the binary opposition between 'persons' and 'things' in the restitutive scenarios. In *LaRose* it is the loss of a child, rather than expropriation of a material object, that activates demands for a restorative procedure. Dusty's killing creates an inter-familial and communal rift that demands a radical response on the part of the culprits of giving up their own son, or, rather, of giving up their 'right' to an exclusive paternal relation to him. This response blurs also other foundational distinctions in the restitutive discourse, namely, between 'restitution', 'compensation' and 'substitution'; the characteristic trait of restitution is the belief in the return of the original love-object, as both compensation and substitution acknowledge the unrestitutability of the loss at hand, and offer surrogates in its place. The narrative of restitutive desires in *LaRose* contains a hopeless wish for preservation and acceptance of substitution; it seeks to preserve the presence of the lost love-object *and* it accepts his symbolic surrogacy. What seems to be occurring at a 'surface' of the ritual is an actualisation of the possibility of the annulment and cancellation of past wrongdoing *as if* it had never taken place. And yet the striking thing about Erdrich's narrative is that the restitution simultaneously repairs *and* destroys; rather than appease the pain of loss, it *doubles the loss*. The interconnected occurrences of the death of one child and of the adoptive translocation of another are echoing wounding events.

In have argued in Chapter 3 that Durkheim's binary distinction between repressive law and restitutive law in *The Division of Labor in Society* is underwritten by a philosophic outlook on modernity whereby the combined ideological forces of individualism and humanitarianism produce an ethical capacity in the modern subject to respond to crime without passionate desires for the wrongdoer's suffering, or what Derrida (2013: 155) in his reading of Nietzsche's remarks about the Roman punishments for unpaid debts has described as 'the voluptuous pleasure of causing the other to suffer'. While in Durkheim's view the repressive function of law in traditional societies is underwritten by 'collective anger', the restitutive operations of law in modern industrialised societies is defined by the absence of such vindictive passions, injurious desires and spectacularised suffering against the wrongdoer. In other words, restitutive norms signify the separation of law from the desire for violence. However, in *LaRose* restitution as an act of doubling the loss of the love-object is the very condition of reparative possibility; here violence and repair are inseparable. As such, *LaRose* is not only an epilogue to the book on tropes, imaginaries and theories of restitution in modern social and political philosophy – it utters 'an additional word', an 'appendage' to the main story – but it also follows the logic of the supplement, which I referenced earlier: it introduces a moment of confusion and instability into the main story, thus threatening to reveal its obscured political logic. The restitutive ritual in *LaRose* offers a narrative pathway for thinking about the other of restitution, or *the other restitution*, a restitution unconnected to the status quo, or the 'original condition', to which the subject longs to 'return'. In Joan Riviere's striking formulation, status quo was preferable to change, because it came to signify to the subject a 'bearable state'. The ethical obligation in *LaRose* to make a shared parental arrangement in order to repair the consequences of an unintended pedicide is very much a departure from such a 'bearable state' – it is something that LaRose's mother *cannot bear*, and yet also something she *survives*, something she *lives through*,[3] by *bearing the unbearable*.

* * *

Another cultural text that illustrates poignantly aporias of restitution theory is Françoise Ozon's film *Frantz* (2016), which narrates events in the aftermath of the First World War, following the killing of a young German soldier, Frantz, by a Frenchman, Adrien.[4] While the killing appears to have been incidental and is warranted both within the norms of *ius bellum* and by the authority of the Catholic faith, Adrien is tormented by guilt and remorse. He visits Frantz's parents, the Hoffmeisters, and his fiancée, Anna, after the war with the intention of revealing his identity as Franz's killer and of asking for their forgiveness. However, Adrien's wish for forgiveness is also imbued with a restitutive fantasy to '[r]eplace the man he's killed', as Adrien's fiancée, Fanny, puts it. While Adrien's motivations are unclear to the other characters, and perhaps even to himself, in a decisive moment of his encounter with the Hoffmeisters, instead of offering an identity disclosure as their son's killer, Adrien impersonates Frantz's fictional friend from pre-war Paris, in an attempt to offer himself to the Hoffmeisters as a 'restitutive object' – a phantasmatic substitute for Frantz – and to bring their mourning to an end. Adrien confabulates a story of his intimate friendship with Frantz and of their shared artistic and intellectual interests and experiences, in an attempt to return Frantz to his family through fictional memories, and thus to *undo* Frantz's killing – to return the parents to the time and condition before the filial death, and the parents' generation to the time and condition from before the war. After one of Adrien's visit to the Hoffmeisters, Frantz's mother exclaims '[t]onight it felt as if Frantz himself was present' (cited in Zolkos 2019: 144). A substitutive 'chain of equivalence' (Marder 2005) between Frantz and Adrien is established and consolidated not only through the translocation of material objects (the Hoffmeisters present Adrien with Frantz's beloved violin), but also through the transfer of affection and erotic attachment as the Hoffmeisters encourage a romantic relationship between Adrien and Frantz's fiancée, Anna. The transfer of Anna's libidinal investment from their one filial love-object to its surrogate signifies the completion of the restitutive process. It also, not unlike in case of Elizabeth in *Frankenstein*, illustrates the gendered dynamics of 'thingification', which produces an object through which the restitutive process is accomplished. However, in Ozon's film the deliberately staged scene of 'filial substitution', whereby the reparation should become complete and the mourning should come to an end, never takes place (Zolkos 2019: 144).[5] Adrien collapses while playing Frantz's violin, unable to continue to provide the Hoffmeisters with the surrogate presence of their dead son. Anna, unlike Elizabeth in *Frankenstein*, is a recalcitrant and unwilling 'restitutive object' that blocks, rather than facilitates, the family's prelapsarian return: even though she develops an erotic attachment to Adrien, she also retains a position of fidelity towards Franz whom she continues to mourn. Anna's visit to France and her encounter with virulent anti-German patriotism is another sign of the Hoffmeisters' (and their generation's) barred return to the time before Frantz's death and before the war. In *Frantz*, like in *LaRose*, restitution does not nullify the past event of loss and dispossession, and it fails to establish the substitutive relationship between restitutive subjects (the Hoffmeisters) and restitutive objects (Adrien, Anna, the violin) in order to open up the passage to the prelapsarian position. The reparative endeavours of the Hoffmeisters and of their generation become synonymous with a failure of responsibility, which also reveals their insurmountable impediment in seeing the continuities of war in the present in the form of raging belligerent nationalist affects. Françoise Ozon presents restitution as deeply transformative and phantasmatic processes, and as a familial scene that becomes a synecdoche of the post-war nation; the restitution consists of compromised ethical positions and of complicated political stakes and struggles, rather than non-violent reparative endeavours.

* * *

Both stories illustrate the operations of undoing by declaring the deaths that have come to pass, *not to have occurred*, or 'not [to have] arrived [*non arrivé*]', as Derrida puts it (1996: 81 n. 16). These 'restitutions without restitution' consist of attempts and gestures of reinstatement, re-acquisition and return that ultimately make the loss ever more pronounced; they evince both the unrestitutability of the love-object *and* the barred gates to the prelapsarian time/place. Referencing Anaximander's parable of *adikia* (archaic injustice), Stephen Ross invokes an 'unending' restitution. This restitution fails to ever satisfy the demands of justice, and aims not at a closure of history, but, rather, at an ethical responsibility that continues and perhaps even increases with time, 'defeating any destiny, growing older and younger than itself, exceeding itself as justice's injustice' (1993: 1, 4). 'What restitution circulates for losses beyond measure, beyond mourning?' Ross asks (1993: 11), '. . . [w]hat of forgotten losses, losses doubly, triply lost?'. In *LaRose* and in *Frantz* restitution can only seek to fill the void by multiplying the loss, and even then it arrives at a position that makes the void ever more obvious, gaping and painful; its restitution is both correction *and* misdirection, repair *and* rupture, cicatrix *and* dehiscence. These aporetic and ambivalent attempts at restitution-making are revealed as sites of deep political tensions, and they are moments where restitution and ethics of responsibility becomes inextricable.

NOTES

Introduction

1. The words of the character of Hubertus Czernin in the film.
2. See, for example, Mbembe's public talk 'Reflections on African Objects and Restitution in the Twenty-First Century' on the occasion of his reception of the Gerda Henkel Prize (2018). See also Mbembe (2017; 2020).
3. Or, in the provenance discourse, of 'legalized theft'. For critical perspectives on provenance research, see, for example, Vrdoljak 2008; Merryman 2010; Azoulay 2019.
4. I take this term from Magdalena Saryusz-Wolska, who writes about 'subcutaneous memory' in cultural representations of the Holocaust (2020). My understanding of this subcutaneous or subterranean location of the prelapsarian and retrocessive motifs in relation to the liberal and juridical restitution discourse also draws on Giorgio Agamben's view of secularisation as a suppression or displacement of theological contents in the realm of public discourse, and not their elimination (see Agamben 2007).
5. The dominant secular and liberal discourse on restitution relies on prior dichotomous conceptualisations of historical time, of the nature of historical events, of the desirability of reparative endeavours as a mode of 'making-good' historical violence, and of the relationship between persons and objects. First, it relies on temporal categories that bifurcate past and present, both in the sense of legitimising the pursuit of historical justice and so-called 'transitional justice', whereby the multiple modalities, instruments and politics of redress are constructed as discontinuous with past atrocity, and thus mark the violent history as *no longer in existence*. This, of course, has the effect of legitimising political initiatives or initiatives by the virtue of their capacity to operate as such 'reversal events' (see, for example, Waldron 1992; Elster 2004; Ohlin 2007; Bevernage 2013; Buckley-Zistel et al. 2013; Corradetti 2013;

Winter 2014; Lu 2018; 2019). Secondly, as I elaborate in the introduction, it relies on a strong distinction between the restitutive subject and restitutive object, which, within the purview of contemporary international law, corresponds largely to the distinction between 'persons' and 'things' as incompatible and mutually exclusive categories (see, for example, Esposito 2015; 2016).

6. While I do not focus on the question of post-atrocity and post-conflict reconciliation, there is a growing body of literature considering the relationship between restitution, reparations and reconciliation. See, for example, Waldron 1992; Wheeler 1997; Barkan 2000; Thompson 2002; Torpey 2003; Brooks 2004; Walker 2010; Hirsch 2013; La Caze 2018; Lu 2018; 2019.

7. As I explain later, that partly happens through the assimilation (and secularisation) of the Christian theme of prelapsarian return, and partly is a reflection of the Aristotelian tradition of corrective justice.

8. I use the term 'trope' in Hayden White's sense of 'modes of employment': tropes are modes and schemes of narrativisation that assemble, interweave and organise elements into a narrative unit that expresses a particular ideological position (White [1973] 2014; 1986). Also, in *Metahistory: the Historical Imagination in Nineteenth-Century Europe* White credits the Enlightenment philosophers with constructing a non-oppositional relationship between reality and imagination. He writes that '[the] philosophes needed a theory of human consciousness in which reason was not set over against imagination as the basis of truth against basis of error, but in which the *continuity* between reason and fantasy was recognized, the mode of their relationship as parts of a more general process of human inquiry into a world incompletely known might be sought, and the process in which fantasy or imagination contributed as much to the discovery of truth as did reason itself might be perceived' ([1973] 2014: 51).

9. The literature on reparative action and the politics of repair has expanded substantially in the recent years in the fields of political theory, political philosophy and moral philosophy. Among others, see Minow 1998; Digeser 2001; Govier 2002; Torpey 2003; 2006; Walker 2006; 2010; 2016; Griswold 2007; Murphy 2010; 2017; Meister 2011; Corradetti, Eisikovits and Rotondi 2015; La Caze 2018.

10. Derrida (1996: 81 n.16) describes the mechanism of *Ungeschehenmachen* as an example of a 'prosthesis of repression' in Freud, which pivots on the question of the meaning of an 'event' in psychoanalysis, or 'the coming of what arrives – or not'. What is peculiar about *Ungeschehenmachen* is that an event that occurred also becomes one that has 'not happened' (*non arrivé*)

11. Jankélévitch (2005: 47; emphasis in the original) writes: '[all] the burn and all that is incurable of remorse lie in the impossibility of integrating that which we cannot . . . renounce. If time does not chew on the *quoddity* of the misdeed, it is because it is impalpable and pneumonic . . . The thing-done falls under the senses, but the fact of having done is of the order of *sense*, since it is an eternal event that is triggered by an intention . . . [the] *fact of the fact* . . . the fact with its exponent . . . evades the corrosive action of duration.' For a discussion of Jankélévitch's incorporation of the concepts of quiddity and quoddity into his philosophic oeuvre, see Kelly 2013; Looney 2015.

12. While reflecting international legal developments in the modern period, the idea of restitution also incorporates elements in law, politics and sociology specific to the modern period. It is in the course of modern legal reforms, and the emergence and consolidation of the institutions of international law, that restitution is tied to the conception of unjust enrichment. The impact of pre-modern traditions of justice, philosophy and theology on the concept of restitution is also undeniable and is visible in its reliance on the dichotomous status of things and persons, which originates in ancient Roman law, in its assumptions in regard to ownership and custodianship, and in the Christian undertones of reparation of harm and wrongdoing. See Koritansky 2011; Corlett 2013.

13. I deliberately do not specify in the book the *kinds* of restitution at hand, because I am interested in mapping out the theoretical developments of restitution as a potent motif, or a political trope, that structures and orients in particular ways texts dealing with the question of reversing and ameliorating (the effects of) unjust enrichment, beyond the formal legal definitions. The broader contexts of this study are thus the on-going debates on post-conflict, post-atrocity and post-colonial restitution. On the typology of restitutive and reparative actions, see Torpey 2005; Rotherham 2007; Paglione 2008; Butt 2009; Sabahi 2011. On land restitution, see Pantuliano and Elhawary 2009; Garcia-Godos 2010. On restitution of cultural property and heritage, see Thompson 2003; Cornu and Renold 2010; Stamatoudi 2011; Azoulay 2019; Robertson 2019.

14. For the discussion of distinction between restitution and compensation in post-conflict and post-atrocity contexts, see Gray 1999; Butt 2009; Cordial and Røsandhaug 2009; Leckie and Huggins 2011.

15. For discussion of the link between property return and the return of displaced populations, see Hathaway 1997; Williams 2007; 2012; 2013; McCallin 2012; Long 2013; Murcia 2014; Souter 2014.

16. Pantuliano and Elhawary (2009) direct such critique at the UN Pinheiro Principle. They write in HPG Policy Brief 'Uncharted Territory': 'In the aftermath of war, humanitarian efforts tend to focus on activities that aim to restore the pre-war status quo. These efforts are based on the assumption that there is a clear distinction between war and peace . . . Violent conflict destroys not only political, economic and social structures, but is itself a process of transformation in which alternative systems of economic accumulation, social regulation and political governance emerge.'

17. The word *hístēmi* is frequently used in the Christian Bible, where it is connotes an activity of placing something or causing it to stand, as well as in the sense of upholding or sustaining the authority or force of something (cf. Revelation 3:20, 'Behold, I stand [ἕστηκα, *hestēka*] at the door and knock; if anyone hears My voice and opens the door, I will come in to him and will dine with him, and he with Me'; Revelation 14:1, '. . . the Lamb was standing [ἑστὸς, *hestos*] on Mount Zion, and with Him one hundred and forty-four thousand, having His name and the name of His Father written on their foreheads'). The concept of *stasis* in mathematics connotes a state of stability in which all forces are equal and opposing, which results in an equilibrium. In political history, Thucydides used *stasis* as a description of

internal disturbances within the state, and has been translated variously as civil war, civil strife, civic disorder, faction, revolution.

18. Intransitive verbs are divided into unaccusatives and unergatives. In unaccusatives, the grammatical subject of the sentence (determined syntactically) is different from the category of semantic agency (determined through relationship to the action or event); in unergatives, the semantic agent voluntarily initiates and/or is actively responsible for the action of the verb.

19. That differentiation within the restitutive lexicon is not to be confused with the polysemy of the concept of 'reparations', defined either as a redressive approach to mass violations more broadly, or, in more specific terms, as a set of measures or programmes, namely, 'benefits [provided] directly to the victims of certain types of crimes' (De Greiff 2006a: 453). See, for example, Corlett 2011; Laplante 2013; Lu 2018.

20. As an idiom of corrective response to wrongdoing, restitution overlaps significantly with reparations insofar as both terms invoke making good after an injury and restoring (something) to its proper place. For instance, Paul M. Hughes (2011: 946) characterises 'reparations' in the language of return, when he writes that '[r]eparations aim at returning victims of injustice to an at least symbolic pre-injury *status quo ante*'.

21. Available at: https://www.ohchr.org/EN/ProfessionalInterest/Pages/RemedyAnd Reparation.aspx.

22. Available at: https://www.unhcr.org/protection/idps/50f94d849/principles-housing-property-restitution-refugees-displaced-persons-pinheiro.html.

23. Note the family resemblance of the interjection 'whenever possible' in the Basic Principles and Guidelines on the Right to a Remedy and of the previously discussed phrase 'so far as possible' in the *Chorzów* ruling of the Permanent Court of International Justice. Both, I suggest, are supplementary, in the Derridean sense, to the formal juridical articulation of restitution as a return to the original state.

24. In addition, restitution has also established itself as a distinctive approach in the field of penology. Eglash (1959) categorises these different restitutive traditions by making a distinction between 'mandatory' (or 'coerced') restitution (in law) and 'spontaneous' restitution (in psychology), and then argues that religion is a field where restitution constitutes a hybrid of the mandatory and spontaneous types (because of the coexistence of ritualised penitence and voluntary expression of religiously inspired moral feelings, such as contrition for wrongdoing). This typology serves Eglash's purpose of articulating a distinctive form of 'guided restitution', or 'creative restitution', in penology, where selected elements of psychological, religious and legal restitution are brought together into a new restitutive '*gestalt*' (1959: 118).

25. On the concept of unjust enrichment in relation to restitution, see Hedley 1985; Dietrich 1998; Giglio 2004; Lodder 2012; Priel 2013; for a juridical focus, Palmer 2016; for a broader and more political focus, Meister 2011.

26. Angelo Corlett (2011), Marie Cornu and Marc-André Renold (2010), Catherine Lu (2018), Giulia Paglione (2008) and Anneke Smit (2012) have argued for more cultural and political insights into the workings of restitutive norms, in recognition

of their complexity and diversity in contemporary global contexts, potentially not only supplementing, but also undermining, the dominant legal approaches to restitution. I agree that the current attention to post-conflict and post-atrocity restitution demands more intersectional and interdisciplinary thinking.

27. Hartman coins the term 'restitutive desire' in his essay 'The Philomena Project' (1991) to point to a sense of finality implied in restitutive acts, and driven by the aim of recreating foundations of lost object, and of thus bringing the violence of dispossession to a 'charismatic closure'.

28. In non-Western legal traditions, including indigenous customary law, one finds a richer and more complex conception of the human subject's relation to the non-human world – the conceptions of 'stewardship', 'guardianship' and 'custodianship' are important alternatives to the notion of 'property'. See Kuprecht 2013; Anderson and Geismar 2017. For an indigenous perspective on the term 'belonging' in the context of cultural heritage restitution, see De Line 2018.

29. In the Roman legal tradition, the status of ownership involves three kinds of rights, or entitlements: *usus* (the right to use and to derive enjoyment from one's property); *fructus* (the right to derive profit from one's property); and *abusus* (the right to alienate one's property through consumption, destruction or transfer to a different owner). See Sarr and Savoy 2018: 29–30 (discussed in the context of cultural heritage restitution).

30. In the Roman law of *mancipium* property was understood as literally that which is taken with one's hand, *manu captum* (Esposito 2015: 19).

31. See Canetti ([1962] 2000); Irigaray (1986); Esposito (2015).

32. A poignant example of such restitutive 'hand gesture' in the Australian Aboriginal and Torres Strait Island context was the return of land to the peoples of Gurindji by the Gough Whitlam government in 1970s in a ceremony including the placing of soil into the hand of a Gurindji elder, Vincent Lingiari, by the prime minister. The ceremony followed a prolonged strike by the Gurindji people against an agricultural company that occupied their land (Wave Hill-Walk Off); the Gurindji land was subsequently purchased by the Whitlam government and returned to its rightful custodians. Interestingly, the ceremonial pouring of soil into Lingiari's hand was a *symbolic undoing* of the (allegedly) 'voluntary' transfer of land custodianship in the 1834 Port Philip land transaction, when the elders were said to have put soil into the hand of John Batman. Whitlam's gesture establishes its importance through the historic referentiality to this 'prior transgression' that it accordingly seeks to *reverse* (Hocking 2018). Restitution understood as a reversal of historic dispossession relies on a particular political epistemology that contrasts past and present as domains of injustice and redress-making, respectively. The binary opposition of past and present potentially distorts the view of Australian settler colonialism as a continuity of violence against the first people, and it also grants greater visibility to those political acts and undertakings that are able to establish themselves as 'reversal events'. As McLaren (2017) argues, there is a danger that the 'iconic handful of sand' will be seen in isolation from the restitutive struggle of the Gurindji.

33. For weaving together traumatic, melancholic and (psychological) restitutive motifs in literature, see Sebald 2002; 2003; 2004; Graham 2011. See also Baxter, Henitiuk

and Hutchinson 2013. In an essay 'An Attempt at Restitution' (2004), first delivered as a public address in 2001 on the occasion of the opening of the House of Literature in Stuttgart, Sebald associates literature with what he calls 'a restitutive attempt [*Ein Versuch der Restitution*]': '[t]here are many forms of writings; only in literature, however, can there be an attempt at restitution over and above the mere recital of facts, and over and above scholarship'. Baxter, Henitiuk and Hutchinson (2013) suggest that with these words Sebald separates restitution from both retribution *and* redemption, and assigns to literature the task of restoring, or returning, agency to 'marginalized historical subjects without seeking to intervene either physically or metaphysically, without prejudicing their alterity'. Interestingly, this restitutive attempt of literature has to do with its imaginary dimension, and with literature's capacity to envision 'alternative, and often elliptical, expressions of historical experience' (Baxter, Henitiuk and Hutchinson 2013, loc. 244).

34. In the Kleinian psychoanalytic tradition, Hanna Segal ([1972] 2005: 50) has made an important distinction between, on the one hand, restitution as reparation, which Klein associated with the depressive position, and which included love and care for the object, and, on the other hand, restitution as an attempted restoration of a 'fantasy world in which dependence on objects is excluded'. See ch. 4 of the book.

35. Jankélévitch also suggested that it was a product of superimposition of a spatial imaginary on the problem of undoing of wrongs, which for him concerned temporality, rather than spatiality. Jankélévitch's philosophy of forgiveness ([1967] 2019; 2005) constitutes a radical departure from the 'myth of symmetry', which governs the law of retaliation and the law of recompense alike. See also Kelly 2013; Looney 2015; Banki 2018; La Caze 2018.

36. In his lectures on the death penalty, Derrida (2013: 351) considers the word 'damnation' (Latin *damnum*), and its cognate terms ('indemnity', 'condemnation') as a wrongdoing and as 'what must be paid to repair the wrong, to remunerate, indemnify, redeem . . .'. In this context Derrida considers Benveniste's shared Germanic etymology of the words '*ghilde*' and '*Geld*', *fra-gildan*, meaning '"to render, restitute" . . . the phenomena of fraternity as convivial communion'.

37. In Polish 'restitution' is a term in biological conservation used to describe attempts at regeneration of endangered species (*restytucja gatunku*), and in architectural and cultural heritage conservation and restoration (*restytucja budynku*). The closest English terms would be 'regeneration' (in regard to biological entities) and 'restoration' (in regard to inanimate entities).

38. The concept of the social imaginary relies on social theory of imagination, its relation to ideology and to fantasy, and its role in subject formation (see, for example, Althusser [1971] 2014; Bachelard 1971; [1988] 2011; Castoriadis 1998).

39. Le Doeuff outlines two possible approaches to the imaginary tropes in philosophy, which she calls, respectively, 'narrow' and 'broad'. In the first approach, the assumption is that the imaginary is a sign of a difficulty or a friction within the argument itself. In the second approach, the emphasis is on possible contradictions, in that the imaginary has the capacity to simultaneously support and undermine the theoretical argument. Le Doeuff argues that 'images work . . . [f]or [the system

that deploys them], because they sustain something which the system cannot itself justify, but which is nevertheless needed for its proper working'; they can also work '[a]gainst [the system when] their meaning is incompatible with the system's possibilities'.

40. In elaborating the conception of fantasy (*Phantasie*) in his meta-psychological writing, Freud helps us grasp its key structural feature: in the process of fantasising (which continues in adult life as day-dreaming, fictional narratives, etc.), the child is in the unique position of occupying a third-person standpoint in relation to their repressed wishes and desires (that is, at once connected to and distanced from them). Lacan elaborates the concept of fantasy as a kind of 'screen' that at the same time reveals something and conceals it; it is impossible for the subject to abandon the fantasy-world, but only to 'traverse' it. In the area of political theory, Janis Stavrakakis argued that fantasies are not domains of the subject's private psychic activity, but, rather, a shared registration of normative symbolic social structures. For Slavoj Žižek, fantasies are collective frameworks of belief, through which the society comes to deal with that which lies outside its norms. Society's fantasy-world can be glimpsed into through observation of ritualistic and symbolic events, such as public spectacles of apology, reconciliation and return. In arguing that restitution in humanitarian and redressive discourses is underpinned by the collective phantasm of returning to a primary and original condition from before the conflict, I suggest that what is at stake is the articulation of desire for a paradisal non-violent life – for the elimination of social strife, conflict and antagonism – and for a harmonious community that is transparent to oneself, through the act of resolving and undoing (the *making-unhappen*) of the violent past. Insofar as restitution remains tied to the humanitarian narratives of violence and dispossessions as a way of compromising or corrupting one's belonging to universal humanity, it also remains invested in recuperating and rescuing the subject's humanity.

41. That highlights another frequently made opposition that the writers of the 'imaginal turn' problematise, namely, between the imaginary and the real, in accordance with the Latin etymology of *imaginari* as 'picturing [only] to oneself' and 'existing only in fancy' (cf. Gatens 1996; Pérez 1999). In the Marxist tradition, it was Louis Althusser who, in his 1971 reading of Lenin's famous definition of ideology as the subject's imaginary relationship to the material conditions of social life, strongly affirmed the binary opposition between the imaginary and the real. Althusser argued that ideology consisted of 'imaginary transposition[s]' of the 'real conditions of existence', thus linking the imaginary with processes of a distortion or falsification of meaning ([1971] 2014: 257). In contrast, Gaston Bachelard, influenced by the Jungian idea that personal imaginaries express the world of the collective archetypical unconscious, saw the imaginary as being in synchronic relation to the real. Bachelard proposed in *Air and Dreams* ([1988] 2011; see also 1971) that the human faculty of imagination should be conceptualised as a *movement*, rather than as a static production of images. For Bachelard, imagination is closely linked to the question of freedom. By defining the imaginary not as a formation of (new) images, but as a transformation and deformation of already existing ones, Bachelard affirmed that the emblematic imaginary gesture is that of surpassing limits and limitations presented to the subject in the now.

CHAPTER 1

1. Larry May differentiates between two mechanisms of *jus post bellum*: restitution and reparation. Whereas restitution concerns 'restoring to the rightful owner what has been lost or taken away', reparations are about 'restoring to good condition of something that has been damage' (2012a: 183; see also Hughes 2011).

2. While Grotius' dramatic life story has been a topic of several studies (see, for example, Dumbauld 1970; van Ittersum 2006), the ironic interplay between his biography and his theorising of restitution resides in something akin to 'restitutive desire' in Grotius' private and political undertakings. Grotius' sentencing in 1619 to life imprisonment in Loevestein castle meant not only loss of freedom, status and reputation, but also confiscation of material property. Following his famous escape in a chest of books, orchestrated by his wife, Maria van Reigersbergen, and maid, Elselina van Houwening, Grotius remained exiled from the States of Holland, serving foreign rulers in France and Sweden, while continuously pursuing (unsuccessful) attempts at negotiating terms of repatriation. The Grotian theory of restitution, resting on the assumption of the sovereign subject acting in accordance with one's will and demanding uninhibited dominion over one's possessions, contrasts curiously with what seems like a defining characteristic of Grotius' life after 1619: that of unrepaired loss, failed restitution and desperation of desire. In contrast to the strong epistemic binary of 'persons' and 'things', on which Grotius' theory of restitution rests and which it in turn reinforces, Grotius' life testifies to the instability of that distinction, and the political precarity that results the 'thingification' of persons.

3. According to Blom (2014), the nineteenth-century 'peace societies . . . traced back to . . . Grotius the evolving conscience of the "civilized" world towards justice and mercy in international conflict'; for instance, at the 1899 Hague Peace Conference, the US delegate Andrew Dickson White invoked Grotius 'as providing "the real foundation of the modern science of international law"'.

4. What tends to be given insufficient recognition in the liberal rights approaches that credit Grotius with the theorisation of 'international society' and international rules of warfare, is his political support for the development of imperial commercial relations by the Dutch in the East Indies (see Keene 2002; Borschberg 2011).

5. In a comparative contextual reading of *De Iure Belli* and *De Iure Praeda*, Edward Dumbauld (1970) points to their 'biographical' differences, as well as their dissimilar goals. While *De Iure Praeda* is underpinned by its author's 'fiery nationalist ardour' (1970: 28), *De Iure Belli*, a work composed during Grotius' imprisonment and exile, seems devoid of patriotic passions. In regard to the intellectual context, Richard Tuck (1999: 78) argues that while *De Iure Praeda* is consistent with the humanist tradition, *De Iure Belli* constitutes a major departure from the tradition, which 'applauded warfare in the interests of one's *res publica*, and saw a dramatic moral difference between Christian, European civilisation and barbarism'. In regard to the question of secularism, while both *De Iure Belli* and *De Iure Praedae* ground social obligations in the principles of natural law, they situate it differently in relation to the divine presence in the world. According to Jerome Schneewind (1998: 66–74), *De Iure Praedae* embraces a distinctively 'voluntarist' account of social obligation, whereby natural law originates in, and derives its authority from,

the commands of the Christian god. This is apparent in the opening statement of the 'Prolegomena', where Grotius states the famous words '[w]hat God has shown to be His Will, that is law' ([1738] 2005: 21). As such, *De Iure Praedae* to a large extent continues the Scholastic conception of natural law. In contrast, *De Iure Belli* has been of great interest for the scholars of Western secularism precisely because it articulates an alternative ('intellectualist') account of social obligations. This is exemplified famously, though not exclusively, in Grotius' *'etiamsi daremus'* passage (so-called 'impious hypothesis'), which states: 'all we have now said would take place, though we should even grant, what without the greatest Wickedness cannot be granted, that there is no God, or that he takes no Care of human Affairs' ([1738] 2005: 89, XI). The binding force of natural law in *De Iure Belli* derives not from its divine origin, but from its recognition as a prerequisite of social life and sociality (cf. Haakonssen 1985; Besselink 1988; Somos 2007). In chapter II of *De Iure Belli* Grotius writes that 'the Law of Nature is so unalterable that God himself cannot change it' and 'the Law of Nature being unchangeable, GOD himself cannot decree any Thing against it' ([1738] 2005: 155, I.10.5, 190, II.1.5). In regard to Grotius' theory of property, Fitzmaurice (2014) discusses Grotius' departure from equating appropriation with occupation in *De Iure Praedae* and his endorsement of a more complex notion of property in *De Iure Belli*; in the latter, Grotius puts a greater emphasis on the contract and mutual consent in the constitution of ownership and property relations (see also Haakonssen 1985).

6. Haakonsen (1985: 250) writes about the 'secularizing effect' of Grotius' work, rather than Grotius' deliberate commitment to reducing the influence of religion upon public life. For Haakonsen (1985: 250), what is at the core of Grotius' secularism is *not* the explicit statements in *De Iure Belli* that separate natural law from the question of divine origins, including the *'etiamsi daremus'* passage, or that authorise secular viewpoints and decision-making in ecclesiastical matters; rather, it is Grotius' contribution to the development of non-theological and empirically testable conception of natural law.

7. On the impact of scholasticism on Grotius' writings, see Tuck 1999; Wauters 2017.

8. For instance, soldiers who voluntarily surrendered to the enemy held no right to return: '[t]hey have no Benefit of Postliminy, [who] . . . being conquered by Arms, yield themselves up to their Enemies' (Grotius [1738] 2005: 1390, IX.II.8, see also [1738] 2005: 1393–4, IX.II.9).

9. See Giglio 2004 for the interpretation of the scholastic and Grotian notions of restitution as 'giving back' the expropriated goods, rather than 'giving up' the unjustly accrued profits. For a contrast between Grotius' and Locke's theory of restitution on this point, see Tuckness 2010.

10. While Geddert (2014: 587) interprets Grotius' theory of restitution as part of expletive ('strict') justice, and thus not as a primarily political issue, but as 'a problem to be solved with finality', May (2012a; 2012b; 2014) discusses Grotius' use of the principle of *meionexia* to present a more political interpretation of restitution in *De Iure Praedae* and in *De Iure Belli*. *Meionexia* is 'the disposition to accord [oneself] less than [one's] due' (Grotius, cited in May 2012a: 206). The corresponding vice to the virtue of *meionexia* is *pleonexia*, often translated as 'greed', 'avarice' or 'insatiability',

by which Aristotle meant the dedication to acquiring the means of good life (wealth) as a goal in itself (in *Leviathan* Hobbes invokes *pleonexia* not as a specific vice, but as a concept of natural law, and interprets it as a universal human inclination to accord oneself more than one's share). For a philosophical overview of the concept of *pleonexia*, see Zolkos 2020. May situates *meionexia* in the *ius post bellum* context to argue for a normative conception of post-conflict reparations as an application of restraint in demanding what, according to the standards of expletive justice, one deserves to receive. *Meionexia* is thus a principle of leniency and moderation in regard to the punitive demands of reparations. The key difference between Geddert and May's interpretations is that for May the Grotian theory of reparations and of punishment belongs to the realm of attributive justice. May emphasises that for Grotius the motivation for *meionexia* originates in humanitarian considerations and 'a sense of honor as well as the duty of humanness and mercy' (2012a: 210). In Book III of *De Iure Belli* Grotius writes that while 'the Goods of an enemy's Subjects may be taken and acquired, not only to reimburse ourselves of the primary Debt, which was the Occasion for the War; but also to make Satisfaction for the subsequent Charges', the prevailing principle is that 'Humanity bids us not use this Right to the utmost' (2005 [1631]: 1477, XII.1.3, 1478, XIII.4.1).

11. In *Summa Theologica*, responding to the question of '[w]hether restitution of what has been taken is necessary for salvation', Thomas Aquinas quotes Augustine's postulate that '[u]nless a man restore[s] what he has purloined, his sin is not forgiven'. He then deliberates that restitution is an act of 'giving back [of a thing unjustly taken] that [re-establishes] equality', and of 'safeguarding of justice', from which it follows that 'it is necessary for salvation to restore what has been taken unjustly' (Aquinas [1888–1906] 2017).

12. Jean Barbeyrac exemplifies Grotius' Aristotelian conception of a medium action in *De Iure Belli* through a discussion of fear. Fear is 'a Passion not evil in its own Nature', rather the problem is the excess or the insufficient amount of fear: 'too much Fear is *Timidity*, or *Cowardice*; too little is *Audacity*, or a rash *Boldness*: [t]he just Medium is *Fortitude*, or rational *Courage*' (in Grotius [1738] 2005: 118, n. XLV (I); emphasis in the original).

13. On the difference between the conception of property in *De Iure Praeda* and in *De Iure Belli*, see Fitzmaurice (2014). Fitzmaurice discusses Grotius' conception of private property as an abandonment of the 'prelapsarian . . . natural state of common property' due to human '[a]mbition, a vice and industry'. This suggests the impact of Reformation theology on Grotius' thinking, namely, 'the association of property with sinfulness [and] . . . fallen [human] nature' (2014: 95). While in *De Iure Praedae* Grotius aligns the event of the emergence of private property closely with the doctrine of occupation and use, which in turn was related to self-preservation, in *De Iure Belli* it 'was no longer simply the taking of things or their use that was the origin of property, but compact' (2014: 96). Importantly, Fitzmaurice notes that Grotius' later departure from the alignment of ownership and occupation, as well as his rejection of 'the right of discovery' potentially gives rise to 'a critique of the [Western] conquest of non-European peoples [because] occupation does not mean bestowing of sovereignty' (2014: 97). See also Wauters 2017.

14. Modern international law makes a distinction between prize-taking, or war booty, which has a narrower definition of enemy property (or land) seized during warfare by the belligerent army, and looting, plunder or pillage, which is not limited to contexts of war, and can be perpetrated by military and civilian actors alike. Pillage has been unequivocally prohibited by international law, including the Fourth Geneva Convention (Art. 33) and the ICC Status (Art. 8(2)(b)), which defined it as a war crime. In contrast, prize-taking has not been fully prohibited by the convention, and is permitted when the confiscation is not about profit-making, but is decisive for the conduct of war, and includes 'objects' such as military documents, military equipment, arms, horses and so on (Geneva Convention III, Art. 18).

15. Grotius' philosophic justification of Dutch imperial ambitions for economic colonial expansion relies on a strong normative and historical binary between peaceful colonial trade and violent conquest. This downplayed the extent to which the advancement of Dutch commercial interests in the East Indies coincided with military expansionism. The historical part of *De Iure Praedae* outlining the history of Dutch trade in the region ('Historica') makes a strong distinction between the violent colonialism of Spain and Portugal, including plunder, physical injury, extermination and institutionalisation of slavery, on the one hand, and the commercial colonialism of the Netherlands – colonial trade relations are for Grotius mutually beneficial, non-exploitative and non-violent (Grotius quotes from a letter by a bishop of Malakka who depicts the Dutch traders as 'most welcome and well liked [by the native populations], because they practiced commerce justly, without resorting to violence and injury' ([1901] 2001: 228). Tuck (1999: 80) emphasises that the political context addressed by Grotius was a 'defensive war' on the part of the Dutch to 'protect either their homeland or existing trade patterns'; rather, the Dutch 'were waging an offensive war, in order to open up trade routes and make a lot of money'. See van Ittersum 2010.

16. Tuck notes an interesting difference between *De Iure Belli* and *De Iure Praeda* in regard to what constitutes lawful causes for war. In his later work Grotius includes among such causes acts of aggression, '[offences] against Nature', which includes 'crimes' of tyranny, cannibalism, piracy and violence against settlers (Grotius, cited in Tuck 1999: 103). Tuck speculates that this development in the direction of justification of interventionist militarism as 'an international right to punish' is linked to the changing character of Dutch colonialism from 1620s onwards, from primarily mercantile activities to territorial annexation (1999: 103, 108).

17. On the difference between 'self-interested sociability' in *De Iure Praeda* and 'sociability as a cause of civil society' in *De Iure Belli*, see Fitzmaurice 2014.

18. That minimalist conception of sociability (and the idea of 'self-interested sociability') is, according to Fitzmaurice (2014: 87–8), a mark of continuing influence of humanist thinking on Grotius' oeuvre, in particular that of Machiavelli.

19. Grotius writes that 'Man above all other Creatures is endued not only with this Social Faculty of which we have spoken, but likewise with Judgement to discern Things pleasant or hurtful, and those not only present but future . . .' (2005 [1631]: 87, IX).

20. Grotius takes the distinction between offensive and defensive war from Luis de Molina's *De Iustitia et Iure* (see Tuck 1999).

21. Note the etymological link between *commandare* ('to order', 'to entrust') and *commendare* ('to commit to the care of keeping').

22. I use the term 'propping' in the psychoanalytic sense of *anaclisis* to depict the relationship between the Grotian theory of restitution and the Roman *ius postlimini* not as a straightforward 'origins story', but, rather, as a narrative of restitutive genesis in which *ius postlimini* is the 'thing' upon which just war theory temporarily rests. Laplanche (1999; see also Laplanche and Pontalis [1967] 1973: 29–32) conceptualises 'propping' with reference to the Freudian term *Anlehnung*, which is frequently rendered by the Greek term *anaclisis*, meaning to 'rest upon' or to 'lean upon'. In the Freudian theory of psychoanalysis, *Anlehnung* was a name used for the process by which sexual instincts are originally attached, or rest on, the source, object and orientation of self-preservative instincts, such as the infant's oral activity at the breast (whereby the sexual pleasure is first linked to the need for nourishment and only secondarily detached and or autonomous from it).

23. According to Ireland (1994) *ius postlimini* developed by gradually broadening its scope from the restoration of liberty, to the return of confiscated possessions, to the revival of other rights and legal relations in operation before the capture (Ireland 1944: 585). It should also be remembered that *ius postlimini* did not solely pertain to the situation of war (even though that is the primary context of Grotius' discussion). For example, *The Digest of Justinian* includes references to the application of *ius postlimini* during peacetime, and Adolf Berger ([1953] 1991: 432) mentions *ius postlimini* in the restoration of the rights of the *deportatio* (convicted criminals permanently exiled from Rome). See also Grotius [1738] 2005: 13, 84–1388, IX.II.4.

24. The law of postliminium has been invoked to support claims of the continuity of statehood, for instance, by post-1989 East European and Baltic states, who argued that their post-war state sovereignty should legally be approached as interrupted and suspended during the period of foreign domination (see Karski 2014; Gotowiecki 2016).

25. There were two Roman divinities of childbirth, Postvorta (oriented at the past) and Antevorta (oriented at the future). At times, they were represented not as two separate divinities, but as two aspects of the goddess of childbirth, childhood and motherhood, Carmenta. Not unlike the two-faced god Janus, the god of ends and beginnings, Carmenta also signifies the capacity of holding together two (only seemingly contradictory) faculties: past-orientation and future-orientation.

26. The root of postliminium is the Latin word *limen*, 'threshold', related to the noun *limitem*, meaning 'a boundary, limit, embankment between fields', and derived from the adjective *limus*, 'transverse' and 'oblique' (*Oxford English Dictionary*).

27. There were institutions in the Roman law exempt from the working of *ius postlimini*, notably the institution of marriage (Watson 1990; 2001). Rather, at the moment of the subject's capture by the enemy army, the marriage was dissolved and the spouse was free to marry another man. With the subject's repatriation, the marriage could be reinstated upon mutual agreement, but not by the virtue of *ius postlimini* (otherwise the spouse who had remarried would have been liable for the crime of adultery).

28. For the elaboration of Austin's notions of illocutionary acts and illocutionary force in the history of political theory, see Skinner 1969. See also Bevir 2002; 2011; Hamilton-Bleakley 2006.

29. The Punic Wars exemplify the concept of political friendship in *ius postlimini*; the Roman soldiers who had escaped war imprisonment by the Carthaginians were not able to claim the right of postliminium in the Greek ports, because Greece remained neutral in the war (2005 [1631]: 1383–4, IX.II.2).

30. *Pomoerium* was demarcated by white marker stones, *cippi*, rather than by a wall, and its primary meaning was not that of separation, but that of creating a trace, or leaving a mark.

31. The creation of the *pomoerium* line was an act of inaugurating *templum* ('sacred section'). Within that line of *pomoerium* any activities and subjects associated with war and with death were prohibited. It was a site where people came into contact and communicated with gods, and where they requested and received divine signs, guidelines and omens, and practiced augury (interpreting the flight of birds as prophetic signs). See Antaya 1980.

32. *Diminutio capitis maxima*, meaning literally 'the decrease of head', was 'the highest and most comprehensive loss of status' that a Roman citizen could suffer during his lifetime (Smith 1875). The Roman law distinguished between three kinds of the loss of status and legal capacity as a consequence of a crime: *maxima* (loss of liberty, citizenship and family); *media* (loss of citizenship and family, but not of personal liberty); and *minima* (loss of familial affiliation, but not of citizenship or liberty).

CHAPTER 2

1. Characteristic of the statement on universal benevolence is a tension between narratives of the modern refinement of morals (with benevolence defined as a distinct cultural achievement) and a Rousseauian position that it is a matter of 'a natural susceptibility to feel sympathy for others' (Taylor 1992: 5).

2. It is sometimes misconstrued that Henry Dunant argued for a social display of charitability and benevolence in response to suffering (specifically, on the battlefield). However, even a cursory reading of his *Un souvenir de Solférino* reveals that it is in fact an accolade for the care and beneficence displayed towards the wounded soldiers by doctors, nurses and civilians, extended equally to enemy soldiers under the slogan 'Tutti fratelli' ('All are brothers'). Dunant was undoubtedly highly impressed by this unanimous display of charitability and benevolence; his proposal to establish a society of emergency relief, the International Committee of the Red Cross/Red Crescent (1863) was thus motivated by a desire to provide an institutional organisation for what he believed was already in existence, but which lacked structure, and hence efficiency, and perhaps also professionalism: a universal human impulse to alleviate the suffering of others. In other words, that humanitarianism was something akin to a universal human 'impulse' presented Dunant both with grounds for optimism and with a challenge, since it relied on spontaneous and instinctive displays of empathy, rather than involved careful thought and planning. The proposal to establish a society for an emergency relief, and, subsequently,

to establish international rules and prohibitions operative during warfare, builds, perhaps paradoxically, on this dual goal to both tap into and to capitalise on the impulsiveness of humanitarian response to suffering, and to 'correct' this impulsiveness through institutionalisation. As much as expressive of belief in universal human benevolence in times of crisis, Dunant's position was also, paradoxically, distrusting of whether it could be relied on without formal organisation and structures.

3. A curious point of resemblance between *Frankenstein* and *A Memory of Solferino* is their figuration of electricity (explicitly in the former, implicitly in the latter). While in Shelley's novel electrification and galvanism becomes the central idiom of animation of lifeless matter (see Gigante 2009: 228, 231; Harkup 2018: 183–206), in Dunant's book the civilians providing relief efforts to the soldiers at Solferino appear galvanised, and the outpouring of care and altruism resembles an electric current or energy field.

4. The concept of benevolence was analysed in the late eighteenth and nineteenth centuries, and now discredited, pseudo-science of phrenology, which held that individual intellectual faculties, propensities and sentiments are causally linked to brain structure (so-called 'phrenological organs'), thus spawning practices of skull measurement etc. to identify mental traits. Phrenologists described benevolence as an example of 'superior sentiments' (not found outside human species), together with hope, imitation, ideality, wit, veneration and wonder. In the 'phrenological chart', benevolence was located in the upper part of the forehead. Silas Jones in *Practical Phrenology*, originally published in 1836, located benevolence in close semantic relation to the idea of universal humanity, by describing it as neither 'adhesive' (not attachable solely to objects of kinship), nor 'philoprogenitive' (not limited to such objects as children or young animals), nor 'inhabitive' (not reducible to objects of close personal knowledge), Rather, Jones described benevolence as 'a broader feeling, going out upon, and embracing the whole human family, and also the suffering brute animal. Excited towards the vicious, it is compassion, towards the suffering, it is sympathy, to all mankind, it is philanthropy. In gifts, it is almsgiving; in needful attentions to the feelings of others, it is kindness or good-will' ([1836] 2011: 71–2).

5. The Latin term *benevolentia* has a corresponding Greek word, *eunoia*, meaning 'beautiful thinking' *or* 'beautiful mind'. For a discussion of the Greek and Roman roots of benevolence in Aristotle's concept of *eunoia*, see, for example, Vivenza 2003. The etymological development of the word kindness (Old English *(ge) cynde*; from Proto-Germanic *kundi-*) derives from the earlier meanings of 'natural', 'native' and 'innate' to 'being well-disposed towards others'. It became synonymous to 'benignancy', 'compassion' and 'tenderness' in *c.* 1300 ('Benevolence', *Online Etymology Dictionary*).

6. Gloria Vivenza (2003: 192) makes a useful distinction between benevolence (*eunoia*) and beneficence (*euergesia*) as corresponding to the distinction between intention and fact. See also Beauchamp 2008, rev. 2019.

7. Mill's stance on British imperialism is an example of how historically philosophy of social benevolence coexisted with, and fuelled, the legitimacy of colonial rule. Mill, who worked for the British East India Company for thirty-five years, coined the idea

of 'benevolent despotism' as part of his defence of the autocratic rule of the British in India. He famously argued in *On Liberty* [1859] 1864: 3) that: '[d]espotism is a legitimate mode of government in dealing with barbarians, provided the end be their improvement'. In *Dissertations and Discussions: Political, Philosophical, and Historical*, Mill stated that '[t]o suppose that the same international customs, and the same rules of international morality, can obtain between one civilized nation and another, and between civilized nations and barbarians, is a grave error' ([1859] 1973). For Mill, the distinction between 'civilised' and 'barbarous' people were an objective and historical category (China and India were once 'civilised' people, who became 'barbarous' due to socio-economic and political stagnation). For a critical discussion of Mill's notion of 'benevolent despotism', see, for instance, Jahn 2005.

8. Cf. Gigante 2000.

9. See Harkup 2018.

10. The Creature's claiming of humanity's protection on the basis of no other identi-fiers or assets than the benevolent foundations of human society, could be read as pre-figurative of the critiques of humanitarianism in the twentieth century, such as Hannah Arendt's doubts about human rights as a legal protection framework for stateless peoples ([1943] 2009). Another contemporary cultural text illustrating the potential dangers of relying on social benevolence for protection is Lars von Trier's film *Dogville* (2003). The similarities between the Creature and *Dogville*'s main char-acter Grace are striking: they both make appeals to the benevolence of the commu-nity without being able to present themselves as political subjects and rights-holders. Both are thus an epitomisation of political vulnerability (Grace, more clearly than the Creature, is a refugee), and both are rejected from human sociability and compan-ionship, and destined to violence. It is also interesting that both undergo a kind of transformation from benevolence into malevolence, and become figures of revenge.

11. Asad associates Taylor's approach with a position of moral progressivism that credits Western modernity with the gradual reduction of violence and human suffering. A somewhat cruder version of that position is found in Steven Pinker's *The Better Angels of Our Nature* (2011), and *Enlightenment Now: the Case for Reason, Science, Humanism, and Progress* (2018). Pinker opens his *Enlightenment Now* with a quote from Alfred North: '[t]he common sense of the eighteenth cen-tury, its grasp of the obvious facts of human suffering, and of the obvious demands of human nature, acted on the world like a bath of moral cleansing'. The impli-cation is that the Enlightenment has been a process of sensitisation to the plight of others, grounded not in kinship or tribal loyalties, but in the ideas of human-ist ethics. However, Pinker ignores the context of Whitehead's statement. While acknowledging the rationalist thinkers for prodigiously using 'scientific abstrac-tions [into the] analysis of the unbounded universe', Whitehead in fact argues that the Enlightenment stands both for a series of original intellectual achievements *and* for a deliberate neglect of what did not neatly fit within the epistemic scheme of rationalism. In *Science and the Modern World* Voltarie in particular features as a proto-humanitarian philosopher who 'hated injustice . . . cruelty, [and] . . . senseless repression', but whose philosophic work also reveals a commitment to an eradication of positions that complicated, and potentially imploded, the rationalist

frame (not only those of irrationalism and medievalism, but also, famously, of Rousseau). Whitehead's point (1948) is not simply that of convenient oversight of content ill-fitted to the rationalist position; rather, he emphasises the uneasy relation that *les philosophes* had to the Gothic aesthetics, which 'symbolizes their lack of sympathy with *dim perspectives*'. At hand is not simply an act of exclusion, but an inability to coexist with modes of thinking that refuse binary opposition in favour of ambiguity, indistinction and hesitation. Whitehead's statement that 'if men cannot live on bread alone, still less can they do so on *disinfectants*', is, paradoxically, perhaps the best critique of Pinker's argument that the culture of universal benevolence, grounded in Western humanism and rationalism, is an unequivocally, and universally, beneficial achievement. To read Pinker's illustrations of his thesis of universal life improvement in modernity as part of the tradition of thought invested in applying the Whiteheadian 'disinfectant', is, then, not only about producing counter-examples, or asking the important question *who have these alleged achievements and benefits have been accessible to* (and at what and whose expense)? It is also about highlighting the historical proximity between the emergence of the 'culture of benevolence' and the philosophical hostility towards ambiguity – the coexistence of two contradictory contents or positions. In arguing that (socially undifferentiated) 'life conditions' have unequivocally and universally improved with time, Steven Pinker is, then, not only ignoring counter facts and statistics, or leaving uninterrogated the issue of racial, neo-colonial, class and gender privilege, but he also, not unlike *les philosophes* that he admires, engaged in the 'disinfecting' – of cleansing, purifying and sterilising – of the messiness of the analysed socio-political realities.

12. In his 1714 *The Fable of the Bees*, Bernard Mandeville considered the principle of self-interest and self-love to be the key determinant of social behaviour. As such Mandeville solidified the early eighteenth-century interpretations of Hobbes as a pioneer of selfish philosophy, which dominated until Hume's more nuanced reading.

13. The contrast between the second and third meaning of 'nature' derives from Butler's juxtaposition of two biblical verses from St. Paul's epistolary writings. In the *Letter to Ephesians*, St. Paul expresses the doctrine of original sin in terms of the vicious or sinful 'nature' of humanity: prior to Christ's redemptive sacrifice, the gentiles 'walked according to the spirit of disobedience' and were 'by nature [*physei*, φύσει] the children of wrath' (Eph. 3:2, quoted in Butler [1726, 1729] 2006: 19–20). This corresponds to Butler's second conception of human nature. The second verse comes from the *Letter to Romans*, where St. Paul writes that 'the Gentiles . . . show that the work of the Law is written on their hearts . . .' (Rom 2:14–15, paraphrased by Butler [1726, 1729]: 2006: 20). Butler takes the figure of the heart to connote 'nature' in the sense 'the natural disposition to kindness and compassion, to do what is of good report' (2006 [1726, 1729]: 20).

14. As Merrill (2011) argues, from Hume's perspective the actions of, for instance, Robinson Crusoe could not be considered as either benevolent or just because they did not procure any advantages to *human* society (this is in spite of the fact that Hume did mention animals, plants and even inanimate objects as 'useful' and 'beneficial . . . to mankind', ([1751] 1998: s. 2, pt 2)).

15. Of course, what the father does not know is that Victor's despair is because Victor had created the brother's real murderer, the Creature, and allowed an innocent person to be convicted for the crime.

16. Hume uses the term 'species' in the modern sense of a distinctive biological class. The notion of 'species' as a classificatory and taxonomic unit, grouping organisms on the basis of common characteristics (capable of breeding with one another and producing sexually fertile offspring). That meaning was established in English in the early 1600s. The earlier meanings were that of 'appearance' and 'outward form' (1550s), and 'distinct class' (1560s) of objects or organisms (from Latin *species*, meaning 'a particular kind', and derived from *specere*, 'to look at', and the Proto-Indo-European *spek-*, 'to observe').

17. An important implication that is found in Hume's writings on race in his essay 'Of National Characters' ([1777] 1994). It is revealing that here the idea of universal humanity appears to be neither devoid of exclusionary procedures, nor to be all-encompassing. Rather, the category of universal humanity is both exclusionary *and* gradational; it both leaves out, or bars, beings designated as *in*human (*sub*human, *non*human or *not-yet*-human) and makes internal distinctions as to who embodies (the condition of) humanity more, or better or more fully. In an infamous note on the racial superiority of whiteness, which Hume added to 'Of National Characters' five years after its first publication in 1748, the category of humanity is split into two: 'I am apt to suspect that negroes, and in general all the other species of men . . . to be *naturally* inferior to whites', and '[s]uch a uniform and constant difference could not happen, in so many countries and ages, if nature had not made an *original distinction* [between] these breeds of men' (cited in Garrett and Sebastiani 2017: 31). What is striking, of course, is that Hume uses the same wording ('natural' and 'original') to speak both about benevolence and about racialised 'national characters'. Contra the interpretation of the note as Hume's unfortunate though momentary departure from his progressive views, including his anti-slavery position, Garrett and Sebastiani use it as an ocular through which they read the larger exclusionary dynamics at work in his philosophy, and in Hume's conceptualisation of 'human nature' more specifically.

18. It is noteworthy that, in as much as Victor seeks redemption and forgiveness for having brought about the Creature, he is also engaged in an active and deliberate process of appealing to and convincing his reader about the purity of his intentions, and, ultimately, about his innocence. In contrast to his earlier regrets and contrition, on his deathbed Victor says to Walton: '[I] do not find [my actions] blamable. In a fit of enthusiastic madness I created a rational creature, and was bound towards him, to assure, as far as it was in my power, his happiness and well-being. This was my duty . . .' ([1818] 2009: 271). He claims that the intention to kill the Creature derives not from vengeful desires, but from a 'higher duty' that trumps parental obligations, namely, Victor says from 'my duties towards beings of my own species' ([1818] 2009: 271). Why species duties should surpass father duties suggests a utilitarian trait in Victor's character; the former 'included a greater proportion of happiness or misery', he states ([1818] 2009: 271).

19. The Creature says to Victor: '[s]till thou canst listen to me and grant me thy compassion. By the virtues that I once possessed, I demand this from you. Hear my tale . . .' ([1818] 2009: 120). Being able to give his maker an account of himself is more important to the Creature than self-preservation: '. . . I ask you not to spare me: listen to me; and then, if you can, and if you will, destroy the work of your hands' ([1818] 2009: 119).

20. O'Rourke (1989) offers a fascinating juxtaposition of *Frankenstein* and Rousseau's *Emile*, where he draws on Mary Shelley's entry on Rousseau, which she contributed to the 1839 *Lives of the Most Eminent Literary and Scientific Men of France* (part of the 133-volume *Cabinet Cyclopaedia*, edited by Dionysius Lardner). O'Rourke's argument is that one should balance the interpretation of *Frankenstein* as a literary illustration of Rousseau's philosophy of education, and in particular of the costs of educators' failure to prevent society's corruptive impact upon the natural qualities of spontaneity, curiosity and benign disposition of children, by taking heed of Shelley's vituperation of what she saw as Rousseau's failure of parental responsibility. Rousseau had five children with Thérèse le Vasseur, with whom he had maintained a non-marital relationship; upon le Vasseur's death, Rousseau is said to have abandoned the children to the care of the Parisian Foundling Hospital. Shelley called this act of withdrawal of paternal responsibility on Rousseau's part a 'secret error'; Rousseau's relegation of the care of his own children to an orphanage was a cruel and ironic act by a man concerned with adverse impacts of social institutions upon children. Shelley described it as Rousseau's failure in 'plainest dictates of nature and conscience', and as a 'distortion of an intellect that blinded him to the first duties of life' (cited in O'Rourke 1989). The Creature's first gesture meets with Victor's rejection; it is an infantile gesture of reaching out to the father for love and protection, as well as expressing happiness at the parental sight, which Victor nevertheless (mis)interprets as an attempt at captivation: '. . . I beheld the wretch – the miserable monster whom I had created. He held up the curtain of the bed; and his eyes, if eyes they may be called, were fixed on me. His jaws opened and he muttered some inarticulate sounds, while a grin wrinkled his cheeks. He might have spoken, but I did not hear; one hand was stretched out, seemingly to detain me, but I escaped, and rushed downstairs' (2009 [1818]: 59).

21. Denise Gigante discusses the Creature's ugliness in the context of the unsuitability of the esthetic categories of the Enlightenment, and in particular of Edmund Burke's treatise on the sublime and the beautiful, to account for the horror and gruesomeness caused by the Creature's unsightly appearance. The dominant Enlightenment aesthetic discourse equates ugly with the absence of beauty; in contrast, Gigante argues (2000: 566) that the ugliness of Frankenstein's Creature is 'positive' in that '[he] not only fails to please, but emphatically displeases'. In other words, Shelley's Frankenstein marks a fundamental shift in cultural imaginary of ugliness from that of a 'lack' or 'privation' (of pleasurable aesthetic experience) to that of 'excess'.

22. Victor's encounters with the Creature have a structural resemblance to the phenomenon of 'lucid nightmare'; for example, on the night of the Creature's creation Victor falls asleep, and it is uncertain whether the vision of the Creature reaching out towards him is a nightmarish image or an actual occurrence. The importance

of dreams and dreaming in *Frankenstein*, including the 'origin-story' of the novel in Mary Shelley's dream, has been analysed in Thomas 1990; Hogle 2014.

23. On *Frankenstein* and the trauma of afterbirth, see Moers [1976] 1985: 77–87.

24. In the same diary entry Shelley notes her response to the dream, 'I awake & find no baby. I think about the little thing all day – not in good spirits' (cited in Schoene-Harwood 2000: 57); a response that is striking for its use of the phrase 'the little thing' to describe the dead child, as a term of endearment, but which also inadvertently invokes the corpse's passage from the status of a person to the status of a thing. Perhaps, too, it is the dream itself that is 'the little thing'; a reverie surfacing of an unconscious desire for the undoing of the daughter's death.

25. It is important to note that Victor's work consists of two components: bioelectric animation *and* the composition of an organic whole from tissue fragments. While the former has received great attention in interpretative and critical literary scholarship of the novel, the latter is yet to be explored in more depth. What is interesting about the latter is how flawed and incomplete Victor's transplantation work is. The Creature appears awkwardly stitched together and continuously fragmented; the narrative focus on selected bodily parts creates an impression of broken sutures and dehiscence.

26. The Creature reflects on his repugnant appearance as 'a figure hideously deformed and loathsome', and describes his superior adaptive skills as inhuman and monstrous: 'I was not even the same nature as man . . . my stature far exceeded theirs . . . Was I, then, a monster, a blot upon the earth, from which all men fled and whom all men disowned?' ([1818] 2009: 144).

CHAPTER 3

1. This 'readerly' approach to Durkheim also requires that one blurs the strict periodisation of his writings into early and late texts, as well as rejects any neat separation between Durkheim structuralism and symbolism, and between his conservative allegiances and his radical political sentiments (Smith and Alexander 2008: 3–8).

2. In speculating about the social implications of the advanced division of labour, Durkheim avoided a direct engagement with Marx's theory of alienation (see, for example, Giddens 1977; 1978). Giddens (1978) notes two main points of difference in the thinking of Marx and Durkheim: first, Durkheim's scepticism about the idea of revolution and his ideological and political commitment to a reformist stance, and, secondly, his ideas about the regulatory role of the state. For Durkheim, the state was not 'a medium of class domination, [but] vehicle for the realization of social reform, through furthering equality of opportunity' (1978: 17; see also Jones 2001: 102–4).

3. The third part of *The Division of Labor in Society* stands in stark contrast to Durkheim's earlier optimistic interpretation about the social effects of industrialisation, division of labour and modern solidarity. In 'The Abnormal Forms' he offers an interpretation of the existing pathologies in the relationship between labour and capital, as well as 'commercial crises . . . bankruptcies . . . normlessness (anomie), lack of regulation, [and] unrestricted play of individual and collective self-interest', in the industrial acquisitive societies' Coser ([1984] 2014: xx). While Durkheim

admittedly thought of these 'pathologies' as transitional rather than inherently systemic, it is important to note that through their identification he linked the division of labour with social justice in ways that revealed strong political commitment to the socialist (reformist) position in the tradition of Henri Saint-Simon and Jean Jaurès. What 'The Abnormal Forms' adds to Durkheim's sociology of modern solidarity is a presupposition that 'organic' solidarity builds on 'social justice and equality of opportunity' (Giddens 1978: 32). As Giddens puts it, for Durkheim the 'pathological' relations between labour and capital are due to two forms of inequality: 'external inequality', which arises from social circumstances of birth, including class belonging, and 'internal inequality', which derives from 'differential distribution of talent and capacity'.

4. The interpretations of Durkheim as a liberal thinker stress that his apparent value-neutral study of individualism as a product of accelerated diversification and social dislocation remains coloured by Durkheim's normative (and political) commitments to values of individual liberty and voluntarism. For examples, Susan Stedman Jones (2001: 49) classifies Durkheim's view of autonomy as 'philosophical liberalism' and situates it in the tradition of Montesqueu, Tocqueville and J. S. Mill, emphasising the centrality of the 'defence of rights, freedom of mind, [and] moral and political individualism' for its conceptualisation. Importantly, Durkheim's liberal view of individualism needs to be differentiated from its contractual and utilitarian variants that advocated a society 'based on exchange transactions . . . in order to maximize personal returns' and constructed an 'isolated, egoistic [and] anarchic' social subject (Giddens 1978: 10, 17). For example, the classical liberal proponent of that view, Herbert Spencer, linked contractual atomistic individualism to the emergence of modern forms of associationism in what he called 'coherent heterogeneous' societies by arguing that 'solidarity in the division of labour is produced automatically by each individual pursuing his own interests in economic exchanges with others' (Giddens 1978: 22). In contrast, Durkheim's view of individualism has been strongly anti-utilitarian (and anti-laissez faire) in his postulate about the existence of a 'non-contractual element in contract' – for Durkheim, it was precisely the successful functioning of contract relations in modern societies that suggested that contracts, regulations and laws were preceded, both chronologically and normatively, by a primary moral order consisting of shared sentiments and value commitments.

5. Some of the works of colonial anthropology that influenced Durkheim were Theodor Waitz's 1864 *Die Anthropologie der Naturvölker* and Gustave Le Bon's 1881 *L'Homme et les sociétés* (see Barnes 1966; Coser [1984] 2014).

6. For example, Waitz writes about African populations that the 'physical resemblance among the natives [derived from] the absence of any strong psychological individuality and from the inferior state of intellectual culture in general' (cited in Durkheim [1984] 2014: 106).

7. Giddens (1977: 66–7) has argued that central to Durkheim's conceptualisation of the collective consciousness was the work of his contemporary German sociologists, and especially that of Albert Schäffle (whose 1875–8 *Bau und Leben des sozialen Körpers* Durkheim reviewed). Schäffle's assumption that 'society has integrated unity comparable to that of a living organism' echoes in *The Division of Labor in Society*, even

though Durkheim's natural references are metaphorical and analogical, rather than a matter of literal application.

8. See, for example, Baxi 1974; Cottorrell 1977; Wityak and Wallace 1981.

9. In Lukes' taxonomy of social solidarity (1972: 158), the morphological basis for mechanical solidarity includes a low degree of social interdependence, a low volume of population, and low material and moral density. It includes formal characteristics of collective consciousness (high volume, intensity and determinateness), and its specific content (religious, transcendental and collectivist). In turn, organic solidarity in described in regard to its morphological characteristics, such as interdependence, high population volume, high material and moral density, and in regard to its expressions of particular features and content of the collective consciousness, including more room for individual action, as well as a low volume, low density and low determination of individual behaviour by the collective ethos (Lukes 1972: 158).

10. See, for example, Crow 2001; Howe 2005; Thijssen 2012.

11. Giddens (1978: 11) writes that for Durkheim 'the role of the sociologist [was] similar to a physician: to distinguish between sickness and health, to diagnose the causes of [sickness] and develop remedial treatment'. This diagnostic approach is conspicuous in the argumentative logic that dominates in *The Division of Labor in Society*; for Durkheim 'the spread of the ideals of individualism [was] not a symptom of a pathological condition of society, but . . . "normal" and healthy expression of the social transformations that [were] engendering a new form of social solidarity'.

12. While my point is that Durkheim theorises restitution within an organicist epistemological framework and through analogy with remedial interventions into pathological bodily developments, it is also important to note his suspicion about social conflict and division in general and his neglect of questions of power within the social (Lukes and Scull, 1983; Lukes [1984] 2014; Garland [2004] 2012).

13. The paradox of Durkheim's suggestion that moral individualism had formed the core of the modern *conscience collective* is that he also related individualism to the sociological processes of the diversification and diffusion of shared moral commitments (see Giddens 1977: 72; 1978: 22–3).

14. This becomes apparent when one views moral individualism not solely in an interlocution with utilitarian philosophy and with classical economic liberalism, but also in conjunction with the tradition of modern humanitarianism, which Durkheim traces back to the philosophies of Kant and Rousseau, to the French Declaration of the Rights of Man, as well as to the French Spiritist movement (*les spiritualistes*), propagated by Allan Kardec (Durkheim 1969: 20–1).

15. Durkheim locates the origins of 'the individualist spirit' in Christianity in that, in contrast to the ancient Greek and Roman systems of beliefs, Abrahamic religions promoted an inward orientation of faith.

16. The broader context of these developments is the categorisation of criminal acts into those against collectives (*dirigés contre des choses collectives*), 'religious criminality' (though Durkheim also includes in this category offences against public authority, ancestral morality and traditions), and criminal acts against individuals, 'human criminality [*criminalité humaine*]' (1983b: 99). Durkheim exemplifies by point with the development of anti-violence legislation in the ancient Rome: while

in the early period, retaliatory and defensive uses of violence were not criminalised, in the classical era and especially as a consequence of the Justinian legal reforms and the development of *Corpus Juris Civilis*, 'man's sympathetic feelings for man were affirmed and developed' (1983b: 99), and the right to retaliation and access to traditional forms of 'self-help' became highly restricted. One of the most 'important antiviolence developments' in the classical and later periods concerned the 'law of possession', whereby special mechanisms (interdicts) were developed to forbid the use of violence in property recovery (Riggsby 2010: 68–9).

17. Important critical interpretations of the global politics of humanitarianism have concentrated on the 'flip side' of mobilising public attention on 'suffering humanity' through feelings of horror as the identification 'monstrous' acts or subjects – be it in reference to so-called 'enemy combatants', 'suicide bombers' or war criminals – thus relegating them outside humanity. Inquiring into the contemporary veneration of human life, Kiarina Kordela has looked at suicide bombing as a political act that coincides with abhorrent affects. Its perpetrators are considered aberrant and monstrous 'not simply [in the sense of being] the other of human – such as animals, plants, and inanimate objects – or just the anti-human – that which wants to destroy humanity – but also that which *must not* be understood by humans' (2016: 196; emphasis in the original; see also Rose 2004; Asad 2007; Arif 2016). The feelings of horror that these acts arouse is interpreted as an 'extra-discursive natural state of being' (Arif 2016: 196), which in turn legitimises 'dehumanizing' politics whereby the perpetrators of suicide bombing, or their sympathisers are divested of the status of (to use a Durkheimian formulation) the 'human person' and of the fellowship in '*l'humanité en général*'. This 'incitement to horror is a *discursive mechanism* that aims at the *construction of a racial divide* between humans and non- or subhumans around the *criterion of the presence or absence of*, precisely, *horror*' (2016: 196; emphasis in the original).

18. In *Life, Emergent* (2016), Yasmeen Arif shows how, within the international legal discourse of the crimes against humanity adopted by the Special Court for Sierra Leone, the empathic constructions of the figure of the child soldier – subject to humanitarian interpretations as an innocent sufferer of violence and a victim of inhuman acts, and filtered through Western middle-class moral sensitivities about childhood – became constituted in relation to its complementary figure, the African warlord: the perpetrator of 'inhuman acts', the monstrous victimiser of children and mutilator of bodies. I suggest that in Durkheim's work one finds the roots of that complementary logic of humanitarianism, which, through its investment in the abstracted notions of humanity as the very precondition of moral action, empathic politics and solidarity with suffering groups, creates a space of constitutive exclusion from the category of the *personne humaine* via the idiom of 'inhuman acts'. Durkheim's argument is based on the assumption that 'humanisation' is an infinitely inclusive process, closely mapped onto the 'civilising' of law and morality, which equally affects victims and perpetrators – his striking omission is then the question of those subjects (and acts) that figure as 'inhuman', and of their relation to the restitutive humanitarian logic insofar as the latter is understood as an operation of undoing of deeds that 'lack humanity', and as a way of instituting solidarity

through sympathy with human suffering. Restitution, in the intrinsic connection to the philosophy of humanitarianism that Durkheim assigns to it, is *aporetic* not simply in the sense of its assumed temporal reversal or in its attachment to phantasmagoric notions of pre-conflict 'normalcy', but also because it intervenes into, and partially constitutes, the terrain of (what counts as) 'acts that lack humanity' – *actes qui manquent d'humanité.*

19. Durkheim writes that '[the] right of property can be far better defined negatively than in terms of positive content, by the exclusion it involves rather than the prerogatives it confers' (1957: 164).

20. On the criticism of Durkheim's extension of the polarity of the sacred and profane beyond the Judeo-Christian religions, see Giddens 1978.

21. Esposito makes a contrary argument about the typology of things, where he argues that the commons and *res sacrae* have a shared logic and common origins in the Roman law, see 2015: 105–6.

CHAPTER 4

1. Schreber's apocalyptic visions are for Freud manifestation of his 'internal catastrophe'; his withdrawal from people, his familial and professional environment, and from 'the external world generally' has been nothing short of 'subjective world [coming] to an end since his *withdrawal of his love from it [seine Welt is untergegangen, seitem er ihr seine Liebe entzogen hat]*' ([1911] 1955: 307; [1955] 2001: 71; emphasis mine).

2. Hegel used the term *Ungeschehenmachen* to capture the power to undo the past (see, for example, Comay 2011; Žižek 2013).

3. Fenichel provides the following explanation for the category of undoing where the second act repeats the first one: '[the] first act was done in connection with a certain unconscious instinctual attitude; it is undone when this same act can be repeated once more under *other inner conditions*. The aim of the compulsion to repeat is to carry out the very same act freed of its secret unconscious meaning, or with the opposite unconscious meaning. If, because of the continued effectiveness of the repressed, some part of the original impulse insinuates itself again into the repetition which was intended as an expiation, a third, fourth, or fifth repetition of the act may become necessary' ([1946] 2014: 154; emphasis mine).

4. Fenichel gives an example of a thrifty person experiencing guilt feelings because of what appears to him to be an extravagant purchase (of a newspaper); while the possibility of returning the purchased object is blocked by shame, he seeks to 'ease his mind' by making an identical purchase, but now with a different attitude. Because the newsstand is closed, he eventually throws the newspaper money away ([1946] 2014: 154).

5. Situating the Freudian and post-Freudian insights into the mechanism of undoing in the broader contexts of restitution theory requires the identification of its operations in post-conflict and post-atrocity narratives as a performative that 'cancels' or 'annuls' the past. For example, official state apologies for crimes committed either during war atrocities or as part of the settler-colonial policies towards indigenous populations posit the apologetic speech as an expression of regret in the face of the

impossibility of undoing the past. The conservative British politician of the nineteenth century, Benjamin Disraeli, expressed that sentiment in his oft-quoted aphorism: '[a]pologies only account for that which they do not alter' (cited in Tavuchis 1991: 5). And yet those studying the social reparative effects of apologies have complicated their relationship to undoing; thus, Tavuchis writes that while apology 'does not and cannot *undo* what has been done [no matter how sincere or effective] . . . in a mysterious way and according to its own logic, this is precisely what it manages to do' (1991: 5; emphasis in the original). Against sociological attempts at explaining that 'mysteriousness' of apology as either dissipation of negative affects or as transformed social relations, I suggest that it points in the direction of psychoanalytic undoing and the way it structures the subject's ambiguous relation to past misdeeds. By seeking to make the past un-happen (and failing spectacularly at this precise task), the Freudian subject reveals itself as internally fractured in its destructive and reparative impulses towards a singular love-object.

6. In the context of restitution, there has been some critical scholarship on how specific acts of material and symbolic restoration point to a collective wish for *Ungeschehenmachen* of their corrective ambitions, especially to the extent that post-conflict restitution has been linked to goals of rehoming displaced populations and 'undoing' the effects of ethnic cleansing (see, for example, McCallin 2012; Ballard 2013; Zolkos 2017). Rhodri C. Williams (2007) analyses critically the current international trends in the field of post-conflict restitution, and persuasively demonstrates how in different cases (Guatemala, Bosnia, South Africa and Czech Republic) restitution has extended beyond the immediate goal of re-acquisition and included *politics of undoing*. In a situation where expropriation has accompanied population displacement, and '[where] entire communities have been scattered, the most satisfying remedy [of restitution] . . . is to *turn back the clock*, *reversing the dislocation*' (Williams 2007: 50; emphasis mine).

7. The principle of *status quo ante bellum* is contrasted to the doctrine of *uti possidetis*, whereby the territory and material possessions acquired during the conflict remain with the new holder (see Sabahi 2011).

8. For the context and analysis of the 'Controversial Discussions' see Rose 1993a; 1993b; Stonebridge and Phillips 1998; King and Steiner 2005.

9. It is important to distinguish between the way that psychoanalysis discusses the psychic situation of the status quo, and the psychological phenomenon of 'status quo bias', which is the emotional bias towards the current (socio-political) state of affairs. The former, as I discuss further, is closely linked with the return to an idealised interpretation of the past, whereas the latter's temporal orientation is the present.

10. Carolyn Laubender (2019a: 60) makes a similar point in regard to Melanie Klein's analysis of Richard. Klein interprets the boy's obsessions with the war as projections of his inner life and his relation to/in his family conflicts. Laubender also suggests that Klein's development of the reparative tendency in children maps onto public debates in Britain about 'the propriety and justness of material reparations after Germany's defeat in World War I', which gives Klein inspiration and a certain sensitivity to the ethical and political stakes of reparations. Laubender argues

that '[regardless] of whether or not Klein had either of these political uses of the [reparations] term in mind when she theorized the way that attack and reparation structure the mind of the child, her ability to even think the subject along the lines of reparation testifies to the broader conception of interwar and wartime justice enabling her theory'.

11. It is interesting, too, that Sharpe turns to the Freudian theory of narcissism at the moment when its psychoanalytic expediency is put into question by some participants of the 'Controversial Discussions' (see Glover, in King and Steiner 1991).

12. Melanie Klein suggests that Sharpe misquotes Freud here (I have not been able to identify the location of that statement in Freud's oeuvre). Also, Klein and Sharpe differ in their interpretation of the subject's separation from the love-object, and of the pre-separation 'situation' that is subject to idealisation: for Sharpe it seems to be an intra-uterine situation (birth as separation or loss), whereas for Klein it is a situation of breast-feeding (weaning as the separation or loss).

13. Sharpe draws indirectly on Freud's theorising of intellectualisation as a defence mechanism in his paper on negation, where he describes it a separation between the 'intellectual function' and the 'affective process', which results in 'a kind of intellectual acceptance of the repressed' ([1950] 1961: 234).

14. For Abraham ([1919] 1948), the resistance against analysis manifests as the subject's refusal to free-associate. Also, the refractory analysands seek to bring the process entirely under the control of the pleasure principle, which is what leads him to suggest the important role of narcissism and of envy in the resistance against the analysis. The negative therapeutic reaction coincides thus with transference of the father figure onto the analysis, and the resistance against the treatment (or, more specifically, against getting better) is a resistance against the father, and a desire to transform the analysis into 'auto-analysis' – a source of pleasure and narcissistic enjoyment, as well as a substitute for masturbation.

15. Riviere's description of the depressive position reveals strong Kleinian influence: '[it is when] all one's loved ones *within* are dead and destroyed, all goodness is dispersed, lost, in fragments, wasted and scattered to the winds; nothing is left *within* but utter desolation. Love brings sorrow, and sorrow brings guilt; the intolerable tension mounts, there is no escape, one is utterly alone, there is no one to share or help. Love must die because love is dead. Besides, there would be no one to feed one, and no one whom one could feed, and no food in the world. And more, there would still be magic power in the undying persecutors who can never be exterminated – the ghosts. Death would instantaneously ensue – and one would choose to die by one's own hand before such a position could be realized' (1936: 144; emphasis in the original).

16. This is not to suggest that in Riviere's paper the psychic and ethical priority of the restitutive commitment to the other over self-repair is devoid of narcissistic or egoistic impulses. In fact, she makes it quite clear that there is an ever-present danger of the subject relating to the other as a vehicle for self-reparation. Likewise, the attention to the other prior to the self can be motivated by an anxiety that, should the analysis bring about some form of self-repair, it would make even more apparent the aporetic nature of reparative engagements with the other: 'the magnitude of the

task would then absorb his whole self with every atom of all its resources, his whole physical and mental powers as long as he lives, every breath, every heartbeat, drop of blood, every thought, every moment of time, every possession, all money, every vestige of any capacity he has – an extremity of slavery and self-immolation which passes conscious imagination' (1936: 150).

17. Salman Akhtar (2009: 239) makes a distinction between undoing and reaction-formation as that between 'season and weather'; while reaction-formation 'works by altering character', undoing operates 'by reversing temporary increases in instinctual impulses'.

18. Susan Isaac's intervention is aimed at demonstrating an inimical intention in Glover's use of the dualist language of 'Freudianism' and 'Kleinianism' in his oeuvre in 1930s, which, she argues, not only naturalises the claims of their difference, but also, interestingly, obfuscates the history of Glover's own (at times critical) engagement with Freud's work at a politically seminal moment in the British Psychoanalytic Society, when adopting a positing of 'Freudian purism' serves as a legitimising tool for the exclusion of non-orthodox theories and methods (Isaac, in King and Steiner 1991: 335–6).

19. In 'The Conception of the Repetition Compulsion' (1943), Bibring distinguishes between repetitive tendencies and restitutive tendencies, and he relates the former to the functioning of id, and the latter to the functioning of ego. Restitution for Bibring is a set of activities and measures that the subject undertakes in order to re-create a pre-traumatic situation.

20. The matter is further complicated by the fact that Klein makes a distinction between, on the one hand, reparation that occurs within the depressive position and consists of attempts at righting wrongs one has brought about upon the love-object, and, on the other hand, a 'manic' or 'obsessive' reparation, which is characterised by continuous belief in the subject's omnipotent control of the object (Klein [1932] 1975).

21. Manic reparation is 'incomplete, self-deceiving and omnipotent'; it involves acts of 'magical reversal or undoing', and it is based on the denial of the 'omnipotent destructive urges' (Bott Spillius et al. 2011: 93, 427). See Klein [1932] 1975.

22. Melanie Klein mentions the importance of Abraham's paper for the theory of reparations in 'Infantile Anxiety Situations Reflected in a Work of Art and in the Creative Impulse' ([1929] 2011: loc. 4966).

23. Abraham includes in his texts an analysis of the language of military reports from the First World War, where, he suggests, the sadistic aims at destruction and elimination roams freely, and result in a striking example of anal erotic discourse of elimination and destruction. The successfully conducted attacks on enemy troops and territorial advancement were described as 'cleaning up', 'mopping up' or 'clearing out' by the British, as '*gesäubert*' and '*aufgeräumt*' by the Germans, and as '*nettoyer*' by the French ([1924] 1994: 76).

24. Abraham writes that 'the psycho-analytic experience and the direct observation of children have established the fact that the set of instincts that aim at destruction and expulsion of the object is ontogenetically older than the impulse that aims at retaining and controlling the object . . . [The] dividing line between [the eliminating and conserving] phases [is where] a decisive change in the attitude of the individual

to the external world [takes place], [and] where "object-love" in the narrower sense begins . . . [In] the normal development . . . the individual ends up being capable of loving his object' ([1924] 1994: 77).

25. On the relation between imaginary and real love-objects, see, for example, Klein ([1935] 2011: loc. 6511): '. . . in the very young children there exist, side by side with its relations to real objects – but on a different plane, as it were – relations to its unreal imagos, both as excessively good and excessively bad figures, and that these two kinds of object-relations intermingle and colour each other to an ever-increasing degree in the course of development'.

EPILOGUE

1. Many thanks to Lia Haro for bringing Erdrich's novel to my attention.
2. It is important to remember that within the Ojibwe tradition of adoption, LaRose does not leave his birth family unit to join the Ravich family, but, rather, becomes *shared* by them. See Wan Mei 2018.
3. Cf. Derrida 2007.
4. I analyse the ethics of remorse and forgiveness in Frantz at the backdrop of Vladimir Jankélévitch moral philosophy in Zolkos 2019.
5. The screenplay of *Frantz* (2016) was adapted, and substantially reworked, from Maurice Rostand's drama *L'Homme que j'ai tué* ([1930] 1950), which was made into a cinematic production in 1932 by Ernst Lubitsch, titled *Broken Lullaby*. The reparative scene closes *Broken Lullaby*; it features a union between Paul and Elsa, which is facilitated by Walter's parents (Adrien, Anna and Frantz, respectively, in Ozon's film). For a comparative discussion of *Frantz* and *Broken Lullaby*, see Zolkos 2019

BIBLIOGRAPHY

Abraham, Karl. [1919] 1948. 'A Particular Form of Neurotic Resistance against the Psycho-Analytic Method', in *Selected Papers of Karl Abraham*, ed. Ernst Jones. London: Hogarth Press and the Institute of Psychoanalysis, 303–11.

Abraham, Karl. [1924] 1994. 'A Short Study of the Development of the Libido, Viewed in the Light of Mental Disorders', in Rita V. Frankel (ed.), *Essential Papers on Object Loss*. New York: New York University Press, 72–93.

Abruzzo, Margaret. 2011. *Polemical Pain: Slavery, Cruelty, and the Rise of Humanitarianism*. Baltimore, MD: Johns Hopkins University Press.

Acorn, Annalise E. 2004. *Compulsory Compassion: a Critique of Restorative Justice*. Vancouver: University of British Columbia Press.

Agamben, Giorgio. 1998. *Homo Sacer: Sovereign Power and Bare Life*, trans. Daniel Heller-Roazen. Stanford, CA: Stanford University Press.

Agamben, Giorgio. 2007. *Profanations*, trans. Jeff Fort. New York: Zone Books.

Akhtar, Salman. 2009. *Comprehensive Dictionary of Psychoanalysis*. London: Karnac.

Alexandrowicz, C. H. [1969] 2017. 'New and Original States: the Issue of Reversion to Sovereignty', in David Armitage and Jennifer Pitts (eds), *The Law of Nations in Global History*. Oxford: Oxford University Press, 390–403.

Althusser, Louis. [1971] 2014. *On the Reproduction of Capitalism: Ideology and Ideological State Apparatuses*, trans. G. M. Goshgarian. London: Verso.

Améry, Jean. 1994. *On Aging: Revolt and Resignation*. Bloomington, IN: Indiana University Press.

Anderson, Jane and Haidy Geismar (eds). 2017. *The Routledge Companion to Cultural Property*. London: Routledge.

Antaya, Roger. 1980. 'The Etymology of Pomerium', *American Journal of Philology* 101(2): 184–9.

Aquinas, Thomas. [1888–1906] 2017. *Summa Theologica*. New York: Mosaicum Books.

Arendt, Hannah. [1943] 2009. 'We Refugees', in Jerome Kohn and Ron H. Feldman (eds), *Hannah Arendt: the Jewish Writings*. New York: Schocken Books, 264–74.

Arif, Yasmeen. 2016. *Life, Emergent: the Social in the Afterlives of Violence*. Minneapolis, MN: University of Minnesota Press.

Arlow, Jacob and Charles Brenner. 1969. 'The Psychopathology of the Psychoses: a Proposed Revision', *International Journal of Psychoanalysis* 50(1): 5–14.

Asad, Talal. 2015. 'Reflections on Violence, Law, and Humanitarianism', *Critical Inquiry* 41(2): 390–427.

Avelar, Idelber. 1999. 'Restitution and Mourning in Latin American Postdictatorship', *boundary 2* 26(3): 201–24.

Azoulay, Ariella. 2019. *Potential History: Unlearning Imperialism*. London: Verso.

Bachelard, Gaston. 1971. *The Poetics of Reverie: Childhood, Language, and the Cosmos*, trans. Daniel Russell. New York: Beacon Press.

Bachelard, Gaston. [1988] 2011. *Air and Dreams: An Essay on the Imagination of Movement*, trans. Frederick Farell. Dallas, TX: Dallas Institute Publications.

Bachmann, Sascha-Dominik and Tom Frost. 2015. 'Justice in Transition: On Territory, Restitution and History', in Natalia Szablewska and Sascha-Dominik Bachmann (eds), *Current Issues in Transitional Justice: Towards a More Holistic Approach*. Heidelberg: Springer, 83–110.

Ballard, Megan J. 2010. 'Post Conflict Property Restitution: Flawed Legal and Theoretical Foundations', *Berkeley Journal of International Law* 28(2): 462–96.

Ballard, Megan J. 2013. 'Relaxing Legal Norms to Restore Rights to Homes and Land in the Aftermath of War', in James Charles Smit (ed.), *Property and Sovereignty: Legal and Cultural Perspectives*. London: Routledge, 9–34.

Banki, Peter. 2018. *The Forgiveness to Come: the Holocaust and the Hyper-Ethical*. New York: Fordham University Press.

Barkan, Elazar. 2000. *The Guilt of Nations: Restitution and Negotiating Historical Injustices*. Baltimore, MD: Johns Hopkins University Press.

Barnes, J. A. 1966. 'Durkheim's Division of Labour in Society', *Man* 1(2): 158–75.

Barnett, Michael. 2011. *Empire of Humanity: a History of Humanitarianism*. Ithaca, NY: Cornell University Press.

Bartels, Anke, Lars Eckstein, Dirk Wiemann and Nicole Waller. 2017. 'Postcolonial Justice: An Introduction', in Anke Bartels, Lars Eckstein, Dirk Wiemann and Nicole Waller (eds), *Postcolonial Justice*. Potsdam: University of Potsdam, vii–xxix.

Bassiouni, Mahmoud C. 2006. 'The Perennial Conflict between International Criminal Justice and Realpolitik', *Georgia State University Law Review* 22(3): 541–60.

Baxi, Upendra. 1974. 'Durkheim and Legal Evolution: Some Problems of Disproof', *Law and Society Review* 8(4): 645–52.

Baxter, Jeannette, Valerie Henitiuk and Ben Hutchinson. 2013. *A Literature of Restitution: Critical Essays on W. G. Sebald*. Manchester: Manchester University Press.

Bazyler, Michael J. 2005. *Holocaust Justice: the Battle for Restitution in America's Courts*. New York: New York University Press.

Bazyler, Michael J. and Roger P. Alford. 2006. *Holocaust Restitution: Perspectives on the Litigation and Its Legacy*. New York: New York University Press.

Beauchamp, Tom L. 2008, rev. 2019. 'The Principle of Beneficence in Applied Ethics', in Edward N. Zalta (ed.), *Stanford Encyclopedia of Philosophy*, available at: https://plato.stanford.edu/entries/principle-beneficence.

Benford, Criscilla. 2010. '"Listen to My Tale": Multilevel Structure, Narrative Sense Making, and the Inassimilable in Mary Shelley's "Frankenstein"', *Narrative* 18(3): 324–46.

Berger, Adolf. [1953] 1991. *Encyclopedic Dictionary of Roman Law*. London: DIANE Publishing.

Besselink, Leonard. 1988. 'The Impious Hypothesis Revisited', *Grotiana* 9(1): 3–63.

Bevernage, Berber. 2013. *History, Memory, and State-Sponsored Violence*. London: Routledge.

Bevir, Mark. 2002. *The Logic of the History of Ideas*. Cambridge: Cambridge University Press.

Bevir, Mark. 2011. 'The Contextual Approach', in George Klosko (ed.), *The Oxford Handbook of the History of Political Philosophy*. Oxford: Oxford University Press, 11–23.

Bewell, Alan. 1988. 'An Issue of Monstrous Desire: Frankenstein and Obstetrics', *Yale Journal of Criticism* 2(1):105–28.

Bibring, Edward. 1943. 'The Conception of the Repetition Compulsion', *Psychoanalytic Quarterly* 12(4): 486–519.

Birks, Peter. 1989. *An Introduction to the Law of Restitution*. Oxford: Clarendon Press.

Blom, Andrew. 2014. 'Hugo Grotius (1583–1645)', *International Encyclopedia of Philosophy*, available at: www.iep.utm.edu/grotius.

Boltanski, Luc. 1999. *Distant Suffering: Morality, Media and Politics*, trans. Graham Burchell. Cambridge: Cambridge University Press.

Borschberg, Peter. 2011. *Hugo Grotius, the Portuguese and Free Trade in the East Indies*. Singapore and Leiden: Singapore University Press and KITLV Press.

Bott Spillius, Elizabeth, Jane Milton, Penelope Garvey, Cyril Couve and Deborah Steiner. 2011. *The New Dictionary of Kleinian Thought*. London: Taylor & Francis.

Bottici, Chiara. 2011. 'From Imagination to the Imaginary and Beyond: Towards a Theory of Imaginal Politics', in Chiara Bottici and Benoît Challand (eds), *The Politics of Imagination*. London: CRC Press, 16–37.

Bottici, Chiara. 2014. *Imaginal Politics: Images beyond Imagination and the Imaginary*. New York: Columbia University Press.

Bowie, Andrew. 2003. *Aesthetic and Subjectivity: From Kant to Nietzsche*. Manchester: Manchester University Press.

Brennan, Tad. 2005. 'Oikeiôsis and Others', in Tad Brennan (ed.), *The Stoic Life: Emotions, Duties, and Fate*. Oxford: Oxford University Press, 154–68.

Broiles, R. David. 2012. *The Moral Philosophy of David Hume*. The Hague: Martinus Nijhoff.

Broken Lullaby. 1932. Film, directed Ernst Lubitsch, screenplay Reginald Berkeley, produced Paramount Pictures.

Bronfen, Elisabeth. 1994. 'Rewriting the Family: Mary Shelley's Frankenstein in its Biographical/Textual Context', in Stephen Bann (ed.), *Frankenstein, Creation and Monstrosity*. London: Reaktion, 16–38.

Brooke, Christopher. 2012. *Philosophic Pride: Stoicism and Political Thought from Lipsius to Rousseau*. Princeton, NJ: Princeton University Press.

Brooks, Roy. 2004. *Atonement and Forgiveness: a New Model for Black Reparations*. Berkeley, CA: University of California Press.

Buckland, William Warwick. [1908] 2010. *The Roman Law of Slavery: the Condition of the Slave in Private Law from Augustus to Justinian*. Cambridge: Cambridge University Press.

Buckley-Zistel, Susanne, Teresa Koloma Beck, Christian Braun and Friederike Mieth. 2013. *Transitional Justice Theories*. London: Routledge.

Bull, Hedley, Benedict Kingsbury and Adam Roberts (eds). 1992. *Hugo Grotius and International Relations*. Oxford: Clarendon Press.

Burrill, Alexander Mansfield. 1860. *A Law Dictionary and Glossary*. London: Baker, Voorhis.

Burrows, Andrew. 2011. *The Law of Restitution*. Oxford: Oxford University Press.

Butler, Joseph. [1726, 1729] 2006. 'Fifteen Sermons Preached at Rolls Chapel', in *The Works of Bishop Butler*, ed. David E. White. Rochester, NY: University of Rochester Press, 33–146.

Butler, Judith and Athena Athanasiou. 2013. *Dispossession: the Performative in the Political*. London: Polity.

Butt, Daniel. 2009. *Rectifying International Injustice: Principles of Compensation and Restitution between Nations*. Oxford: Oxford University Press.

Buyse, Antoine. 2008. 'Lost and Regained? Restitution as a Remedy for Human Rights Violations in the Context of International Law', *Zeitschrift für ausländisches öffentliches Recht und Völkerrecht* 68(1): 29–153.

Canetti, Elias. [1962] 2000. *Crowds and Power*, trans. Carol Steward. New York: Continuum.

Carnoy, Martin. 2014. *The State and Political Theory*. Princeton, NJ: Princeton University Press.

Caruth, Cathy. 1996. *Unclaimed Experience: Trauma, Narrative and History* Baltimore, MD: Johns Hopkins University Press.

Cassin, Barbara, Emily Apter, Jacques Lezra and Michael Wood. 2014. *Dictionary of Untranslatables: a Philosophical Lexicon*. Princeton, NJ: Princeton University Press.

Castoriadis, Cornelius. 1998. *The Imaginary Institution of Society*, trans. Kathleen Blamey. Cambridge, MA: MIT Press.

Chatty, Dawn. 2016. 'Anthropology and Forced Migration', in Elena Fiddian-Qasmiyeh et al. (eds), *The Oxford Handbook of Refugee and Forced Migration Studies*. Oxford: Oxford University Press, 74–85.

Celermajer, Danielle. 2009. *The Sins of the Nation and the Ritual of Apologies*. Cambridge: Cambridge University Press.

Cladis, Mark S. 2012. 'Suffering to Become Human: a Durkheimian Perspective', in W. S. F. Pickering and Massimo Rosati (eds), *Suffering and Evil: the Durkheimian Legacy*. New York: Berghahn, 81–100.

Clemens, Justin and Ben Naparstek. 2011. 'An Interview with Jacqueline Rose', in Justin Clemens and Ben Naparstek (eds), *The Jacqueline Rose Reader*. Durham, NC: Duke University Press, 341–60.

Comay, Rebecca. 2011. *Mourning Sickness: Hegel and the French Revolution*. Stanford, CA: Stanford University Press.

Cordial, Margaret and Knut Røsandhaug. 2009. *Post-conflict Property Restitution*. Leiden: Martinus Nijhoff.

Corlett, Angelo J. 2011. 'Reparations', in William Edelglass and Jay L. Garfield (eds), *The Oxford Handbook of World Philosophy*. Oxford: Oxford University Press, 596–608.

Corlett, Angelo J. 2013. *Responsibility and Punishment*. Heidelberg: Springer.

Cornu, Marie and Marc-André Renold. 2010. 'New Developments in the Restitution of Cultural Property: Alternative Means of Dispute Resolution', *International Journal of Cultural Property* 17: 1–31.

Corradetti, Claudio. 2013. 'Philosophical Issues in Transitional Justice Theory: a (Provisional) Balance', *Politica e Società* 2: 185–220.

Corradetti, Claudio, Nir Eisikovits and Jack Volpe Rotondi. 2015. *Theorizing Transitional Justice.* London: Routledge.

Coser, L. A. 1977. *Masters of Sociological Thought: Ideas in Historical and Social Context.* New York: Harcourt Brace Jovanovich.

Coser, L. A. [1984] 2014. 'Introduction to the 1984 Edition', in Steven Lukes (ed.), *Émile Durkheim: the Division of Labour in Society.* New York: Free Press, xi–xxiii.

Cottorrell, Roger. 1977. 'Durkheim on Legal Development and Social Solidarity', *British Journal of Law and Society* 4(2): 241–52.

Cox, Murray. 1999. *Remorse and Reparation.* Philadelphia, PA: Jessica Kingsley.

Cristi, Marcela. 2012. 'Durkheim on Moral Individualism, Social Justice and Rights: a Gendered Construction of Right', *Canadian Journal of Sociology* 37(4): 409–38.

Crow, Graham. 2001. *Social Solidarities: Theories, Identities and Social Change.* London: Open University Press.

David, René. 1972. *International Encyclopedia of Comparative Law, vol. II: the Legal Systems of the World / Their Comparison and Unification.* London: Brill.

De Greiff, Pablo. 2006a. 'Justice and Reparations', in Pablo De Greiff (ed.), *The Handbook of Reparations.* Oxford: Oxford University Press, 451–72.

De Greiff, Pablo. 2006b. 'Repairing the Past: Compensations for Victims of Human Rights Violations', in Pablo De Greiff (ed.), *The Handbook of Reparations.* Oxford: Oxford University Press, 1–16.

De Line, Sebastian. 2018. 'Weaving Reflections: On Museology and the Rematriation of Indigenous Beings from Ethnological Collections', *bauhaus imaginista.*

Derrida, Jacques. [1976] 2016. *Of Grammatology*, trans. Gayatri Chakravorty Spivak. Baltimore, MD: Johns Hopkins University Press.

Derrida, Jacques. 1992. *Given Time: I. Counterfeit Money*, trans. Peggy Kamuf. Chicago, IL: University of Chicago Press.

Derrida, Jacques. 1996. *Archive Fever: a Freudian Impression*, trans. Eric Prenowitz. Chicago, IL: University of Chicago Press.

Derrida, Jacques. 2007. *Learning to Live Finally: An Interview with Jean Birnbaum*, trans. Pascale-Anne Brault and Michael Naas. New York: Melville House.

Derrida, Jacques. 2013. *The Death Penalty.* Chicago, IL: University of Chicago Press.

Deutscher, Max (ed.). 2001. *Michele Le Doeuff: Operative Philosophy and Imaginary Practice*. New York: Humanity Books.

Dietrich, Joachim. 1998. *Restitution: a New Perspective*. Sydney: Federation Press.

Digeser, P. A. 2001. *Political Forgiveness*. Ithaca, NY: Cornell University Press.

Diner, Dan and Gotthard Wunberg. 2007. *Restitution and Memory: Material Restoration in Europe*. New York: Berghahn.

Dogville. 2003. Film, directed Lars von Trier, screenplay Lars von Trier, produced Filmek AB, Zoma Films UK, Canal 3, France 3 Cinéma.

Dumbauld, Edward. 1970. *The Life and Legal Writings of Hugo Grotius*. Norman, OK: University of Oklahoma Press.

Dunant, Henry. [1962] 2013. *A Memory of Solferino*, trans. American Red Cross. Geneva: International Committee of the Red Cross.

Durkheim, Émile. [1893] 2007. *De la division du travail social*. Paris: Alcan.

Durkheim, Émile. 1893. 'Review. Gaston Richard, Essai sur l'origine de l'idée de droit', *Revue Philosophique* 35: 290–6.

Durkheim, Émile. 1898. 'L'individualisme et les intellectuelles', *Revue Ble* 4(10): 7–13.

Durkheim, Émile. [1890–1900] 1950. *Leçons de sociologie: physique des moeurs et du droit*. Paris: Les Presses universitaires de France.

Durkheim, Émile. 1901. 'Deux lois de l'évolution pénale', *Année sociologique* 4: 65–95.

Durkheim, Émile. 1957. *Professional Ethics and Civic Morals*, trans. C. Brookfield. Glencoe, IL: Free Press.

Durkheim, Émile. ([1957] 1983). 'The Nature and Origins of the Right of Property', in *Durkheim and the Law*, ed. Steven Lukes and Andrew Scull, trans. C. Brookfield. Oxford: Martin Robertson, 158–91.

Durkheim, Émile. 1969. 'Individualism and the Intellectuals', trans. Steven Lukes, *Political Studies* 17(1): 19–30.

Durkheim, Émile. 1983a. 'From Repressive to Restitutive Law', in *Durkheim and the Law*, ed. Steven Lukes and Andrew Scull, trans. Steven Lukes. Oxford: Martin Robertson, 62–77.

Durkheim, Émile. 1983b. 'The Evolution of Punishment', in *Durkheim and the Law*, ed. Steven Lukes and Andrew Scull, trans. Anthony Jones and Andrew Scull. Oxford: Martin Robertson, 78–102.

Durkheim, Émile. 1983c. 'The Origins of Law', in *Durkheim and the Law*, ed. Steven Lukes and Andrew Scull, trans. Andrew Scull. Oxford: Martin Robertson, 164–75.

Durkheim, Émile. [1984] 2014. *The Division of Labor in Society*, trans. Steven Lukes. New York: Free Press.

Eglash, Ambert. 1959. 'Creative Restitution: Its Roots in Psychiatry, Religion and Law', *British Journal of Delinquency* 10(2): 114–19.

Elster, Jon. 2004. *Closing the Books: Transitional Justice in Historical Perspective*. Cambridge: Cambridge University Press.

Eng, David. 2016. 'Colonial Object Relations', *Social Text* 34(1): 1–19.

Englard, Izhak. 2009. *Corrective and Distributive Justice: From Aristotle to Modern Times*. Oxford: Oxford University Press.

Erdrich, Louise. 2016. *LaRose*. New York: HarperCollins.

Esposito, Roberto. 2015. *Persons and Things: From the Body's Point of View*, trans. Zakiya Hanafi. London: Polity.

Esposito, Roberto. 2016. 'Persons and Things', *Paragraph* 39(1): 26–35.

Fackenheim, Emil L. 1994. *To Mend the World: Foundations of Post-Holocaust Jewish Thought*. Bloomington, IN: Indiana University Press.

Feldman, Shelley, Charles Geisler and Gayatri A. Menon. 2011. *Accumulating Insecurity: Violence and Dispossession in the Making of Everyday Life*. Athens, GA: University of Georgia Press.

Fenichel, Otto. [1946] 2014. *The Psychoanalytic Theory of Neurosis*. London: Routledge.

Figlio, Karl. 2017. *Remembering as Reparation: Psychoanalysis and Historical Memory*. London: Palgrave Macmillan.

Fitzmaurice, Andrew 2014. *Sovereignty, Property and Empire, 1500–2000*. Cambridge: Cambridge University Press.

Fitzpatrick, Peter. 2002. *The Mythology of Modern Law*. London: Routledge.

Florescu, Radu. 1999. *In Search of Frankenstein: Exploring the Myths Behind Mary Shelley's Monster*. London: Robson.

Freud, Anna. [1937] 1993. *The Ego and the Mechanisms of Defence*. London: Karnac.

Freud, Sigmund. [1896] 1962. 'The Aetiology of Hysteria', in *The Standard Edition of the Complete Psychological Works of Sigmund Freud, vol. III (1893–1899): Early Psycho-Analytic Publications*, ed. James Strachey, trans. C. M. Baines. London: Hogarth Press and the Institute of Psychoanalysis, 187–221.

Freud, Sigmund. [1909] 1955. 'Notes Upon a Case of Obsessional Neurosis', in *The Standard Edition of the Complete Psychological Works of Sigmund Freud, vol. X: (1909): Two Case Histories (Little Hans and the Rat Man)*, ed. and trans. James Strachey. London: Hogarth Press and the Institute of Psychoanalysis, 153–317.

Freud, Sigmund. [1911] 1955. 'Psychoanalytische Bemerkungen über einen autobiographisch beschriebenen Fall von Paranoia', in *Gesammelte Werke (Band 8): Werke aus den Jahren 1909–1913 von Sigmund Freud*. London: Imago, 237–320.

Freud, Sigmund. [1923] 2000. 'Das Ich und das Es', in *Studienausgabe, Bd. 3. Psychologie des Unbewussten*, ed. S. Fischer. Frankfurt: Fischer Taschenbuch-Verlag, 273–330

Freud, Sigmund. [1926] 2010. *Hemmung, Symptom und Angst*. Berlin: Nikol Verlag.

Freud, Sigmund. [1927] 1961. 'The Ego and the Id', in *The Standard Edition of the Complete Psychological Works of Sigmund Freud, vol. XIX: 1923–1925: The Ego and the Id and Other Works*, ed. James Strachey, trans. Joan Riviere. London: Hogarth Press and the Institute of Psychoanalysis, 1–66

Freud, Sigmund. [1949] 1959. 'Inhibitions, Symptoms and Anxiety', in *The Standard Edition of the Complete Psychological Works of Sigmund Freud. Volume XX*, ed. James Strachey, trans. Alex Strachey. London: Hogarth Press and the Institute of Psychoanalysis, 77–175.

Freud, Sigmund. [1950] 1961. 'Negation', in *The Standard Edition of the Complete Psychological Works of Sigmund Freud, vol. XIX*, ed. James Strachey, trans. Joan Riviere. London: Hogarth Press and the Institute of Psychoanalysis, 233–9.

Freud, Sigmund. [1958] 2001. 'Psychoanalytic Comments on an Autobiographical Account of a Case of Paranoia', in *The Standard Edition of the Complete Psychological Works of Sigmund Freud, vol. XII: 1911–1913*, ed. and trans. James Strachey. London: Hogarth Press and the Institute of Psychoanalysis, 3–84.

Frey, R. G. 1992. 'Butler on Self-love and Benevolence', in Christopher Cunliffe (ed.), *Joseph Butler's Moral and Religious Thought: Tercentenary Essays*. Oxford: Oxford University Press, 243–67.

Frantz. 2016. Film, directed Françoise Ozon, screenplay Françoise Ozon and Philippe Piazzo, produced Mars Films.

Frim, Landon. 2019. 'Impartiality or Oikeiôsis? Two Models of Universal Benevolence', *Symposion* 6(2): 147–69.

Frosh, Stephen. 2013. *Hauntings: Psychoanalysis and Ghostly Transmissions*. London: Springer.

Galaway, Burt and Joe Hudson. 1972. 'Restitution and Rehabilitation: Some Central Issues', *Crime and Delinquency* 18(4): 403–10.

Gane, Mike. 2002. 'Durkheim: Woman as Outsider', in Mike Gane (ed.), *Radical Sociology of Durkheim and Mauss*. London: Routledge, 85–134.

Garcia-Godos, Jemima. 2010. 'Addressing Land Restitution in Transitional Justice', *Nordic Journal of Human Rights* 28(2): 122–42.

Garland, David. [2004] 2012. 'Frameworks of Analysis in the Sociology of Punishment, in Joseph E. Jacoby, Theresa A. Severance and Alan S. Bruce (eds), *Classics of Criminology*. Long Grove, IL: Waveland Press, 675–83.

Garrett, Aaron. 2018. 'Joseph Butler's Moral Philosophy', in Edward Zalta (ed.), *The Stanford Encyclopedia of Philosophy*, available at: https://plato.stanford.edu/archives/spr2018/entries/butler-moral.

Garrett, Aaron and Silvia Sebastiani. 2017. 'David Hume on Race', in Naomi Zack (ed.), *The Oxford Handbook of Philosophy and Race*. Oxford: Oxford University Press, 31–43.

Gatens, Moira. 1996. *Imaginary Bodies: Ethics, Power and Corporeality* London: Routledge.

Geddert, Jeremy Seth. 2014. 'Beyond Strict Justice: Hugo Grotius on Punishment and Natural Right(s)', *Review of Politics* 76(4): 559–88.

Germany v. *Poland* (Factory at Chorzow), PCIJ Ser. A, No. 9, 1927.

Geuss, Raymond. 2009. *Politics and the Imagination*. Princeton, NJ: Princeton University Press.

Giddens, Anthony. 1977. *Capitalism and Modern Social Theory: an Analysis of the Writings of Marx, Durkheim and Max Weber*. Cambridge: Cambridge University Press.

Giddens, Anthony. 1978. *Durkheim*. Hassocks: Harvester.

Gigante, Denise. 2000. 'Facing the Ugly: the Case of "Frankenstein"', *ELH* 67: 565–87.

Gigante, Denise. 2009. *Life: Organic Form and Romanticism*. New Haven, CT: Yale University Press.

Giglio, Francesco. 2004. *The Foundation of Restitution for Wrongs*. London: Hart.

Glance, Jonathan C. 1996. '"Beyond the Usual Bonds of Reverie?" Another Look at the Dreams in "Frankenstein"', *Journal of the Fantastic in the Arts* 7(4): 30–47.

Goldberg, M. A. 1959. 'Moral and Myth in Mrs. Shelley's Frankenstein', *Keats-Shelley Journal* 8: 27–38.

Gotowiecki, Paweł 2016. 'Restitutio ad integrum – prawno-polityczna doktryna ośrodka legalistycznego polskiej emigracji politycznej na Zachodzie (1945–1990)', *Miscellanea Historico-Iuridica* 15(1): 205–20.

Gottesman, D. M. 1975/6. 'Working Through: a Process of Restitution', *Psychoanalytic Review* 62(4): 639–45.

Govier, Trudy. 2002. *Forgiveness and Revenge*. London: Routledge.

Graham, Eliza. 2011. *Restitution*. London: Pan Books.

Gray, Christine. 1999. 'The Choice between Restitution and Compensation', *European Journal of International Law* 10(2):413–23.

Greenleaf, Monica and Stephen Moeller-Sally. 1998. *Russian Subjects: Empire, Nation, and the Culture of the Golden Age*. Evanston, IL: Northwestern University Press.

Grewe, Wilhelm G. [1984] 2014. 'Status Quo', in Rudolf Bernhardt et al. (eds), *Encyclopedia of Public International Law, vol. 7: Foundations and Principles of International Law*. Amsterdam: Elsevier Science, 438–442.

Griswold, C. L. 2007. *Forgiveness: a Philosophical Exploration*. Cambridge: Cambridge University Press.

Grotius, Hugo. [1738] 2005. *The Rights of War and Peace*, trans. Jean Barbeyrac. Indianapolis: Liberty Fund.

Grotius, Hugo. [1901] 2001. *Commentary on the Law of Prize and Booty*, trans. Gwladys L. Williams. Indianapolis: Liberty Fund.

Haakonssen, Knud. 1985. 'Hugo Grotius and the History of Political Thought', *Political Theory* 13(2): 239–65.

Hamilton-Bleakley, Holly. 2007. 'Linguistic Philosophy and *The Foundations*', in Annabel Brett and James Tully (eds), *Rethinking the Foundations of Modern Political Thought*. Cambridge: Cambridge University Press, 20–36.

Harkup, Kathryn. 2018. *Making the Monster: the Science behind Mary Shelley's Frankenstein*. New York: Bloomsbury.

Harrison, Jonathan. 1976. *Hume's Moral Epistemology*. Oxford: Clarendon Press.

Hartman, Geoffrey H. 1991. 'The Philomela Project', in Geoffrey H. Hartman (ed.), *Minor Prophecies: the Literary Essay in the Culture Wars*. Cambridge, MA: Harvard University Press, 164–75.

Hathaway, James C. 1997. 'The Meaning of Repatriation', *International Journal of Refugee Law* 9(4): 551–8.

Hedley, Steve. 1985. 'Unjust Enrichment as the Basis of Restitution: an Overworked Concept', *Legal Studies* 5(1): 56–66.

Hirsch, Alexander. 2013. *Theorizing Post-Conflict Reconciliation: Agonism, Restitution and Repair*. London: Routledge.

Hocking, Jenny. 2018. '"A Transforming Sentiment in this Country": the Whitlam Government and Indigenous Self-determination', *Australian Journal of Public Administration* 77: 5–12.

Hogle, Jerrold E. 2014. 'Romantic Contexts', in Andrew Smith (ed.), *The Cambridge Companion to 'Frankenstein'*. Cambridge: Cambridge University Press, 41–55.

Howe, Adrian. 2005. *Punish and Critique: Towards a Feminist Analysis of Penality*. London: Routledge.

Hughes, Paul M. 2011. 'Reparations', in Deen K. Chatterjee (ed.), *Encyclopedia of Global Justice*. Dordrecht: Springer, 945–6.

Hume, David. [1739] 1973. *A Treatise of Human Nature*. Oxford: Clarendon Press.

Hume, David. [1751] 1998. *An Enquiry concerning the Principles of Morals*, trans. Tom L. Beauchamp. Oxford: Oxford University Press.

International Center for Transitional Justice, the, available at: https://www.ictj.org.

Ireland, Gordon. 1944. 'Jus Postlimini and the Coming Peace', *Tulane Law Review* 18: 584–96.

Irigaray, Luce. 1986. 'Fecundity of the Caress', in Richard A. Cohen (ed.), *Face to Face with Levinas*. New York: State University of New York Press, 231–56.

Israel, Jonathan. 1995. *The Dutch Republic: Its Rise, Greatness, and Fall, 1477–1806*. Oxford: Clarendon Press.

Jahn, Beate. 2005. 'Barbarian Thoughts: Imperialism in the Philosophy of John Stuart Mill', *Review of International Studies* 31(3): 599–618.

Jankélévitch, Vladimir. [1967] 2019. *Le pardon*. Paris: Flammarion.

Jankélévitch, Vladimir. 2005. *Forgiveness*, trans. Andrew Kelly. Chicago, IL: University of Chicago Press.

Johnstone, Gerry. 2002. *Restorative Justice: Ideas, Values, Debates*. Portland, OR: Willan Publishing.

Jones, Susan Stedman. 2001. *Durkheim Reconsidered*. Cambridge: Polity.

Jones, Robert Alun. 1986. *Émile Durkheim: An Introduction to four Major Works*. Beverly Hills, CA: Sage.

Jones, Silas. [1836] 2011. *Practical Phrenology*. Toronto: Read Books.

Justinian. [1903] 2014 *The Digest of Justinian*, trans. Charles Henry Monro. Cambridge: Cambridge University Press.

Kalinowska, Izabela. 2004. *Between East and West: Polish and Russian Nineteenth-century Travel to Orient*. Rochester, NY: University of Rochester Press.

Karski, Karol. 2014. '"Ius Postlimini" jako podstawa uznania ciągłości przedwojennych i dzisiejszych państw bałtyckich', *Zeszyty Prawnicze* 14(1): 7–52.

Kaufman, Will. 2007. 'On the Psychology of Slavery Reparation', *Atlantic Studies* 4(2): 267–84.

Keene, Edward. 2002. *Beyond the Anarchical Society: Grotius, Colonialism and Order in World Politics*. Cambridge: Cambridge University Press.

Kelly, Andrew. 2013. 'Jankélévitch and the Metaphysics of Forgiveness', in Alan Udoff (ed.), *Vladimir Jankélévitch and the Question of Forgiveness*. Lanham, MD: Lexington Books, 27–46.

King, Pearl and Riccardo Steiner (eds). 1991. *The Freud–Klein Controversies 1941–45*. London: Brunner-Routledge.

Klein, Melanie. [1929] 2011. 'Infantile Anxiety Situations Reflected in a Work of Art and in the Creative Impulse', in *Love, Guilt and Reparation: and Other Works 1921–1945*, Kindle edn. London: Vintage Digital. Location 4921-5079.

Klein, Melanie. [1932] 1975. *The Psychoanalysis of Children*, trans. Alexis Strachey. London: Hogarth Press.

Klein, Melanie. [1933] 2011. 'An Early Development on Conscience in the Child', in *Love, Guilt and Reparation: And Other Works 1921–1945*, Kindle edn. London: Vintage Digital. Location 5732-5930.

Klein, Melanie. [1935] 2011. 'A Contribution to the Psychogenesis of Manic-Depressive States', in *Love, Guilt and Reparation: And Other Works 1921–1945*, Kindle edn. London: Vintage Digital. Location 6034-6619.

Klein, Melanie. [1936] 2011. 'Weaning', in *Love, Guilt and Reparation: And Other Works 1921–1945*. Kindle edn. London: Vintage Digital. Location 6651-6974.

Klein, Melanie. [1937] 2011. 'Love, Guilt and Reparation', in *Love, Guilt and Reparation: And Other Works 1921–1945*. Kindle edn. London: Vintage Digital. Location 7001-7810.

Klein, Melanie. 1948. *Contributions to Psycho-Analysis 1921–1945*. London: Hogarth Press.

Kordela, Kiarina A. (2016). 'Monsters of Biopower: Terror(ism) and Horror in the Era of Affect', *Philosophy Today* 60(1): 193–205.

Koritansky, Peter Karl. 2011. *The Philosophy of Punishment and the History of Political Thought*. Columbia, MO: University of Missouri Press.

Koskenniemi, Martti. 2019. 'Imagining the Rule of Law: Rereading the Grotian "Tradition"', *European Journal of International Law* 30(1): 17–52.

Kravitz, Leonard S. and Kerry M. Olitzky. 1995. *The Journey of the Soul: Traditional Sources on Teshuvah*. Northvale, NJ: Jason Aronson.

Kuprecht, Karolina. 2013. *Indigenous Peoples' Cultural Property Claims: Repatriation and Beyond*. Heidelberg: Springer.

Kyriakakis, Joanna. 2012. 'Justice after War: Economic Actors, Economic Crimes, and the Moral Imperative for Accountability after War', in Larry May and Andrew T. Forcehimes (eds), *Morality, Jus Post Bellum, and International Law*. Cambridge: Cambridge University Press, 113–39.

La Caze, Marguerite. 2002. *The Analytic Imaginary*. Ithaca, NY: Cornell University Press.

La Caze, Marguerite. 2003. 'Michèle Le Doeuff and the Work of Philosophy', *Australian Journal of French Studies* 40(3): 244–56.

La Caze, Marguerite. 2008. 'Michele le Doeuff, Feminist Epistemology, and the Unthought', *Hecate: An Interdisciplinary Journal of Women's Liberation* 34(3): 62–79.

La Caze, Marguerite. 2018. *Ethical Restoration after Communal Violence*. Lanham, MD: Lexington Press.

Langford, Malcolm and Khulekani Moyo. 2010. 'Right, Remedy or Rhetoric?' *Nordic Journal of Human Rights* 28(2): 143–76.

Laplanche, Jean. 1992. 'Interview. Jean Laplanche Talks to Martin Stanton', trans. Martin Stanton, in John Fletcher and Martin Stanton (eds), *Jean Laplanche: Seduction, Translation and the Drives*. London: Institute of Contemporary Arts, 3–20.

Laplanche, Jean. 1999. *Essays on Otherness*. London: Routledge.

Laplanche, Jean, and J-B. Pontalis. [1967] 1973. *The Language of Psycho-analysis*, trans. Donald Nicholson-Smith. New York: W. W. Norton

Laplante, Lisa J. 2013. 'The Plural Justice Aims of Reparations', in Susanne Buckley-Zistel et al. (eds), *Transitional Justice Theories*. London: Routledge, 66–84.

Laubender, Carolyn. 2019a. 'Beyond Repair: Interpretation, Reparation, and Melanie Klein's Clinical Play-Technique, Studies in Gender and Sexuality', *Studies in Gender and Sexuality* 20(1): 51–67.

Laubender, Carolyn. 2019b. 'Empty Space: Creativity, Femininity, Reparation, Justice', *Free Associations: Psychoanalysis and Culture, Media, Groups, Politics* 75(19): 27–48.

Lear, Jonathan. 2014. 'Mourning and Moral Psychology', *Psychoanalytic Psychology* 31(4): 470–81.

Le Doeuff, Michèle. 1989. *The Philosophical Imaginary*, trans. Colin Gordon. Stanford, CA: Stanford University Press.

Le Doeuff, Michèle. 2007. *Hipparchia's Choice: An Essay Concerning Women, Philosophy, etc.*, trans. Trista Selons. New York: Columbia University Press.

Leckie, Scott and Chris Huggins. 2011. *Conflict and Housing, Land and Property Rights: a Handbook on Issues, Frameworks, and Solutions.* Cambridge: Cambridge University Press.

Lehmann, Jennifer M. 1994. *Durkheim and Women.* Lincoln, NE: University of Nebraska Press.

Lesaffer, Randall. 2010. 'Alberico Gentili's *ius post bellum* and Early Modern Peace Treaties', in Benedict Kingsbury and Benjamin Straumann (eds), *The Roman Foundations of the Law of Nations: Alberico Gentili and the Justice of Empire.* Oxford: Oxford University Press, 210–40.

Levine, Samuel J. 2000. 'Teshuva: a Look at Repentance, Forgiveness and Atonement in Jewish Law and Philosophy and American Legal Thought', *Fordham Urban Law Journal* 27(5): 1677–93.

Levy, Ernst. 1943. 'Captivus Redemptus', *Classical Philology* 38: 159–76.

Likierman, Meira. 2002. *Melanie Klein: Her Work in Context.* New York: Continuum.

Lodder, Andrew. 2012. *Enrichment in the Law of Unjust Enrichment and Restitution.* New York: Bloomsbury.

Loewald, Hans. 1953. 'Psychoanalysis and Modern Views on Human Existence and Religious Experience', *Journal of Pastoral Care* 7: 1–15.

Loewald, Hans. 1989. *Papers on Psychoanalysis.* New Haven, CT: Yale University Press.

Long, Katy. 2013. *The Point of No Return: Refugees, Rights, and Repatriation.* Oxford: Oxford University Press.

Looney, Aaron. 2015. *Vladimir Jankélévitch: the Time of Forgiveness.* New York: Fordham University Press.

Lu, Catherine. 2018. 'Reconciliation and Reparations', in Seth Lazar and Helen Frowe (eds), *The Oxford Handbook of Ethics and War.* Oxford: Oxford University Press, 538–556.

Lu, Catherine. 2019. *Justice and Reconciliation in World Politics.* Cambridge: Cambridge University Press.

Luckhurst, Roger. 2013. *The Trauma Question*. London: Routledge.

Lukacher, Ned. 1988. *Primal Scenes: Literature, Philosophy, Psychoanalysis*. New York: Cornell University Press.

Lukes, Steven. 1972. *Émile Durkheim: His Life and Work*. New York: Harper & Row.

Lukes, Steven and Andrew Scull. 1983. 'Introduction', in Steven Lukes and Andrew Scull (eds), *Durkheim and the Law*. Oxford: Martin Robertson, 1–32.

Lyotard, Jean-Françoise. [1991] 2001. *The Inhuman*, trans. Geoffrey Bennington and Rachel Bowlby. Cambridge: Polity Press.

Mackie, J. L. 1981. *Hume's Moral Theory*. London: Routledge.

Marder, Michael. 2005. 'Sure Thing? On Things and Objects in the Philosophy of Jacques Derrida', *Postmodern Culture* 15(3), available at: http://pmc.iath.virginia.edu/text-only/issue.505/15.3marder.txt.

May, Larry. 2012a. *After War Ends: a Philosophical Perspective*. Cambridge: Cambridge University Press.

May, Larry. 2012b. 'Reparations, Restitution, and Transitional Justice', in Larry May and Andrew Forcehimes (eds), *Morality, Jus Post Bellum, and International Law*. Cambridge: Cambridge University Press, 32–48.

May, Larry. 2014. 'Jus Post Bellum, Grotius, and Meionexia', in Carsten Stahn, Jennifer S. Easterday and Jens Iverson (eds), *Jus Post Bellum: Mapping the Normative Foundations*. Oxford: Oxford University Press, 15–25.

May, Larry and Elizabeth Edenberg. 2013. 'Introduction', in Larry May and Elizabeth Edenberg (eds), *Jus Post Bellum and Transitional Justice*. New York: Cambridge University Press, 1–25.

Mbembe, Achille. 2017. *Critique of Black Reason*, trans. Laurent Dubois. Durham, NC: Duke University Press.

Mbembe, Achille. 2018. 'Reflections on African Objects and Restitution in the Twenty-First Century', public talk on the occasion of the Reception of Gerda Henkel Prize 2018, available at: https://lisa.gerda-henkel-stiftung.de/reflections_on_african_objects_and_restitution_in_the_twenty_first_century?nav_id=7933&language=en.

Mbembe, Achille. 2020. *Out of the Dark Night: Essays on Decolonization*. New York: Columbia University Press.

McCallin, Barbara. 2012. 'Restitution and Legal Pluralism in Contexts of Displacement', Research Case Study. International Centre for Transitional Justice.

McLaren, Annemarie. 2017. 'Review of A Handful of Sand: The Gurindji Struggle, After the Walk-Off by Charlie Russell Ward', *Native American and Indigenous Studies* 4(2): 115–16.

Mégret, Frederic and Raphael Vagliano. 2017. 'Transitional Justice and Human Rights', in Cheryl Lawther, Luke Moffett, and Dov Jacobs (eds), *Research Handbook on Transitional Justice*. Cheltenham: Edward Elgar, 95–116.

Mei, Wan. 2018. 'Culture Survivance and Religion Healing: On Ojibwe Spirituality in Healing Trauma in *LaRose*', *Journal of Literature and Art Studies* 8(8): 1181–7.

Meister, Robert. 2011. *After Evil: a Politics of Human Right*. New York: Columbia University Press.

Meron, Theodor. 1998. *War Crimes Come of an Age*. Oxford: Oxford University Press.

Merrill, Jacqueline Pfeffer. 2011. 'David Hume and the Virtue of Benevolence', *Philanthropy Daily*, 3 December, available at: https://www.philanthropydaily .com/david-hume-and-the-virtue-of-benevolence.

Merryman, John Henry. 2010. *Imperialism, Art and Restitution*. Cambridge: Cambridge University Press.

Mill, John Stuart. [1859] 1864. *On Liberty*. London: Longman, Green, Longman Roberts & Green.

Mill, John Stuart. [1859] 1973. *Dissertations and Discussions: Political, Philosophical, and Historical*. London: Haskell House.

Minow, Martha. 1998. *Between Vengeance and Forgiveness: Facing History After Genocide and Mass Violence*. Boston, MA: Beacon Press.

Moers, Ellen. [1976] 1985. 'Female Gothic', in George Levine and U. C. Knoepflmache (eds), *The Endurance of Frankenstein*. Berkley, CA: University of California Press, 77–87.

Moore, Burness and Bernard Fine. 1990. 'Restitution', in Burness Moore and Bernard Fine (eds), *Psychoanalysis: the Major Concepts*. New Haven, CT: Yale University Press, 169–70.

Mulhall, Stephen. 2004. 'Taylor's Political Philosophy', in Ruth Abbey (ed.), *Charles Taylor*. Cambridge: Cambridge University Press, 105–26.

Murcia, Luis Eduardo Pérez. 2014. 'Social Policy or Reparative Justice? Challenges for Reparations in Contexts of Massive Displacement and Related Serious Human Rights Violations', *Journal of Refugee Studies* 27(2): 191–206.

Murphy, Ann. 2012. *Violence and the Philosophical Imaginary*. New York: State University of New York Press.

Murphy, Colleen. 2010. *A Moral Theory of Political Reconciliation*. Cambridge: Cambridge University Press.

Murphy, Colleen. 2017. *The Conceptual Foundations of Transitional Justice*. Cambridge: Cambridge University Press.

Naranch, Laurie E. 2003. 'The Imaginary and a Political Quest for Freedom', *differences: A Journal of Feminist Cultural Studies* 13(3): 64–82.

Nichols, Robert. 2018. 'Theft is Property! The Recursive Logic of Dispossession', *Political Theory* 46(1): 3–28.

Nietzsche, Friedrich Wilhelm. [1889] 2009. *Twilight of the Idols, or, How to Philosophize with a Hammer*, trans. Thomas Common. New York: Dover.

Norton, David Fate and Jacqueline Taylor (eds). 2008. *The Cambridge Companion to Hume*, 2nd edn. Cambridge: Cambridge University Press.

Ohlin, Jens David. 2007. 'On the Very Idea of Transitional Justice', *Whitehead Journal of Diplomacy and International Relations* 8(1): 51–68.

O'Mahony, Lorna Fox and James A. Sweeney. 2013. *The Idea of Home in Law: Displacement and Dispossession*. Farnham: Ashgate.

Online Etymology Dictionary, available at: https://www.etymonline.com.

O'Rourke, James. 1989. '"Nothing More Unnatural": Mary Shelley's Revision of Rousseau', *ELH* 56(3): 543–7.

Pagden, Anthony. 2012. 'Conquest and the Just War: the "School of Salamanca" and the "Affair of the Indies"', in Sankar Muthu (ed.), *Empire and Modern Political Thought*. Cambridge: Cambridge University Press, 30–60.

Paglione, Giulia. 2008. 'Individual Property Restitution: from Deng to Pinheiro – and the Challenges Ahead', *International Journal of Refugee Law* 20(3): 391–412.

Palmer, Jessica. 2016. 'Unjust Enrichment, Proprietary Subrogation and Unsatisfactory Explanations', *Singapore Academy of Law Journal* 28: 955–83.

Pantuliano, Sara and Samir Elhawary. 2009. 'Uncharted Territory: Land, Conflict, and Humanitarian Action', *HPG Policy Brief 39*.

Paoletti, Giovanni. 2012. 'Some Concepts of "Evil" in Durkheim's Thought', in W. S. F. Pickering and Massimo Rosati (eds), *Suffering and Evil: the Durkheimian Legacy*. New York: Berghahn, 63–80.

Pederson, Joshua. 2018. 'Trauma and Narrative', in J. Roger Kurtz (ed.), *Trauma and Literature*. Cambridge: Cambridge University Press, 97–109.

Pelinka, Anton. 2019. *Austria: Out of the Shadow of the Past*. London: Routledge.

Pensky, Max. 2003. 'The Relevance of the Past: Between Construction and Debt', *Intertexts* 7(2): 131–43.

Pérez, Emma. 1999. *The Decolonial Imaginary: Writing Chicanas into History*. Bloomington, IN: Indiana University Press.

Pinker, Steven. 2011. *The Better Angels of Our Nature: Why Violence Has Declined*. London: Penguin.

Pinker, Steven. 2018. *Enlightenment Now: the Case for Reason, Science, Humanism, and Progress*. New York: Viking.

Priel, Dan. 2013. 'The Law and Politics of Unjust Enrichment', *University of Toronto Law Journal* 63(4): 1–40.

Rabey, David Ian. 2013. *David Rudkin: Sacred Disobedience: An Expository Study of His Drama 1959–1994*. London: Routledge.

Republic of Austria v. *Altmann*, 541 US 677 2004.

Rieder, John. 2003. 'Patriarchal Fantasy and the Fecal Child in Mary Shelley's Frankenstein and Its Adaptations', in Jerrold E. Hogle (ed.), *Frankenstein's*

Dream. A Romantic Circles Praxis Volume, June, available at: https://romantic-circles.org/praxis/frankenstein/rieder/rieder.html.

Riggsby, Andrew M. 2010. *Roman Law and the Legal World of the Romans*. Cambridge: Cambridge University Press, 135–42.

Riviere, Joan. 1936. 'A Contribution to the Analysis of the Negative Therapeutic Reaction', *International Journal of Psychoanalysis* 17: 304–20.

Roberts, Tom Aerwyn. 1973. *The Concept of Benevolence: Aspects of Eighteenth-Century Moral Philosophy*. London: Macmillan.

Robertson, Geoffrey. 2019. *Who Owns History? Elgin's Loot and the Case for Returning Plundered Treasure*. London: Knopf.

Rochlin, Gregory. 1953. 'Loss and Restitution', *Psychoanalytic Studies of the Child* 8(1): 288–309.

Rose, Jacqueline. 1993a. 'Negativity in the Work of Melanie Klein', in *Why War? Psychoanalysis, Politics, and the Return to Melanie Klein*. Oxford: Blackwell, 137–90.

Rose, Jacqueline. 1993b. 'War in the Nursery', in *Why War? Psychoanalysis, Politics, and the Return to Melanie Klein*. Oxford: Blackwell, 191–230.

Rose, Jacqueline. 1993c. 'An Interview with Jacqueline Rose', in *Why War? Psychoanalysis, Politics, and the Return to Melanie Klein*. Oxford: Blackwell, 231–55.

Rose, Jacqueline. 1996. *States of Fantasy*. New York: Clarendon Press.

Rose, Jacqueline. 2004. 'Deadly Embrace', *London Review of Books* 24(21): 21–4.

Ross, Stephen. 1993. *Injustice and Restitution: the Ordinance of Time*. New York: SUNY Press.

Rostand, Maurice. [1930] 1950. *L'Homme que j'ai tué*. Paris: Nagel.

Rotherham, Craig. 2000. 'Restitution and Property Rites: Reason and Ritual in the Law of Proprietary Remedies', *Theoretical Inquiries in Law* 1(2): 204–31.

Rotherham, Craig. 2007. 'The Conceptual Structure of Restitution for Wrongs', *Cambridge Law Journal* 66(1): 172–99.

Rutherforth, Thomas. [1754–6] 1832. *Institutes of Natural Law: Being the Substance of a Course of Lectures on Grotius de Jure Belli et Pacis*. Cambridge: J. Bentham, printer to the University.

Sabahi, Borzu. 2011. *Compensation and Restitution in Investor–State Arbitration: Principles and Practice*. Oxford: Oxford University Press.

Sarr, Felwine and Bénédicte Savoy. 2018. *The Restitution of African Cultural Heritage: Toward a New Relational Ethics*, trans. Drew S. Burk, vol. 26, Ministry of Culture of the French Republic, available at: http://restitutionreport2018.com.

Saryusz-Wolska, Magdalena. 2020. 'Travelling Memories of the Holocaust in the Occupied Soviet Union: Hans Scholz's *Through the Night* and Its Remediation', *German Studies Review* 43(4).

Savoy, Bénédicte. 2018. 'Property and Possession: Some Considerations on the History of Ideas Relating to a Pair of Legal Concepts', *Völkerrechtsblog*, 18 September, available at: https://voelkerrechtsblog.org/property-and-possession.

Schneewind, Jerome B. 1998. *The Invention of Autonomy: a History of Modern Moral Philosophy*. Cambridge: Cambridge University Press.

Schnier, Jacques. 1957. 'Restitution Aspects of the Creative Process', *American Imago* 14(3): 211–23.

Schoene-Harwood, Berthold. 2000. *Mary Shelley, Frankenstein: a Reader's Guide to Essential Criticism*. Cambridge: Icon Books.

Scholz, Sally. 2012. *Political Solidarity*. University Park, PA: Penn State University Press.

Sebald, W. G. 2002. *Austerlitz*, trans. Anthea Bell. London: Short Books.

Sebald, W. G. 2003. *On the Natural History of Destruction*, trans. Anthea Bell. London: Hamish Hilton.

Sebald, W. G. 2004. 'An Attempt at Restitution: a Memory of a German City', trans. Anthea Bell, *The New Yorker*, 20 December, available at: https://www.newyorker.com/magazine/2004/12/20/an-attempt-at-restitution?verso=true.

Segal, Hanna. [1972] 2005. 'A Delusional System as a Defence against the Re-emergence of a Catastrophic Situation', in Hanna Segal (ed.), *Psychoanalysis, Literature and War: Papers 1972–1995*. London: Routledge, 39–50.

Shelley, Mary. [1818] 2009. *Frankenstein, or The Modern Prometheus*. London: Penguin.

Sherwin-White, Susan. 2018. *Melanie Klein Revisited: Pioneer and Revolutionary in the Psychoanalysis of Young Children*. London: Routledge.

Skinner, Quentin. 1969. 'Meaning and Understanding in the History of Ideas', *History and Theory* 8(1): 3–53.

Slater, Thomas. 1911. 'Restitution', in *Catholic Encyclopedia*. New York: Robert Appleton, available at: http://www.newadvent.org/cathen/12788a.htm.

Smit, Anneke. 2012. *The Property Rights of Refugees and Internally Displaced Persons: Beyond Restitution*. London: Routledge.

Smith, Phillip and Jeffrey C. Alexander. 2008. 'Introduction: the New Durkheim', in Jeffrey C. Alexander and Phillip Smith (eds), *The Cambridge Companion to Durkheim*. Cambridge: Cambridge University Press, 1–37.

Smith, William. 1875. *A Dictionary of Greek and Roman Antiquities*. London: John Murray.

Somos, Mark. 2007. 'Secularization in *De Iure Praedae*: from Bible Criticism to International Law', *Grotiana* 26(1): 147–91.

Souter, James. 2014. 'Durable Solutions as Reparation for the Unjust Harms of Displacement: Who Owes What to Refugees?' *Journal of Refugee Studies* 27(2): 171–90.

Stamatoudi, Irini A. 2011. *Cultural Property Law and Restitution*. Cheltenham: Edward Elgar.

Steger, Manfred B. and Paul James. 2013. 'Levels of Subjective Globalization: Ideologies, Imaginaries, Ontologies', *Perspectives on Global Development and Technology* 12(1/2): 17–40.

Steinmetz, George. 2006. 'Decolonizing German Theory: An Introduction', *Postcolonial Studies* 9(1): 1–13.

Sterrenburg, Lee. 1979. 'Mary Shelley's Monster: Politics and Psyche in Frankenstein', in George Levine and U. C. Knoepflmache (eds), *The Endurance of Frankenstein*. Berkeley, CA: University of California Press, 143–71.

Stonebridge, Lyndsey and John Phillips. 1998. *Reading Melanie Klein*. London: Psychology Press.

Straumann, Benjamin. 2003–4. 'Oikeiosis and Appetitus Societatis. Hugo Grotius' Cicernonian Argument for Natural Law and Just War', *Grotiana* 24/25: 41–66.

Straumann, Benjamin. 2015. *Roman Law in the State of Nature*, trans. Benjamin Cooper. Cambridge: Cambridge University Press.

Streiker, Gisela. 1996. *Essays on Hellenistic Epistemology and Ethics*. Cambridge: Cambridge University Press.

Tavuchis, Nicholas. 1991. *Mea Culpa: a Sociology of Apology and Reconciliation*. Stanford, CA: Stanford University Press.

Taylor, Charles. 1992. *Sources of the Self*. Cambridge, MA: Harvard University Press.

Taylor, Jacqueline. 2013. 'Hume on the Importance of Humanity', *Revue Internationale de Philosophie* 1(263): 81–97.

Thijssen, Peter. 2012. 'From Mechanical to Organic Solidarity and Back: with Honneth beyond Durkheim', *European Journal of Social Theory* 15(4): 454–70.

Thomas, Ronald R. 1990. *Dreams of Authority: Freud and the Fictions of the Unconscious*. New York: Cornell University Press.

Thompson, Janna. 2002. *Taking Responsibility for the Past: Reparation and Historical Injustice*. Cambridge: Polity Press.

Thompson, Janna. 2003. 'Cultural Property, Restitution and Value', *Journal of Applied Philosophy* 20(3): 251–62.

Torpey, John C. 2001. '"Making Whole What has been Smashed": Reflections on Reparations', *Journal of Modern History* 73(2): 333–58.

Torpey, John C. 2003. *Politics and the Past: On Repairing Historical Injustices*. Lanham, MD: Rowman & Littlefield.

Torpey, John C. 2005. 'Victims and Citizens: the Discourse of Reparation(s) at the Dawn of the New Millennium', in Koen Feyter, Marc Bossuyt, Stephan Parmentier and Paul Lemmens (eds), *Out of the Ashes: Reparation for*

Victims of Gross and Systematic Human Rights Violations. Antwerp: Intersentia, 35–50.

Torpey, John C. 2006. *Making Whole What has been Smashed: On Reparation Politics*. Cambridge, MA: Harvard University Press.

Trotter, Amber M. 2019. *Psychoanalysis as a Subversive Phenomenon: Social Change, Virtue Ethics, and Analytic Theory*. Langham, MD: Lexington Press.

Tuck, Richard. 1983. 'Grotius, Carneades and Hobbes', *Grotiana* 4(1): 43–62.

Tuck, Richard. 1987. 'The "Modern" Theory of Natural Law', in Anthony Pagden (ed.), *The Languages of Political Theory in Early-Modern Europe*. Cambridge: Cambridge University Press, 99–119.

Tuck, Richard. 1993. *Philosophy and Government 1572–1651*. Cambridge: Cambridge University Press.

Tuck, Richard. 1999. *Rights of War and Peace: Political Thought and the International Order*. Oxford: Oxford University Press.

Tuck, Richard. 2003. 'The Making and Unmaking of Boundaries from the Natural Law Perspective', in Allen Buchanan and Margaret Moore (eds), *States, Nations and Borders: the Ethics of Making Boundaries*. Cambridge: Cambridge University Press, 143–70.

Tuckness, Alex. 2010. 'Retribution and Restitution in Locke's Theory of Punishment', *Journal of Politics* 72(3): 720–32.

United Nations. 2005. 'Basic Principles and Guidelines on the Right to a Remedy and Reparation for Victims of Gross Violations of International Human Right Law and Serious Violations of International Humanitarian Law'. General Assembly of the United Nations. Resolution 60/147. December 16, available at: https://www.ohchr.org/EN/ProfessionalInterest/Pages/RemedyAndReparation.aspx.

United Nations. 2005. 'Principles on Housing and Property Restitution for Refugees and Displaced Persons' (Pinheiro Principles). Economic and Social Council of the United Nations. E/CN.4/Sub.2/2005/17, available at: https://www.unhcr.org/protection/idps/50f94d849/principles-housing-property-restitution-refugees-displaced-persons-pinheiro.html.

van Gelderen, Martin. 2011. '"*So meerly humane*": Theories of Resistance in Early Modern Europe', in Annabel Brett and James Tully (eds), *Rethinking the Foundations of Modern Political Thought*. Cambridge: Cambridge University Press, 149–70.

van Ittersum, Martine Julia. 2006. 'Introduction', in Martine Julia van Ittersum (ed.), *Commentary on the Law of Prize and Booty*. Indianapolis, IN: Liberty Fund, xiii–xxii.

van Ittersum, Martine Julia. 2010. 'The Long Goodbye: Hugo Grotius' Justification of Dutch Expansion Overseas, 1615–1645', *History of European Ideas* 36(4): 386–411.

Vivenza, Gloria. 2003. 'The Classical Roots of Benevolence in Economic Thought', in B. B. Price (ed.), *Ancient Economic Thought*. London: Routledge, 191–210.

Vrdoljak, Ana Filipa. 2006. *International Law, Museums and the Return of Cultural Objects*. Cambridge: Cambridge University Press.

Waldron, Jeremy. 1992. 'Superseding Historical Justice', *Ethics* 103(1): 4–28.

Walker, Margaret Urban. 2006. *Moral Repair: Reconstructing Moral Relations after Wrongdoing*. Cambridge: Cambridge University Press.

Walker, Margaret Urban. 2010. *What is Reparative Justice?* Milwaukee, WI: Marquette University Press.

Walker, Margaret Urban. 2016. 'Making Reparations Possible: Theorizing Reparative Justice', in Claudio Corradetti, Nir Eisikovits and Jack Volpe Rotondi (eds), *Theorizing Transitional Justice*. London: Routledge, 211–24.

Waller, James. 2016. *Confronting Evil: Engaging Our Responsibility to Prevent Genocide*. Oxford: Oxford University Press.

Watson, Alan. 1987. *Roman Slave Law*. Baltimore, MD: Johns Hopkins University Press.

Watson, Alan. 1990. *Studies in Roman Private Law*. London: A. & C. Black.

Watson, Alan. 2001. 'Thinking Property at Rome', in Paul Finkelman (ed.), *Slavery and the Law*. New York: Rowman & Littlefield, 419–36.

Wauters, Bart. 2017. 'Grotius, Necessity and the Sixteenth-Century Scholastic Tradition', *Grotiana* 38(1): 129–47.

Wheeler, Samuel C. 1997. 'Reparations Reconstructed', *American Philosophical Quarterly* 34(3): 301–18.

Whelan, Frederick G. 1980. 'Property as Artifice: Hume and Blackstone', *Nomos* 22: 101–29.

White, Hayden. [1973] 2014. *Metahistory: the Historical Imagination in Nineteenth-Century Europe*. Baltimore, MD: Johns Hopkins University Press.

White, Hayden. 1986. *Tropics of Discourse: Essays in Cultural Criticism*. Baltimore, MD: Johns Hopkins University Press.

Whitehead, Alfred North. 1948. *Science and the Modern World*. New York: New American Library of World Literature.

Wertz, Frederick. 2003. 'Freud's Case of the Rat Man Revisited: An Existential-Phenomenological and Socio-Historical Analysis', *Journal of Phenomenological Psychology* 34(1): 47–78.

Williams, Rhodri C. 2007. 'The Contemporary Right to Property Restitution in the Context of Transitional Justice', International Center for Transitional Justice, Occasional Paper Series, May.

Williams, Rhodri C. 2012. 'Protection in the Past Sense: Restitution at the Junction of Humanitarian Response to Displacement and Transitional Justice', in Roger Duthie (ed.), *Transitional Justice and Displacement*. New York: Social Justice Research Council, 85–138.

Williams, Rhodri C. 2013. 'Restitution at the Juncture of Humanitarian Response to Displacement and Transitional Justice'. New York: International Center for Transitional Justice, Brookings-LSE Project on Internal Displacement.

Winkel, Laurence. 2005. 'Problems of Legal Systematization from *De iure praedae* to *De iure belli ac pacis*', *Grotiana* 26–8: 61–78.

Winter, Stephen. 2013. 'Towards a Unified Theory of Transitional Justice', *International Journal of Transitional Justice* 7(2): 224–44.

Wityak, Nancy L. and Ruth A. Wallace. 1981. 'Durkheim's Non-Social Facts about Primitives and Women', *Sociological Inquiry* 51(1): 61–7.

Wodak, Ruth. 2009. *Discursive Construction of National Identity*. Edinburgh: Edinburgh University Press.

Woman in Gold. 2015. Film, directed Simon Curtis, screenplay Alexi Kaye Campbell, produced BBC Films and Origin Pictures.

Ziolkowski, Theodore. 1981. 'Science, Frankenstein and Myth', *Sewanee Review* 89(1): 34–56.

Žižek, Slavoj. 2013. *Interrogating the Real*. New York: A. & C. Black.

Žižek, Slavoj, Eric L. Santner and Kenneth Reinhard. [2006] 2013. *The Neighbor: Three Inquiries in Political Theology*. Chicago, IL: University of Chicago Press.

Zolkos, Magdalena. 2010. *Reconciling Community and Subjective Life. Trauma Testimony as Political Theorizing in the Work of Jean Améry and Imre Kértesz*. New York: Continuum.

Zolkos, Magdalena. 2017. '"The Return of Things as They Were": New Humanitarianism, Restitutive Desire and the Politics of Unrectifiable Loss', *Contemporary Political Theory* 16(3): 321–41.

Zolkos, Magdalena. 2019. 'The Work of Remorse: Vladimir Jankélévitch's Conception of the Ethical Subject and Françoise Ozon's *Frantz*', in Marguerite La Caze and Magdalena Zolkos (eds), *Contemporary Perspectives on Vladimir Jankélévitch: On What Cannot be Touched*. Lanham, MD: Lexington, 137–56.

Zolkos, Magdalena. 2020 (forthcoming). '"Le pardon clos" at le pléonexie dans *Le Pardon* de Jankélévitch', *Les Cahiers de l'Herne*.

INDEX